URBAN HOUSING IN HILL STATE
Demand and Determinants

About the Authors

Utpal Kumar De (M.Sc., Ph.D.) is currently a Professor of Economics at the North-Eastern Hill University, Shillong, India. Prof. Dehas been engaged in teaching at post-graduate level since 1994. Prof. Dehas delivered keynote and invited lectures in over 100 international and national conferences in India and abroad, and published 155 research articles in reputed national and international journals. Besides completing six research projects, he has so far published 15 authored books and edited volumes from various reputed publishers and successfully guided 14 research scholars for Ph.D.

Vitsosie Vupru (M.A., Ph.D.), did his Masters in Economics from Gokhale Institute of Politics &Economics, Pune and Ph.D. in Economics from North-Eastern Hill University, Shillong. Dr. Vupru taught Economics at Dimapur Government College, Dimapur from 2004 to 2022. At present he is a Principal of Sao Chang College, Tuensang, Nagaland, India. He has published half-a-dozen research articles in various international and national journals and presented papers in half-a-dozen conferences. However, this is his maiden venture.

URBAN HOUSING IN HILL STATE
Demand and Determinants
An Experience in North-East India

Utpal Kumar De
Vitsosie Vupru

CONCEPT PUBLISHING COMPANY PVT. LTD.
NEW DELHI - 110 059

ISBN: 978-93-5594-624-9

First Published 2023

Published and Printed by

Since 1974

Concept Publishing Company Pvt. Ltd.
A/15-16, Commercial Block, Mohan Garden
New Delhi-110059 (India)
T : +91-11-41101460
E: publishing@conceptpub.com, *W*: www.conceptpub.com

Cataloging in Publication--Courtesy: D.K. Agencies (P) Ltd. <docinfo@dkagencies.com>

De, Utpal Kumar, 1968- **author.**
Urban housing in hill state : demand and determinants : an experience in North-East India/Utpal Kumar De, Vitsosie Vupru.
pages cm
Includes bibliographical references and index.
ISBN 9789355946249

1. Housing--India--Dimāpur. 2. Housing--India--Dimāpur--Statistics. I. Vupru, Vitsosie, author. II. Title.

LCC HD7361.D56D48 2023 | DDC 338.47690830954165 23

Preface

Housing is a basic requirement of human well-being. The status of housing sector is also an important indicator of the wealth and economic health of a nation. It has been observed that a high demand for housing triggers faster growth than many other economic sectors. Therefore, Government of India has laid great emphasis on the infrastructure sector, especially the housing sector, to meet the growing housing requirements of the burgeoning population. Access to required housing is however dependent on the affordability of the individuals and the price of houses. Thus, proper pricing of houses and other variables that exert an influence on house prices entails vital policy implication.

Price of residential properties varies across space and time depending upon the characteristics of the houses as well as on the preferences of the potential buyers and their capabilities. The purchase of a residential property, from the individual's point of view, is both a consumption decision as well as an investment decision. In an endeavour to model the housing prices, two approaches have been widely used by the researchers. The first approach is the **mono-centric model**, where housing price is assumed to be a function of proximity to a single employment centre or workplace. It was first employed by Von Thunen (1825) and then it was applied to residential locations by Alonso (1964), Muth (1969) and Mills (1972), (Koomen and Buurman, 2002). This theory tries to capture the relative housing prices through the relative savings from commuting costs associated with different locations. However, unlike other consumption goods, the housing market is unique because it manifests the characteristics of durability, heterogeneity, and spatial fixity. Hence, to model this differentiation effectively, the second approach, namely **the hedonic price model** has been developed.

The hedonic price model posits that goods are typically sold as a package of inherent attributes (Rosen, 1974). Therefore, the price of a house in relation to another differs with the additional unit of the different attributes inherent in it, depending upon their desirability to the potential buyers. The relative price of a house is then the summation of all its *marginal or implicit* prices estimated through the regression analysis. After Rosen (1974), several studies have also utilized this technique to examine the relationship between attribute preference and the price of properties (Li & Brown, 1980; Walden, 1990; Sirpal, 1994; and Garrod and Willis, 1999). This is due to the fact that the market price of a housing unit can be determined not only through the cost of construction, but also by the buyers' evaluations of the housing unit's bundle of inherent attributes, such as *locational, structural, or neighbourhood* attributes (Freeman, 1979). Most of these studies were carried out to analyze the housing markets in the West; particularly in America and Europe. However, a few were conducted in the East till the end of the 20th century, such as Edmonds (1984) in Japan, Mok, Chan and Cho (1995), So, Tse and Ganesan (1997), Chau, Ma and Ho (2001), and Chau, Ng and Hung (2001) in Hongkong and Hsueh (2000) in Taiwan (see Chin and Chau, 2003).

Dimapur, the commercial hub of Nagaland, was the ancient capital of the erstwhile Dimasa Kachari kingdom, whose rule existed before the 13th century A.D. It was often described as the "Brick City" by European scholars and also by the Ahoms because the seat of capital of the kingdom was originally surrounded by brick walls of four feet wide and sixteen feet high. During the World War II, it was the staging post for the Allied offensive against the Japanese forces during the Battle of Kohima. Reinforcement and supplies were all routed through Dimapur since it was the only place in Nagaland connected with railways and airways, besides better roadways. It is also regarded as the 'gateway' to Nagaland. It is one of the fastest growing cities in India (GoI-UNDP Project, 2013).

Dimapur was constituted as a town on August 8, 1954 with the promulgation of the Constitution of Town Committee Rules, 1954, when Nagaland State was administratively under Assam State as Naga Hills District. Unlike other places in the state, Dimapur city has a heterogeneous mix of people from all over India, and for which it is also known as "mini India" (DMC). The population of Dimapur (municipal area) in 1991 was only about 57,000 and it increased to 1,23,777 in the span of 20 years (Census, 2011). Up to 2004, Dimapur was under the administrative control of Dimapur Town Committee. With the passing of the Nagaland Municipal Act, 2001, the Dimapur Municipal Council was constituted on January 19, 2005. Dimapur Municipality covers an area of 18.32 sq. km. Till 2001, Dimapur town had only 21 wards with a population of 98,096 as per 2001 Census Report. According to 2011 Census Report,

Dimapur Municipal area houses 27,870 households under 23 wards consisting of 87 colonies. Thus, there has been a population growth of about 26 per cent during the first decade of the 21st century in the Dimapur Municipality. A rapid urban sprawl in Dimapur has been observed over the years.

Residential houses in Dimapur have witnessed a rapid increase in the recent years. Construction of cottages and some independent houses has been a very common feature of the city, besides the commercial complexes constructed by private individuals and groups. It is apparent that both construction of houses and population of Dimapur have increased rapidly over the years. Also, there is a close relation between rising urban population and rising demand for houses in and around its urban fringe. The rise in population consequently increases the demand for residential properties and indirectly affects the demand for housing attributes in accordance with the needs and desires of the inhabitants.

Over the years, prices of house are also observed to increase at a rapid rate along with the increase in demand which is also associated with a spatial variation. This variation within Dimapur itself is due to multiplicity of factors including proximity to business centres, congeniality and nearness to working places, and other civic facilities as well as variations in security situation. As far as residential houses are concerned, variations in the price of a house (through sale/purchase) or rented houses arise in addition to these former attributes, due to variation in cost of construction, age of the building (which may not be a case for rented house), size of the house, availability and quality of water, proper drainage facility, and other environmental amenities. However, no concrete analysis has been made so far on the nature of variation in demand for housing and its characteristics across various socio-economic groups in Dimapur, even though the residential property demand has unprecedentedly risen in the city in recent times.

The present study investigates the people's preferences for *locational, structural, and neighbourhood housing* attributes in connection with the choice of residence and the variation in price due to the variation of such attributes. All three categories of attributes have been considered in the statistical exposition of housing demand through a hedonic pricing analysis that offers a newer dimension of house pricing for a small hill town in India's North East. Further, the role of socio-economic-cultural and religious background of the neighbours in the selection of housing location has been analysed statistically.

The outcome of this volume thus provides an important addition to the academic discourses and policy implication. The volume would be a valuable acquisition by the academicians, researchers and policy makers involved in housing design, management and development.

Utpal Kumar De
Vitsosie Vupru

Acknowledgements

We are thankful to Concept Publishing Company for accepting and bringing out our research work. Also, we are indebted to North-Eastern Hill University for providing necessary infrastructure to conduct this research in the Department of Economics.

Our special thanks are also due to all the respondents and officials who had helped us generously during the time of Primary Survey as well as in the collection of official data at different stages of this research work. Further, we express our profound gratitude to all those persons who have directly or indirectly helped in the course of undertaking this research.

We hope that this book will be helpful to researchers, policy makers and students of post-graduate level. Therefore, it can be a good acquisition by the academic libraries. We, however, welcome comments and ideas from the readers that would be helpful for conducting further research in this line.

Utpal Kumar De
VitsosieVupru

Contents

List of Tables

List of Figures

List of Abbreviations/Acronyms

CBD	Central Business District
CGI	Corrugated Galvanised Iron
CMO	Chief Medical Officer
CPI	Consumer Price Index
CV	Coefficient of Variation
DEO	District Education Officer
DMC	Dimapur Municipal Council
GBs	Gaon Buras
GoI	Government of India
GOI-UNDP	Government of India-United Nations Development Project
HPM	Hedonic Pricing Method
HS	High School
ILP	Inner Line Permit
LCI	Locational Convenience Index
LPG	Liquid Petroleum Gas
NE	North East (India)
NPWD, R&B	Nagaland Public Works Department, Roads and Bridges
NSDP	Nagaland State Domestic Product
PCI	Per Capita Income
SD	Standard Deviation
SEK	Swedish Krona
SSA	Sarva Shiksha Abhiyan
VIF	Variance Inflation Factor
WTP	Willingness to Pay

1
Prologue

Introduction

Housing is a basic necessity of human well-being. It is universally accepted as one of the indispensable needs of human being along with food and clothing. This explains why it represents the single largest investment of majority of households across the countries. The status of housing sector is also an important indicator of the wealth and economic health of a nation. It has been observed that a high demand for housing triggers faster growth in many other economic sectors (Glossop, 2014). The "housing revolution" that followed in the post-independence era in India also points to the importance of studies directed towards the problems related to housing in India. In addition, the importance of studies dealing with housing markets in India is even greater when one considers that these markets revolve around the role of the various governments (both central and states) in the housing markets, resulting in rent controls, direct provision of housing and infrastructures, and poor planning (Tiwari & Rao, 2016). In recent years, the Government of India has laid great emphasis on the infrastructure sector, especially the housing sector, to meet the burgeoning housing requirements of the growing population, in particular, and their welfare, in general. Thus, proper pricing of houses and other variables that exert an influence on house prices entails vital policy implication.

Price of residential properties varies across space and time depending upon the characteristics of the houses as well as on the preferences of the potential buyers and their capabilities. The purchase of a residential property, from the individual's point of view, is both a consumption decision as well as an investment decision (Shiller, 2008). In an endeavour to model the housing prices, two approaches have been widely used by the researchers. The first approach is the **mono-centric model**, where housing price is assumed to be a function of proximity to a single employment centre or workplace. It was first applied to residential locations by Alonso (1964), and then by Muth (1969), Mills (1972) and Koomen and Buurman, (2002) among many others. This theory tries to capture the relative housing prices through the relative savings from commuting costs associated with different locations. However, unlike other consumption goods, the housing market is unique because it manifests the characteristics of durability, heterogeneity, and spatial fixity. Hence, to model this differentiation effectively, the second approach, namely, **the hedonic price model** has been developed.

The hedonic price model is based on the concept of demand for attributes (Becker, 1965; Lancaster, 1966). The model posits that goods are typically sold as a package of inherent attributes (Rosen, 1974). Therefore, the price of a house in relation to another differs with the additional unit of the different attributes inherent in it, depending upon the desirability of the potential buyers for them. The relative price of a house is, therefore, the summation of all its *marginal or implicit* prices estimated through the regression analysis. After Rosen (1974), several studies have also utilized this technique to examine the relationship between attribute preference and the price of properties (Li & Brown, 1980; Walden, 1990; Sirpal, 1994; Garrod and Willis, 1999; Bajari and Benkard, 2005; Shimizu, 2014; and Hulagu, *et al.*, 2016). This is due to the fact that the market price of a housing unit can be determined not only through the cost of construction, but also by the buyers' evaluations of the housing unit's bundle of inherent attributes, such as *locational, structural, or neighbourhood* attributes (Freeman, 1979). Most of these studies were carried out to analyze the housing markets in the Western world; particularly in America and Europe. However, in recent past a few studies have been carried out in Asian and African countries, such as Edmonds (1984) in Japan, Mok, Chan and Cho (1995), So, Tse and Ganesan (1997), Chau, Ma and Ho (2001), and Chau, Ng and Hung (2001) in Hongkong and Hsueh (2000) in Taiwan.

Residential Housing in Dimapur Town

Residential houses in Dimapur have witnessed a rapid increase in recent years. Construction of cottages and some independent houses has been a very common feature of the city, besides the commercial complexes constructed by private individuals and groups. Apart from being already an important centre of commerce and education with good schools and colleges, Dimapur houses a fairly literate population (87.48%) with a large proportion of them employed in services and private enterprises (GoI, 2011). These factors are known to be closely associated with rural-urban and intra-regional migration. Nonetheless, faster economic growth and development have also been observed to be related to the growth of housing sector in urban areas, which can be ascribed to a business town like Dimapur in Nagaland (Jud and Watts, 1981; and Clauretie and Neill, 2000).

It is apparent that both construction of houses and population of Dimapur have increased rapidly over the years. Also, there is a close relation between rising urban population and rising demand for houses in and around its urban fringe. The rise in population consequently escalates the demand for residential properties and also indirectly affects the demand for housing attributes in accordance with the needs and desires of the inhabitants.

Over the years, prices of houses are also observed to increase at a rapid rate along with the increase in demand, which is also associated with a spatial variation. This variation within Dimapur itself is due to multiplicity of factors including proximity to business centres, congeniality and nearness to working places, and other civic facilities as well as variations in security situation. As far as residential houses are concerned, variations in the price of a house (through sale/purchase) or rented houses arise in addition to these former attributes, due to the variation in the cost of construction, age of the building (which may not be in the case of a rented house), size of the house, availability and quality of water, proper drainage facility, and other environmental amenities. However, no concrete study has been made on the nature of variation in demand for housing and its characteristics across various socio-economic groups in Dimapur, even though the residential property demand has unprecedently risen in the town in recent times.

Therefore, it is pertinent to seriously investigate the people's preferences for *locational, structural, and neighbourhood housing* attributes in connection with the choice of residence and the variation in price due to the variation of such attributes. Since Dimapur remains the most populous and unequalled town in Nagaland, it follows that housing for the people should be adequately researched, as shelter is one of the foremost priorities of life in urban development.

In the light of the above statement, this volume attempts to bring out the role of various housing attributes on people's residential choices in a North-East Indian town, Dimapur, which can be called a mini-India. This study tries to address the following questions as noted below.

The Questions

The findings of this study are expected to provide answers to the following specific research questions:

1. What are the different attributes of housing demand in this small hill town?
2. Why do we observe variations in housing prices or house rent even when they possess similar locational and structural attributes?
3. What are the impacts of the changes in the attributes on sales/ purchase of houses and house rent?

This study, therefore, examines:

(a) If there is a significant relationship between distance of a residential property from the centre of importance (workplace, school, market, etc.) and its nature.

(b) Whether housing price (purchased or rented) is positively related to the income of the house buyers/tenants.

(c) If the homogeneity of culture and religion significantly affect the demand for housing and its price (which are also known as the neighbourhood attributes of housing demand).

Brief Profile of Dimapur Town

Dimapur town is situated on latitude 25°54′30″ degree North and longitude 93°44′15″ degree East in the state of Nagaland, India. It is bounded on the north by the Lengri River and Mikhir Hills (Assam) and on the south by the highlands including the Rangapahar Cantonment. On the east, the boundary throughout is formed by the Dhansiri river (Town Planning Organization, 1975). Dimapur, the commercial hub of Nagaland, was the ancient capital of the erstwhile Dimasa Kachari Kingdom, whose rule existed before the 13th century A.D. It was often described as the "Brick City" by European scholars and also by the Ahoms because the seat of capital of the kingdom was originally surrounded by brick walls of four feet wide and sixteen feet high. During the World War II, it was the staging post for the Allied offensive against the Japanese forces during the Battle of Kohima. Reinforcement and supplies were all routed through Dimapur since it was the only place in Nagaland connected with railways and airways, besides better roadways. It is also regarded as the 'gateway' to Nagaland. It is one of the fastest growing cities in India (GoI-UNDP Project, 2013). Dimapur town occupies a position of great importance not only within the state of Nagaland but also for the adjoining districts of Assam and the state of Manipur. Besides, the town also performs the function of a transportation nodal point.

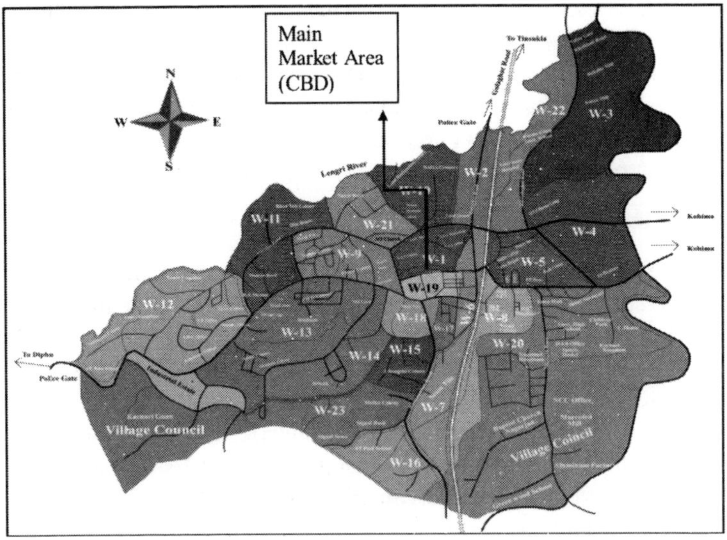

Fig. 1.1: Map of Dimapur Town, Nagaland

Source: Dimapur Municipal Council.

Dimapur was constituted as a town on August 8, 1954 with the promulgation of the Constitution of Town Committee Rules, 1954, when Nagaland was administratively under Assam state as Naga Hills District. Dimapur attained the status of an urban area only in 1961 when the census records designated it as a town with a population of 5,753 persons (Census Report, 1961). The statehood of Nagaland in the year 1963, which brought a flow of immigrants, has been the most important event in the history of Dimapur (Town Planning Organization, 1975). The high influx of immigrants to Dimapur is also accentuated by the fact that it is the only place in Nagaland where Inner Line Permit (ILP) is relaxed. Unlike other places of the state, Dimapur has a heterogeneous mix of people from all over India, and for which it is also known as "mini India" (DMC).

The population of Dimapur (municipal area) in 1991 was only about 57,000 and it increased to 1,22,834 during next 20 years (Census, 2011). Up to 2004, Dimapur was under the administrative control of Dimapur Town Committee. With the passing of the Nagaland Municipal Act, 2001, the Dimapur Municipal Council was constituted on January 19, 2005. Dimapur Municipality covers an area of 25.54 sq. km. Till 2001, Dimapur town had only 21 wards with a population of 98,096 as per 2001 Census Report. According to 2011 Census Report, Dimapur Municipal area houses

27,165 households under 23 wards consisting of 87 colonies. Population figure increased to 1,31,955 in 2015 (as per the projection on the basis of previous growth rates). Thus, there has been a population growth of about 34 per cent during the first one and half decade of the 21st century in the Dimapur Municipality. It is thus, clear that there is a rapid urban sprawl in Dimapur over time.

Scope of this Study

The whole volume has been arranged into six chapters. Besides this first chapter that provides the background and objectives of the study, chapter two reviews the available literature pertaining to the studies on (i) Development of hedonic method of housing prices, (ii) Impact of housing attributes on housing prices, and (iii) Also, the methodology adopted for the purpose of analysis and collection of data is outlined in this section. In chapter three, the trends of residential properties, amenities and demand for housing are analyzed based on available secondary data. Based on the primary data collected through field survey, chapter four and chapter five analyze the socio-economic characteristics of the respondents as well as the determinants of housing demand in Dimapur Municipal Area. Chapter six summarizes the findings of the whole study and provides policy implications coming out of the study.

REFERENCES

Alonso, A. (1964). *Location and land use: towards a General Theory of Land Rent*. Harvard University Press, Cambridge, Massachusetts.

Bajari, P. and Benkard, C.L. (2005). "Demand estimation with heterogeneous consumers and unobserved product characteristics: A hedonic approach". *Journal of Political Economy*, 113(6), 1239-1276.

Becker, G.S. (1965). "A theory of the allocation of time". *Economic Journal*, 75(299), 493-517.

Chau, K.W., Ma, V.S.M. and Ho, D.C.W. (2001). "The pricing of 'luckiness' in the apartment market". *Journal of Real Estate Literature*, 9(1), 31-40.

Chau, K.W., Ng, F.F. and Hung, E.C.T. (2001). "Developer's goodwill as significant influence on apartment unit prices". *Appraisal Journal*, 69(1), 26-34.

Clauretie, T.M. and Neill, H.R. (2000). "Year-round school schedules and residential property values". *Journal of Real Estate Finance and Economics*, 20(3), 311-322.

DMC official website – dmcnagaland.nic.in/SSL/login.aspx

Edmonds, R. (1984). "A theoretical basis for hedonic regression: A research primer", *AREUEA Journal*, 12(1), 72-85.

Freeman, A.M. (1979). "Hedonic prices, property values and measuring environmental benefits: A survey of the issues". *Scandinavian Journal of Economics*, 81(1), 154-171.

Garrod, G. and Willis, K.G. (1999). *Economic Valuation of the Environment: Methods and Case Studies*, Edward Elgar Publishing Ltd., UK.

Glossop, C. (2014). *Housing and Economic Development: Moving forward together*. Centre for Research and Market Intelligence. Retrieved from www.centreforcities.org/wp-content/uploads/2014/09/08-11-06-Housing-and-economic-development.pdf on 21/02/2017.

Government of India, Census of India 2011, New Delhi. Retrieved from: www.census2011.co.in/census/city/183-dimapur.htmlon 12/11/2013.

Government of India, UNDP Project. (2013). *District Human Development Report, Dimapur, Nagaland*. Government of Nagaland, Department of Planning and Coordination.

Hsueh, L.M. (2000). "The relationship between housing price, tenure choice and saving behavior in Taiwan". *International Real Estate Review*, 3(1), 11-33.

Hugalu, T. *et al.* (2016). *A hedonic house Price Index for Turkey*. Working Paper No. 16/03, Central Bank of the Republic of Turkey. Retrieved from: https://www.unece.org/fileadmin/DAM/stats/documents/ece/ces/ge.22/2016/Session_6_Hedonic_House_Price_Index_for_Turkey.pdf on 22/08/2016

Jud, G.D. and Watts, J.M. (1981). "Schools and housing value". *Land Economics*, 57(3), 459-470.

Koomen, E. and Buurman, J. (2002). "Economic theory and land prices in land use Modeling". *Paper presented at the 5th AGILE Conference on Geographic Information Science, Palma* (Balearic Islands, Spain) 2002.

Lancaster, K.J. (1966). "A new approach to consumer theory". *Journal of Political Economy*, 74(2), 132-157.

Li, M.M and Brown, H.J. (1980). "Micro-neighbourhood externalities and hedonic housing prices". *Land Economics*, 56 (2), 125-141.

Mills, E.S. (1972). *Studies on the Structure of the Urban Economy*. John Hopkins University, Baltimore.

Mok, H.M.K., Chan, P.P.K. and Cho, Y.S. (1995). "A hedonic price model for private properties in Hong Kong". *Journal of Real Estate Finance and Economics*, 10, 37-48.

Muth, R.F. (1969). *Cities and Housing: The Spatial Pattern of Urban Residential Land Use*. Chicago, University of Chicago Press.

Rosen, S. (1974). "Hedonic prices and implicit markets: Product differentiation in pure competition". *Journal of Political Economy*, 82(1), 35-55.

Shiller, R.J. (2008). *The Subprime solution: How today's global financial crisis happened, and what to do about it*. Princeton: Princeton University Press.

Shimizu, C. (2014). "Estimation of hedonic single-family house price function considering neighborhood effect variables". *Sustainability*, 6, 2946-2960. DOI: 10.3390/su6052946.

Sirpal, R. (1994). "Empirical modeling of the relative impacts of various sizes of shopping centres on the value of surrounding residential properties". *Journal of Real Estate Research*, 9 (4), 487-505.

So, H.M., Tse, R.Y.C. and Ganesan, S. (1997). "Estimating the influence of transport on house prices: Evidence from Hong Kong". *Journal of Property Valuation & Investment*, 15 (1). 40-47.

Tiwari, P. and Rao, J. (2016). *Housing markets and housing policies in India*. ADBI Working Paper 565. Tokyo: Asian Development Bank Institute. Retrieved from: http://www.adb.org/publications/major-challenges-facing-small-and-medium-sizedenterprises-asia-and-solutions/ on 21/02/2017

Town Planning Organization. (1975). *The Master Plan for Dimapur*, Department of Urban Development, Government of Nagaland.

Walden, M.L. (1990). "Magnet schools and the differential impact of quality on residential property values". *Journal of Real Estate Research*, 5(2), 221-230.

2
Studies on House Pricing and Method of Analysis

Review of Literature

According to the subjective theory of value, the value of a good is not determined by any inherent property of the good, nor by the amount of labour necessary to produce the good, but instead value is determined by the importance an acting individual places on a good for the achievement of his desired ends (Menger, 1871). Thus, there is no unambiguous meaning to the word "value" as it may denote different things to different people. The goods under consideration embody varying amounts of attributes and are differentiated by the particular attribute composition that they possess. In most cases, the attributes themselves are not explicitly traded, so that one cannot observe the prices of these attributes directly. In such a case, hedonic pricing models are useful in order to determine how the price of a unit of commodity varies with the changes in set of attributes it possesses. As the demand varies with the variation in inherent qualities or attributes of a commodity like house, it is matter of behavioural aspects of individual economic agents like buyers, which is reflected in their choices for various attributes. Both the academia and real estate professionals have, therefore, accepted behavioural research as a valid and appropriate aspect of real estate market analysis (Gibler and Nelson, 2003; Bello and Bello, 2007; Rahadi *et al.,* 2012). Much work has been done on the relative impact of factors that influence house prices in the last few decades.

The review of relevant literature has been made under the following broad themes. At first review of studies applying various techniques for house pricing has been made. Then studies related to the theoretical and empirical development of hedonic technique are reviewed. Thereafter, studies on the impact of various housing attributes on housing price have been re-examined.

Methods Applied for Analysing House Pricing

The recent literature has been primarily concerned with estimating determinants of the demand for various housing characteristics inherent in a housing property and those are sold along with the whole property. Studies reveal how compositional and qualitative changes can affect the median or mix-adjusted measures (that adjust only for specicfic types of compositional change) of house prices. However, these methods cannot capture the impacts of qualitative changes in housing attributes and other social and environmental attributes associated with different houses on price. In order to overcome such limitations, several regression-based approaches have been proposed in the literature.

The *hedonic pricing method* has been applied in this study, which uses regression technique and explains price as a function of house attributes (Freeman, 1979; Li & Brown, 1980; Hulagu *et al.*, 2016). In many of the commonly used hedonic models these characteristics are being categorized into three groups: structural, neighbourhood, and environmental (Akpon, 1996). The second approach is *repeat sales method*, which applies changes of house selling price variation of the same housing unit at different points of time (Follain and Calhoun, 1997). The third one is a Hybrid approach, a combination of elements in the former two approaches and that was first recommended by Quigley (1995). The composition, which he imposes, result in more proficient factor estimates, if the hypothesized error is acceptable. However, only the first two approaches are commonly used. The results from a study of Australian house prices suggest that regression-based methods can provide a useful control for compositional effects (Hansen, 2006). In the present study, the hedonic approach is used because the repeat sales method is inappropriate due to two reasons. Data on house sale is not readily available and houses are not frequently transacted in the area.

Hedonic Analysis of Housing Demand

The theoretical and empirical developments in the use of the hedonic technique in the analysis of the demand for housing characteristics have been extensive. A housing unit is considered to be a heterogeneous commodity and each unit being different from others because of the different attributes. When a house is purchased or rented, the various attributes that go with it are also purchased or rented. Here, these attributes are broadly classified into structural, locational and neighbourhood characteristics. Surrounding environmental attributes are included in neighbourhood characteristics.

Relationships between a commodity and its characteristics have been studied by Lancaster (1966), who discussed the utility-bearing characteristics of the commodity, and Rosen (1974) who later extended the study to include a market between buyers and sellers to obtain the equilibrium-implicit prices of the characteristics. Although the work of Lancaster (1966) provided an implicit theoretical base for empirical estimates of hedonic housing price equations, Rosen (1974) developed a theoretical model for the structural analysis of hedonic prices.Now-a-days, Rosen's approach has been frequently used in analyzing the demand for housing attributes in literature.

Theoretical and Empirical Development of Hedonic Technique

The first formal contribution to hedonic price theory was made by A.T. Court in 1939, although there were some other informal studies. However, more than 15 years prior to Court, Haas (1922) had conducted a hedonic study that has been ascribed to have first published the term "hedonic", which is derived from the Greek word *hedonikos*, which simply means pleasure. In the economic context, it refers to the utility or satisfaction that one derives through the consumption of goods and services. The work of Haas (1922) has been regarded as the first among the applications of hedonic indices. He determined the prices of agricultural areas in Minnesota (USA) during the time period 1916-1919 on the basis of a linear regression model (Colwell and Dilmore, 1999). In another early work, Waugh (1928) provided evidences of the factors influencing vegetable prices by using hedonic pricing model.

One of the most influential studies was done by A.T. Court (1939), who was probably the first to estimate a quality-adjusted price index based on the hedonic price model. By many standards of contemporary hedonic price analysis, Court's work stands up quite well. It deals with problems of non-linearity and with changes in underlying goods bundles. It addresses a substantive methodological problem with circumspect analysis and interpretation. In his work, he explained that the marginal cost of the characteristics generates the prices of automobiles. Also, L.M. Court (1941) introduced the 'entrepreneurial and consumer demand theories for commodity spectra'. He derived the inverse utility function and *via* inverse utility function, he defined the counterparts of the Hicks-Allen elasticity of (quantity) substitution, which measures the substitutability of changes in pairs of commodity prices. He based his analysis on the linear continuum of commodities called 'commodity spectrum'. In the commodity spectrum, he considered infinite number of commodities into account. The points of the spectrum represent point-goods and the totality of point-goods within certain subinterval of the commodity spectrum that can be regarded as composing a particular grossly *differentiated* class of commodities. Housing, according to him, is considered as a good item to be used in the commodity-spectrum concept, even though the number of types of buildings is finite. But he claimed that the number is large enough to construct a continuous distribution or spectrum of such types to facilitate the treatment of any economic study of housing. Houthakker (1952) carried out a research on the 'compensated changes in quantities and qualities consumed'. He pointed out that quality variations of a commodity are ignored and the varieties (if any) of an item are evaluated as different commodities. To correct this, he introduced qualities as separate variables in the utility function, in addition to quantities. He examined compensated changes both in qualities and quantities *via* the Slutsky equation. However, his consumer theory was restricted in the sense that the quality of a commodity was described by one variable. However, he claimed that the methods he proposed could be easily extended to the multi-quality case.

Regression techniques were also applied to analyze the effects of quality changes on the price of cars (Griliches, 1961; and Maurer, Martin and Sebastian, 2004). Muth (1966) introduced the 'household production and consumer demand functions' for similar study. Introducing houses as intermediate inputs in the household production function, he derived the consumer demand function whose arguments are real income, relative prices of other goods and the ratios of relative prices of all commodities used to produce the final good to its price.

However, the two main approaches which contributed greatly to the theoretical development of hedonic prices are based on the works of Lancaster (1966) and Rosen (1974). The first approach was derived from Lancaster's (1966) consumer theory, and the second comes from the hedonic price model postulated by Rosen (1974). The chief technical novelty of Lancaster's theory lies in breaking away from the traditional approach that goods are the direct objects of utility and, instead, supposing that it is the properties or attributes of the goods from which utility is derived. Both approaches aimed to impute prices of attributes based on the relationship between the observed prices of differentiated products and the number of attributes associated with these products. Their models surmised that goods possess a myriad of attributes that combine to form bundles of characteristics (or objectively measurable, utility-affecting attributes), which the consumer values. However, these models have some fundamental differences.

The Lancastrian model presumes that goods are members of a group and that some or all of the goods in that group are consumed in combinations, subject to the consumer's budget. It also assumes a linear relationship between the price of goods and the characteristics contained in those goods. Implicit prices are constant over ranges of characteristic amounts. They can only change when there is a change in the combination of goods consumed. In comparison, Rosen's model assumes that there is a range of goods, but that consumers typically do not acquire preferred attributes by purchasing a combination of goods. Rather, each good is chosen from the spectrum of brands and is consumed discretely. The hedonic price approach also does not require joint consumption of goods within a group. Rosen postulated that unless it is possible for consumers to arbitrage attributes by untying and repackaging them, a non-linear relationship between the price of goods and their inherent attributes would be more probable. A non-linear price function implies that the implicit price is not a constant, but a function of the quantity of the attribute being bought and depending on the actual functional form of the equation, on the quantities of other attributes associated with the good as well. Thus, Lancaster's approach is more suited to consumer goods, whereas Rosen's model can be associated with durable goods like housing.

Over the past four decades, the hedonic-based regression approach has been employed extensively in housing market literature to investigate the relationship between house prices and housing characteristics. Specifically, the technique has been employed to achieve three main goals: (i) to explain the price formation of property assets (mainly residential) by identifying the main determinants of property prices, (ii) to isolate and quantify the impact of different structural (physical), locational and neighbourhood characteristics on property prices, and (iii) to account for changes in the price formation process across regions or over time (Lorenz, 2006).

Impact of Housing Attributes on Housing Price

Residential properties are multidimensional commodities characterized by durability, structural inflexibility, and spatial fixity (Chau, Ng and Hung, 2001). Typically, housing attributes are classified into locational attributes, structural attributes, and neighbourhood attributes. These attributes encompass both quantitative and qualitative attributes (Goodman, 1989). The market prices of the property can, therefore, be expressed as a function of locational, structural, and neighbourhood variables. The implicit price of each housing attribute, *ceteris paribus*, can be derived from the regression coefficients (Rosen, 1974). Several empirical studies have been conducted to examine the relationship between attribute preference and housing price. The marginal implicit values of the attributes are obtained by differentiating the hedonic price function with respect to each attribute (McMillan, Reid and Gillen, 1980). This function is known as the hedonic price function; hedonic because it is determined by the different qualities of the differentiated good and the pleasure (in economic terms utility) these would bring to the purchaser.

Locational Attributes

With respect to the locational attributes, distance to the central business district (CBD) and job accessibility has been found to significantly affect housing prices. Accessibility variables define the ease with which local amenities can be reached from the property where the individual live or is expected to stay. The early model developed by Kain and Quigley (1970) included distance to Central Business District, but it was not statistically significant. Waddell (2011) challenged the familiar assumption that a workplace is determined prior to the residence location. He endorsed for some interaction between these two variables by using a joint model specification. Moreover, he asserted that the degree to which residence location is driven by workplace location (or the opposite) depends on the degree to which workplace locations are distributed in a city, as well as on individual's socioe-conomic characteristics. One drawback of Waddell's study is that it does not incorporate transit and highway accessibility measures.

But several later studies found significant negative impact of distance to city or job centre on house prices. For instance, Soderberg and Janssen (2001) using the market as the city centre in Stockholm found significant negative impact on property price with increasing distance. Frew and Wilson (2002) found a significant connection between apartment location and rents in Portland Oregon Metropolitan Area in USA during 1993. They showed that rental values drop substantially for the first ten miles outside of the city centre, indicating that the downtown area is the central urban hub. Frew and Jud (2003) also estimated the value of a sample of apartment properties sold during 1996–99 in the greater Portland, Oregon area and found that property values decline with increasing distance from the city centre. Grimes and Liang (2007) also found that land is highly valued near the city centre, declining (non-linearly) as distance from the CBD increases. In the same way, Zou (2015) found house prices to decrease with distance from the CBD and walking distance to the nearest transit station. Nunns, Hitchins and Balderston (2015) further found evidence of spatial dependence in Auckland's housing market. In other words, the sale price of a single house is significantly correlated with neighbouring property values.

Hedonic price methods can be applied to separate parts of metropolitan areas to measure price differences both within and among such submarkets. It was observed that judicious subdivision of the metropolitan market using separate equations reveals valuable information about price variation within the metropolitan area (Goodman, 1978). McMillen and McDonald (1998) used distances to multiple employment centres in models to predict both population and employment densities in Los Angeles and suburban Chicago, respectively. Orford (cited in Ottensmann, Payton and Man, 2008) also combined distances to multiple employment centres with distances to other regional amenities in predicting housing prices (Orford *op. cit.*).

Cost of travel, travelling time, availability and convenience of different modes have all been employed to measure accessibility to CBD. Vessali (1996) consolidated the empirical evidence of 37 studies on accessibility and concluded that accessibility to transit tends to appreciate residential property value by 6 to 7 per cent. So, Tse and Ganesan (1997) showed that the accessibility to minibuses emerges as the most influential in determining house prices based on a sample of a large residential area of the middle-income class in Hong Kong. In this case, the use of minibuses as a daily transport mode is important because minibuses pick up commuters close to their homes and are widely used for connecting to other transport modes. Welch (2010), in a study of Atlanta, reaffirmed that accessibility to rail station appreciates property value. However, he found that property located in economically strong area benefit much more as compared to those located in economically weak area for similar transit proximity.

Changes in accessibility were found to affect total property prices significantly – both in a statistical and practical sense. Kockelman (1997) found that changes in accessibility and travel costs affect land and dwelling-unit values in highly significant ways both statistically and economically. Srour, Kockelman and Dunn (2002) used location accessibility as a major explanatory variable for property-valuation and residential location modelling. Access to jobs, shopping centre and parks were found to be statistically and practically significant (Musa, 2016; Nakamura, 2018). They also reveal relations of interest with land rent estimates, which are calculated based on normalized residuals of property-valuation models. Such an association has not been made so clear before, and it suggests that rent formulations may prove an important measure of access, since they follow consumers' willingness to pay for location. Savings in transportation costs and the frequency of transport services appear to have positive impacts on housing prices. However, Kain and Quigley (1970) found that better educated and higher income households tend to reside farther away from CBD, which may be due to preference for tranquility and cleaner environment.

There are studies that used the hedonic price model to estimate the implicit price of views (Jayasekare, Herath, Wickramasuriya and Perez, 2019). Li and Brown (1980) asserted that higher on-site visual quality is strongly associated with higher sales price of residential properties. They estimated that the implied price differential between the highest and the lowest index amounts to $2520. Rodriguez and Sirmans (1994) examined the role of scenic view in housing market in Fairfax County, Virginia and found that a good scenic view adds about 8 per cent to the value of a single-family house.

Tse (2002) affirmed that there is a strong preference for a sea view in Hong Kong indicating that residents are willing to pay a higher price for a sea facing house with a readily sea view. Fleischer (2011) calculated the room prices of hotels situated along the Mediterranean Sea and found that hotels charge higher prices (by about 10%) for a room with a sea view compared to a room without sea view. Lansford and Jones (1995) in their study of the implicit price of recreational and aesthetic benefits found proximity to Lake Travis (with better view of the lake) in Texas command a high premium on residential property prices. Kruse and Ahmann (2009) also observed that Lake Adjacency does have a positive and significant impact on residential property values and that, all else being equal, properties with lake proximity or with a lake view are worth more than properties without these characteristics. Benson, Hansen, Schwartz and Smersh (1998) employed a detailed classification system that categorizes views on the basis of both type and quality of view to estimate the value of the view amenity. They estimated that ocean view and lake view command a high premium in single-family residential prices in Bellingham, Washington and the study also found a positive relationship between the quality of view and property prices.

Corell, Lillydahl and Singell (1978) found that green views have a significant positive impact on adjacent property values. They estimated that distance from the greenbelt has a statistically significant negative impact on the price of residential property. Other things being identical, there is a $42 decrease in the residential property price for every 10 feet distance away from the greenbelt. Jim and Chen (2006) also estimated that view of green spaces and proximity to water bodies increase housing price, contributing notably at 7.1 per cent and 13.2 per cent, respectively in Haizhu district in the core area of Guangzhou (China). Rohani (2012) on the other hand combined view and access to amenity and found that views and amenity of the Hauraki Gulf together has significant impact on property prices in the study area. On an average, other things remaining the same, a broad water view increased the mean land value by 50 per cent while locations on the coastline increased land value by 43 per cent. Similarly, Bourassa *et al.* (2003) found that the hedonic value of aesthetic externalities increased more rapidly than house prices from 1986 to 1996 in Louisville's neighbourhoods. On the other hand, Tse and Love (2000) found that the attribute of a cemetery view has a significant negative impact on property value in the Hong Kong real estate market.

Interestingly, the hedonic price model has also been employed in the study of the influence of superstitious beliefs on housing prices, especially in the Chinese community. It has been observed that apartments with lucky number (example, number 3, 6, 8 or 9) have been found to be sold at significantly higher prices in comparison to those with unlucky numbers such as 4 (Bourassa and Peng, 1999; and Fortin, Hill and Huang, 2013). Although Chau, Ma and Ho (2001) found that a lucky floor number is a valuable housing attribute, the demand for flats with lucky numbers is found to highly volatile in another study by Ho (2008).

Structural Attributes

Structural variables define the fabric of each building and the plot upon which it is built. A wide range of structural variables were calculated for each property including ground floor area, garden area and property type. Several empirical studies have found that structural attributes such as floor area or size has a significant positive impact on house prices (Carroll, Clauretie and Jensen, 1996; Selim, 2008; Zou, 2015; and Nunns, Hitchins & Balderston, 2015). Interestingly, prices seem to be more responsive to building size (floor space) than they are to land area (Bourassa *et al.*, 2003; Samarasinghe and Sharpe, 2010). Rodriguez and Sirmans (1994) also estimated that number of rooms; bedrooms and bathrooms significantly affect the house prices positively. So, Tse and Ganesan (1997) in their study of seven housing estates for 1994 in Hong Kong found that the valuation of a higher-level floor turns out to be more expensive than that of a middle floor. This observation was reaffirmed by Conroy, Narwold and Sandy (2013). The results of their study also suggest that there is a higher-floor premium for condominiums in San Diego. Specifically, an increase in the floor level is associated with about a 2.2 per cent increase in sale price. But the higher-floor premium appears to be quadratic in price, suggesting that price increases at a decreasing rate above the mean floor level. However, Wong *et al.* (2006) based on a sample of highly homogeneous housing units in buildings of varying heights, found that (1) the floor-level premium was not constant, but diminished as floor level increases; and (2) there was a positive and significant premium for units in low-rise buildings over those in high-rise ones. Chau, Wong and Yiu (2004) established that a balcony has a value enhancement effect on high-rise residential properties, regardless of the view outside.

Good architectural design also commands a price premium (Millhouse, 2005). Ahlfeldt and Maennig (2011) have also shown that large architectural structures, like arenas, emanate positive externalities that improve location desirability in their neighbourhoods. Researchers also concluded that age of house is negatively related to the prices of properties (Kain and Quigley, 1970; Rodriguez and Sirmans, 1994; and Zou, 2015). However, Li and Brown's (1980) study found a positive effect of age on some buildings due to historical significance or vintage effects of the buildings. Nunns, Hitchins & Balderston (2015) also pointed out that people place a higher value on 'heritage' buildings (pre-1940) in Auckland, Australia.

The provision of other housing attributes such as garage significantly appreciates housing prices (Forrest, Glen and Ward, 1996). Moreover, Samarasinghe and Sharpe (2010) pointed out that provision of more garages is associated with higher housing sale prices. Garrod and Willis (1992) also pointed out that presence of patio, air and water heating systems, and the numbers of fireplaces positively affect house prices. Other empirical works found that structural quality, such as exterior structure, condition of floors, windows; walls and levels of housekeeping have an impact on housing prices (Kain and Quigley, 1970; Morris, Woods and Jacobson, 1972; and Nunns, Hitchins & Balderston, 2015). Improved quality of infrastructural facilities associated with the house such as water, electricity, access road, drainage, fence etc. also enhance the rental values of residential properties (Augustina, 2015).

Neighbourhood Attributes

Neighbourhood variables describe the characteristics of local area (surrounding) in which the property is located (De and Vupru, 2018). The hedonic pricing approach has also been used to explore the impacts of neighbourhood attributes on the property prices. However, the concept of 'neighbourhood' is contentious and there is no consensus in the literature regarding, which variable best proxy neighbourhood quality, an unobservable variable (De and Vupru, 2017).

Several empirical studies have found that the qualities of schools in the neighbourhood tend to appreciate the value of residential property (Haurin and Brasington, 1996; Black, 1999; and Max, 2004). However, it was pointed out in some other studies that there are also negative externalities of 'year-round school' on the residential properties in the neighbourhood areas (Clauretie and Neill, 2000). Proximity to shopping complexes generates both positive and negative externalities (Des Rosiers, Lagana, Theriault and Beaudoin, 1996). But the size of a shopping centre is found to have a positive contributory effect on the values of surrounding residential properties (Sirpal, 1994; and Des Rosiers, Lagana, Theriault and Beaudoin, 1996). Also, places of worship, such as churches, appears to affect residential houses in a positive way (Carrol, Clauretie and Jensen, 1996). Urban forests also exert positive externalities (Tyrvainen, 1997).

On the other hand, despite beneficial effect of easy access for treatment, availability of hospital in the neighbouring area is found to have a negative impact due to superstitious beliefs of house buyers in Seoul, South Korea (Huh & Kwak, 1997). As opposed to this, Tatt, Yi & Lin (2015) found that condominium price is increased for every kilometre nearer to a hospital in Kuala Lumpur. However, Peng and Chiang (2015) asserted that hospitals exert both positive and negative impacts of residential property prices and suggested that hospitals would only be highly evaluated in a 'close-but-not-too-close' geographic location. From urban planning perspective, hospitals, which are crucial in ageing societies, may reduce its negative externalities by creating spatial barriers such as scenic roads to keep distance from adjacent properties.

Ambient air quality also comes into play in the determination of house prices or rents of apartments. Ridker and Henning (1967), Anderson and Crocker (1971), Chay and Greenstone (1998), Chattopadhyay (1999), Zabel and Kiel (2000), and Murty and Gulati (2004) using hedonic technique examined the relationship between air quality and property values and established that air pollution turns out to be relatively significant variable in explaining residential property values. All these studies found significant willingness to pay for improvement in ambient air quality and thus the increased house prices. Thus, preference for environmental or natural resource quality can be reflected in the variation in house prices, and would be suitably estimated by using hedonic pricing techniques, as shown by Ketkar, 1992 (cited in Kiel,1995), Leggett and Bockstael (2000), and Hoehn and Deaton (2002).

The questions of hazards, security etc., are also important criteria in case of people's preference of residential houses. There is a clear indication that crime has a statistically significant negative impact on house prices (Thaler, 1978; and Frischtak and Mandel, 2012). Though crime is predominantly a local issue, Pope and Pope (2012) pointed out that a nationwide decrease in crime has a statistically significant impact on property prices and suggested that decreasing crime leads to increase in property values.

Over time, with population growth and technological development coupled with higher living standards, travel frequency has tremendously increased. This has also resulted in increase in noise pollution across all urban areas. Nelson (1982) reviewed nine empirical studies conducted previously in Canada and United States and concluded that the price of a house located adjacent to a major highway depreciates on an average by 8 to 10 per cent. Wilhelmsson (2000) also found significant negative effect of noise pollution on house prices in Angby, a suburb of Stockholm, Sweden. He estimated that a single-family house of SEK 9,75,000 would sell for SEK 6,50,000 if located near a road where noise is loud. Theebe (2004) estimated that noise levels above 65 db appear to be capitalized into house prices, with a maximum discount of approximately 12 per cent. However, the discount varies across sub-markets and is a non-linear function of the noise level. Several other empirical studies have also specifically analyzed the impact of airport noise and found significant negative impact of airport noise on housing prices (Nelson, 1980; Pennington, Topham and Ward, 1990; Espey and Lopez, 2000; Bell, 2001; and Cohen and Coughlin, 2008). However, Rahmatian and Cockerill (2004) pointed out that there exist two distinct measurable price gradients that distinguish large airports from small airports. They estimated that houses located near a large airport have a price gradient that is significantly larger than houses located near small airports.

Researches on hedonic method also indicate that residential property values are reduced by increased proximity to hazardous waste sites (Deaton and Hoehn, 2002, 2004; Braden, Feng and Won, 2011). However, it was also shown that people's perception about hazardous waste sites might also change sometimes. Kohlhase (1991) pointed out that a significant discount in the price of houses in Houston's housing market located close to toxic waste dumps. The result was found only after the sites have been identified and publicized by the Environmental Protection Agency (EPA). Before that knowledge coming to public, neighbouring people hardly gave any importance to it. Vor and Groot (2011) also found industrial sites to have a statistically significant negative impact on property values.

Interdependence of various attributes has also been highlighted in some studies. It was found that consumers of rented house consider floor area, water supply and power supply to be complementary to each other and the other characteristics of house as substitutes of the floor area (Mishra and Ngullie, 2008). But the study suffers from the limited sample size with many coefficients to estimate and they found the coefficients of most of the relevant explanatory variables insignificant.

Besides, hedonic pricing technique has also been applied to the valuation of a wide variety of products including durable consumer products such as computers and cars, agricultural commodities and wildlife related recreation resources too while other applications have involved the estimation of the benefits of environmental improvements.

Limitations of Hedonic Models

Despite its wide and popular uses, hedonic measures are not without their limitations. In particular, the use of regression techniques implies that hedonic models are only as good as the specications used to derive them, and often depend on the quality of the data available. If hedonic regressions omit variables that have signicant impacts on house prices that can result in biased estimates of pure price changes. Analogously, if the relationships between the attributes of houses and their effect on prices are incorrectly specified, for instance through an incorrect functional form, this could also result in biased estimates (Hansen, 2006). Meese and Wallace (1997) said that drawbacks to the hedonic regression approach are ignorance of both the functional form of the relation and of the appropriate set of house characteristics to include in the analysis, which can result in conflicting estimates in the model. However, the functional form issue is resolved by taking different techniques. Even if this model has been widely used, misspecification of models, multicollinearity, independent variable interactions, heteroskedasticity, non-linearity and outliers can affect the efficiency of hedonic price model in real estate appraisals (Limsombunchai, 2004). Els and Fintel (2008) also pointed out that difficulty in identifying the neighbourhood characteristics due to similarity in a specific neighbourhood is an important drawback of hedonic pricing method. Moreover, these characteristics are measured based on the willingness to pay of the buyer for that specific attribute provided that the buyer is aware of its existence. They further noted that hedonic method considers the combined characteristics of the property transacted. This method is more complicated than other methods and needs skill in statistics on interpreting variables and selecting functional forms, which are not a direct process.

The weaknesses of the hedonic method and the assumptions behind it relate to problems of individual perception, subjectivity, continuity, aversion behaviour, market segmentation and the assumption of equilibrium (Maddison, 2001). Another weakness of hedonic pricing method (HPM) is that it can only estimate user benefits, in particular with respect to the recreation value of the area (Garrod and Willis, 1999). HPM also suffers from several analytical problems such as omissions of important characteristics, doubts about the correct mathematical specification of the model, and so on (Garrod, 1994). However, if the limitations of HPM are properly taken into account, the method can be useful in revealing valuable information about the values of attributes. Therefore, these limitations need to be addressed prior to confronting the model with real-world data (Vanslembrouck, Huylenbroeck and Meensel, 2005).

Advantages of the Hedonic Approach

The primary problem related with the evaluation of real estate price is its "heterogeneity" (Follain and Calhoun, 1997). In housing market, it is not easy to get many houses with similar quality. The facilities provided and the standard of construction may vary greatly between houses. They also added that bigger heterogeneity is more complicated in valuing, due to variation in quality. Even if buildings have the same facilities, the rate of usage depends on the building's age. Besides, the house price has complex individuality (Shimizu & Nishimura, 2007). As a result, we need to adapt a method in order to manage change in quality of real estate through time. One way to avoid these difficulties is to estimate quality differences using regression analysis (Rosen, 1974).

Several empirical studies show that hedonic approach is more preferable relative to other methods. Mark and Goldberg (1984) evaluated hedonic and repeat sales methods for neighbourhoods in Vancouver and concluded that hedonic approach is better relative to repeat sales that become visible to undervalue increase in price. Meese and Wallace (1997) also argued in favour of the hedonic approach when they applied it for US housing market. The reason is that it is less affected by sample-selection bias and captures better the inherent prices of housing attributes compared to repeat sales approach. Clapham *et al.* (2006) also discovered that indices developed by Swedish data set using hedonic approach are less prone to adjustments than repeat sales. Moreover, hedonic approach is less sensitive to tiny segmented markets (Francke, Vos and Janssen, 2000). A study by Wilhelmsson (2008) to construct a price index for the segmented housing market also shows that hedonic regression method is more suitable than the repeated sales method.

The main advantage of hedonic price method is that it is based on real market selection by professionals and theoretical background (Els and Fintel, 2008). Besides, real estate data tend to be easily available, as real estate is a huge investment in many countries, which requires appropriate record keeping. Limsombunchai (2004) also added that managing property attributes is one of the advantages of hedonic method. He further noted that this allows a person to differentiate the impact of the real property appreciation and changing observation composition.

• Another key advantage of the hedonic pricing method is that one only needs to have certain information, such as the property price, the composition of housing attributes, and a proper specification of the functional relationships. The marginal attribute prices are obtained by estimating the parameters of the hedonic price function. It is a straightforward approach because only the coefficients of the estimated hedonic regression are needed to indicate the preference structure.

Despite the disputable assumptions associated with hedonic approach, which involve substantial simplification and abstraction from a complex reality, the hedonic price model has been deployed extensively in housing market research (Freeman, 1979; Leggett & Bockstael, 2000; Chau, Ma and Ho, 2001). As astutely observed by Freeman (1979), the data may be inadequate; variables are measured with error; and the definitions of empirical variables are seldom precise, but these do not render the technique invalid for empirical purposes.

Thus, in spite of the limitations of the hedonic pricing method, it is also seen that this method has several advantages especially in the housing market. It has been found to be most widely accepted and hence used method in estimation of housing prices. Therefore, in this present study the hedonic approach is used.

Methodology

The study on the determinants of demand for housing in Dimapur town has been completed in successive steps. In this chapter, methodology used for the purpose of analysis has been described in detail. First of all, nature and sources of data used in the analysis of the trends of residential properties, amenities and demand for housing in Dimapur town, and various tools and techniques that have been employed in analyzing data for the purpose of the study have been discussed. Thereafter, the nature of primary data collected through field survey to analyse the socio-economic characteristics of the surveyed respondents and estimate the impact of various housing attributes (determinants) on the demand for housing, sampling technique adopted, and techniques of analysis of data have been described. Here, the methods of analysis of the socio-economic characteristics of respondents/ households are discussed first. Thereafter, various tools and techniques used for analyzing the determinants of demand for housing, and factors affecting choice of housing have been discussed. From these analyses, we tried to bring out some policy implications for the purpose of better housing policy.

Trends of Residential Properties, Amenities and Demand for Housing

Development of residential properties in any area generates both positive and negative impacts. Economic prosperity of an urban centre attracts people of various categories who ultimately require appropriate housing facilities to pursue their urban lives. Moreover, owners of rental housing also benefit from the housing market. However, unplanned growth of residential buildings in many cases causes environmental hazards like hazardous waste dumped in various sites, air and noise pollution, and road congestions leading to vehicular traffic problems and several other issues.

The development of residential properties and amenities are both demand-pushed and demand-pulled phenomena. Availability of adequate and affordable housing and better amenities increases the demand for housing by attracting new entrants. Also, higher demand for housing and other amenities due to rise in population exerts a positive growth of residential houses and amenities. In order to examine the trends of residential properties and amenities, secondary data from the various census reports and Government offices were collected and analyzed. This gives a picture of the changing population, residential properties and amenities over the decades 1971 to 2011.

Collection of Data

In order to examine the trends of residential properties and amenities, both primary and secondary data have been collected. The secondary data on growth of population in Dimapur over time, its density, number of households, and number of buildings, availability and quality of amenities like source of drinking water and its supply, cooking fuel, structural variations of housing in the town etc. have been collected from urban development authority, municipal authority, census reports and other government reports. The demand for housing and land/property prices are positively related. However, due to the absence of Government administered prices in Dimapur, secondary data available with the Revenue Branch of the district administration cannot throw any light on the actual value of land prevalent across the town or over time. The actual value of the transaction is not projected in the official records because the buyers are found to have paid the revenue for much lesser value than the actual value of land prevalent in Dimapur town. Since there are no reliable secondary data on land prices, the information has been collected through direct personal interviews from Councillors, Gaon Buras (G.Bs.), Colony Chairmen and prominent citizens across the 23 wards.

Mode of Analysis

The data on population along with residential properties and amenities have been taken from secondary sources and tabulated. Then their decadal growth rates have been calculated and presented using appropriate diagrams. Increase in land prices over the years have been considered to reflect the rising requirement and scarcity of housing and thereby housing prices. Directly growth of scarcity of houses is difficult to get since houses are scarcely sold independently in the area. Ward-wise differences in the land prices and its growth both at current prices and constant prices during 2000–2015 have been analysed to understand the spatio-temporal variation. The constant prices have been computed by using the CPI to adjust for the inflation with 2004-05 as the base year. The analysis has been carried out on the basis of land use which has been categorized into six parts as per the classification adopted by Land Records and Survey Department, Dimapur. As per the importance, these categories are Special Commercial, Commercial A, Commercial B, Residential A, Residential B, and Homestead and barren or agricultural. The temporal and periodic growth of the prices for each category of land has also been estimated.

Socio-economic Characteristics and Determinants of Demand for Housing

A primary survey has been conducted during 2015-16 in the study area for collecting information on socio-economic, demographic and various housing attributes at household level and use them to analyze the impacts of various determinants and/or attributes of housing demand.

Selection of Sample and Data Collection

As mentioned earlier, Dimapur Municipal Council area comprised 27,857 households across 23 wards (GoI, 2011). Out of 27,857 households in the town, 19,051 (68.39%) households are in rented houses while 7,403 (26.58%) households reside in their own houses.

The sample size is approximated by using Cochran's (1963) formula

$$n_0 = \frac{z^2pq}{e^2}$$

Here, n_0 is sample size, z^2 is the desired confidence level, p is estimated proportion of an attribute that is present in the population and it is assumed to be 0.5 for maximum variability, q is 1-p. Here, 95 per cent level of confidence is considered and on the basis of the above formula, e^2 or margin error or confidence interval is 4.38 per cent. Thus, 490 can be the representative sample size.

On an average, twenty (20) households each were selected by simple random sampling without replacement from all the 23 wards in the study area. However, from the larger ward proportionately more numbers were also selected. The details of sample selection are shown in Table 2.1. After proper scrutiny for the erratic and incomplete information, finally, 490 interview schedules are used for the analysis.

Table 2.1: Ward-wise distribution of Sample Households in 2011 and Selection of Sample Size

Ward	Total Households	Sample Households	Rejected	Sample Used
1	1249	22	1	21
2	723	20	Nil	20
3	1258	22	2	20
4	1952	25	1	24
5	1676	24	2	22
6	584	20	Nil	20
7	1814	24	1	23
8	847	20	Nil	20
9	1410	22	1	21
10	906	20	Nil	20
11	952	20	Ni!	20
12	1582	23	1	22
13	1572	23	Nil	23
14	1428	22	Nil	22
15	1193	21	Nil	21

(Contd.)

Ward	Total Households	Sample Households	Rejected	Sample Used
16	1785	24	1	23
17	508	20	Nil	20
18	1026	21	Nil	21
19	268	20	Nil	20
20	1331	22	Nil	22
21	1149	21	Nil	21
22	1043	21	Nil	21
23	1614	23	Nil	23
Total	**27,870**	**500**	**10**	**490**

Note: (i) A minimum of 20 samples from each ward is used. However, for every ward with more than 1000 households, 1 extra sample for up to every 200 households (e.g. 1 sample for 1 to 200 additional households). (ii) Some questionnaires were rejected due to incomplete, erratic and inconsistent information.

Source: Economic Census Report, 2011 & Field Survey Conducted during 2015-16.

Out of 490 total sample units, 414 are tenant households and 76 are owner occupied households. The information has been collected through an interview schedule from the respective sample respondents in each ward. In most cases, the head of the household (respondent) were given an explanation of what information we needed from them. Sometimes, the respondent had to seek assistance of other members of the family to provide the appropriate information.

Information on demographic and socio-economic characteristics of the households such as age, sex, marital status, family size, community, domicile, religion, education of head and spouse, type of employment of head and spouse, and income of head and the family have been collected through an interview schedule. Other details like number of families living in the same building, possession and type of personal vehicle, and employment of domestic servant have also been collected. For the tenant respondents, duration of stay in the town (in years), time taken for arranging first rented accommodation (in months), and desire to change accommodation and the reasons thereof have been recorded. For rental units, we observe rental prices, but not housing and land values. For owner-occupied units, we observe both housing and land values as well as implicit rental prices (equivalent market rent value). The implicit rent is taken as a proxy for house price (rent in this case) because data on actual sale/purchase is not readily available. It may be noted that transactions of houses are not made frequently in the survey area. Hence, the current monthly rent paid (equivalent market rent value for owner-occupied houses) of the sample respondents are recorded and the relation of rent with various socio-economic, structural, neighbourhood and locational characteristics is examined for hedonic pricing analysis. With regard to the tenants, monthly rents at two points of time (ten years wherever available) are collected so that the average annual growth of rent across the wards can be explained. In respect of owner-occupied respondents, the size and the current prices of their respective plot/land and house along with its prices a decade before (wherever available) are also collected. This is also done in order to get an idea of average annual growth rate of price per unit (per square feet).

From both the tenants and owners, information on structural attributes, locational attributes and neighbourhood attributes in regard to the residential building have been collected. Availability and quality of floor, wall, roof, number of rooms, toilet, water supply in the house, sewer type, overall condition of house etc. (structural characteristics), quality of approach road, location of the house near river, distance from workplace, business centre, rail station, shopping centre etc. (locational characteristics), household perception of security, pollution and proximity to local amenities such as departmental shop, worship place, educational institution etc. (neighbourhood characteristics) are collected from each respondent.

Description of Data

As mentioned above, information is collected consisted of both categorical as well as numeric data. Some of the variables like sex, marital status, domicile status, attached toilet, flower bed, garage, proximity to garbage dumping site, heavy traffic noise and veranda or balcony have binary values 1 and 0. Variables, such as education, occupation, vehicle type, external wall material, floor material, roof material, fencing, compound, quality of approach road, sewer type, water supply, overall house condition and quality of approach road have ordinal values starting from 0 and following the Likert scale higher value indicate better situation/quality. Educational attainment has been categorized into five categories, viz. illiterate, literate, secondary, higher secondary and graduate and above. Illiterate represents those who cannot read and write, literate for those who studied up to class 7, secondary for those who passed class 10 but less than class 12, higher secondary for those who passed class 12 but less than graduation degree, and graduate and above for those with graduate and above degrees. Occupation has been classified as unemployed, private employment, self-employed/business, government service and others. Here, in the others category, all those who cannot be included in any of the former categories are considered such as retired servicemen. Religion of the respondents is categorized into Muslim, Hindu, Christian, Buddhist, Jain and Sikh. Religion and occupation are ranked on the basis of average rent paid by the respective groups. Information on the monthly income were collected as numerical data and grouped in various ranges. Vehicle owner has been categorized into no vehicle, two-wheeler, three-wheeler and four-wheeler (car).

Some variables such as availability of certain attributes (location near river, garbage dumping site and heavy traffic noise) are binary having values of 0 and 1. Similarly, variables such as material of external wall, floor, roof, water connection, water supply, sewer type, overall house condition and quality of approach road to the house are represented by ordinal values from 0 onwards with higher values indicating better condition. The exterior wall material used for the house has been categorized into bamboo or wood, combination of bamboo/wood with concrete (bricks), and the whole concrete. The floor material has been categorized into earth, wood, cement and marble/tiles. Roof has been categorized into tin/asbestos and concrete. Water supply is categorized like insufficient, just sufficient, reasonably good and 24 hours supply respectively. Overall condition of the housing unit has been classified according to the respondent's opinion as unsatisfactory, medium or excellent. Quality of approach road to the residence is categorized into no approach road, road with earthen surface, stone and earth, and cemented/ blacktopped.However, in case of security standard, a 5-point Likert scale has been employed where 2 represents very good, 1 for good, 0 for normal, -1 for not up to the mark and -2 for very bad. The size of house and land area is measured in terms of square feet. The distances from various places of importance and other local amenities (workplace, school, market, places of entertainment and leisure etc.) are measured in terms of metres. The data collected has been utilized for analysis after segregating the sample units between owner occupied and tenant households.

Mode of Data Analysis

For analyzing various socio-economic and demographic characteristics of sample respondents across the wards, ward-wise percentage distribution of various characteristics has been tabulated and analysed for both owner and tenant categories. Percentage distribution of various socio-economic characteristics is also portrayed using appropriate diagrams (pie chart or bar diagrams). To get an idea about the economic conditions of the surveyed respondents across the wards, per capita income (PCI) has been computed for each sample household and ward-wise average of that has been computed for both the groups. To analyse income disparity, ward-wise coefficients of variation (CV) in PCI and overall CV of the surveyed tenant and owner households have been computed for the purpose of analysis. In order to check whether housing is becoming scarcer and more time is required to find rented accommodation in recent years, the duration of stay (year) in Dimapur among the tenants and the time required to get their first rented house (month) has been analyzed through tabular presentation and correlation as well as regression analysis.

Ward-wise percentage distribution of various structural attributes and civic amenities possessed by the sample residential buildings in Dimapur town is analyzed. Each attribute has been categorized into a number of available options representing quality of house and availability of facilities. Ward-wise percentage distribution of various structural attributes and civic amenities have been computed and from the average percentages of the best options so calculated for each attribute, and then ranking of wards in terms of percentage of the availability and quality of the various structural attributes and civic amenities has been computed by simple summation of the percentages of all the available attributes in a particular category (structural or civic amenities) and dividing it by the total number of attributes and amenities. This is done to have a better idea about the overall variations in the structural attributes, and coefficient of variation as well as Chi-square test have been applied for examining the variability across the respondents and wards. In order to check the correlation among the selected attributes or amenities that helps in understanding whether the quality of one structural attribute or amenity (say, better floor material), possessed by a housing unit is related to quality of other structural attributes or amenities involved in the same unit, Fisher's intra-class correlation has been employed (Fisher, 1954).

In order to know the variation in temporal growth of house price, a comparison of average growth rates of the houses built before and after the year 2000 has been analyzed. Also, categorizing houses on the basis of its structural quality, viz. houses built with bamboo/wood wall, concrete wall but with tin roof and concrete wall with concrete roof, a comparative analysis of average annual growth rates of their prices have been carried out. Also, coefficients of variations of rent, land prices and house prices have been computed.

Analysis of Impacts of Various Housing Attributes on Housing Price (Rent)

Sale and purchase of house in market is different from that of other commodity as houses are not sold or purchased frequently or on a regular basis. Hence, sale or purchase value of house is inadequate and rental value, which also depends on choice of tenants and on the basis of various facilities and housing structures, is considered for the analysis. The hedonic pricing method has provided a framework for the analysis of differentiated goods like housing units, whose individual features may not have distinctive observable market prices. Over the past four decades, this method has been utilized extensively in the housing market literature to investigate the relationship between house prices or pricing of housing attributes.The hedonic approach looks at the price or rent as being determined by the attributes of the housing unit and the surrounding neighbourhood, on which the potential buyer or tenant in this case depends for revealing their choice. The hedonic regression methodology recognizes that housing is a composite product and that housing units are heterogeneous. While the attributes are not sold separately, regressing sales price or rent of this composite product on those attributes yields the marginal contribution of each attribute to the sales price. Of course, there is a basic difference for the purchase and become owner of a house and taking a house on rent. The residential owners look at various attributes for the long term stay and hence may insist on some attributes more like availability of water in the long run, location as the family has to commute for the whole life or over generations, surrounding environment etc. On the other hand, despite some limitation tenant choose a house for residence where the primary objectives are fulfilled like nearness to the workplace, security of family as he will leave women at home during working hours, but can compromise with some attributes like surrounding environment for temporary stay and for smaller rent. So, there may be a variation in emphasis given to various attributes by the owner purchasers and tenants. However, the major considerations for choosing a house for purchase or rent remain same.

Typically, the housing attributes are classified into locational attributes (L), structural attributes (S), and neighbourhood attributes (N). These attributes encompass both quantitative and qualitative variables (Goodman, 1989). The implicit market prices (P) of the property can be expressed as: $P = f(L, S, N)$. The partial derivative of this price function with respect to any attribute is the implicit marginal attribute price, *ceteris paribus* (Rosen, 1974). This implicit price of the housing attribute is revealed in the regression coefficient. As mentioned in the previous paragraph, all buyers/tenants perceive the amounts of attributes embodied in the housing product to be identical, but their subjective valuations of each component attribute may differ. The price of the house, then, is the sum of the implicit prices for the attributes that are contained in it. It, thus, enables us to test and analyze the possible influence of each of the many attributes on the house price.

Rosen's model, which is employed in this analysis, involves two steps. The first stage hedonic estimates may be used to calculate the implicit price of housing characteristics.Thereafter, using implicit prices a demand function is estimated in the second stage of analysis. However, Rosen also proposed a second stage that involved regression of marginal prices of each characteristic at the bundles actually purchased by consumers on the characteristics of the good and consumer demographic variables. This second stage was intended to recover a demand function for each characteristic. However, it was later discovered (Brown and Rosen, 1982; Follain and Jimenez, 1985; Bartik, 1987; Epple, 1987; Brasington and Hite, 2005) that the second-stage regression had a simultaneity problem because consumers with a high preference for certain characteristics would naturally purchase bundles that contain large amounts of those characteristics (Bajari and Benkard, 2005). This simultaneity problem causes inconsistent estimates in the second stage. Epple suggests that this problem can be solved if data are available on many markets in which tastes can be assumed to be the same. However, data of this kind have proved difficult to find, and as a result, Rosen's second stage is not as widely used today. Therefore, for the estimation of the impacts of the various attributes on demand for housing and housing price (or rent), the first step of Rosen's model has been used in the present analysis.

However, for the sake of convenience, we shall retain the basic notations of Rosen. Let z be a vector of housing attributes $(z_1, z_2, \ldots, z_k)$ and x be the composite good, which includes all other goods except housing. Suppose that consumers have the utility function U(x, z, C), where C represents household demographic characteristics that may affect preferences. Assuming that is the numeraire good and that a consumer buys only one house, he maximizes his utility subject to the budget constraint,

$$x + \mathrm{P(z)} = \mathrm{Y},$$

where Y is income and P(z) is the price of a house with attributes z. The consumer chooses and z to satisfy the equation,

$$\frac{\partial P}{\partial z_i} = \frac{\frac{\partial U}{\partial z_i}}{\frac{\partial U}{\partial x}} \quad \text{......(2.1)}$$

which states that marginal price of attribute z equals the marginal willingness to pay (WTP), or the marginal rate of substitution. The marginal WTP function on the right-hand side of (2.1) is also referred to as the inverse demand function for attribute z_i.

The first stage of the Rosen's two-step procedure involves specification of the form of the housing price function P(z) and econometric estimation of its parameters. Marginal bids for a housing attribute are then determined by taking the derivative of the hedonic price function with respect to the attribute in question. The hedonic slope, which depends on the attribute levels, can be used to measure the WTP for a small increase in an attribute.

Morancho (2003) asserted that though Rosen (1974) provided the theoretical foundation for the development of the hedonic house pricing, however, the theory does not give a basis to know the functional form to be used. Cropper, Deck and McConnell (1988) suggest linear form, semi-logarithmic and double logarithmic forms instead of quadratic forms when some relevant explanatory variables are omitted. They concluded that the linear form performs one of the best in the presence of misspecification.

Data, which have been employed for the purpose of the analysis, have been grouped into structural, locational and neighbourhood attributes. The value of Variance Inflation Factor (VIF) has been considered to check the incidence of multi-collinearity, and the variables with high VIF values have been dropped. Next, in order to avoid the problem of heteroskedasticity, the numeric variables have been transformed into their natural log forms (Wooldridge, 2015).

The functional form of the hedonic equation employed for the analysis of impacts of various housing attributes for both the tenants and owner-occupied households is

$$\log P_i = \alpha_1 + \sum_{i=1}^{n} \beta_i \log z_i + \sum_{i=1}^{n} \gamma_i X_i + U_i \quad \dots\dots\dots (2.2)$$

where P_i represents monthly rent paid by the ith respondent, z_i represents quantitative explanatory variables like age of house, carpet area, distances from places of importance etc. and X_i represents categorical variables like floor material, quality of approach road, security standard, etc., α_1 represents the intercept and U_i the random disturbance term with usual classical regression properties. Here β_i represents the elasticity of P_i with respect to ith explanatory variable Z, while γ_i is the impact of a marginal change in the ith categorical variable on the rate of changes in P_i.

Along with the estimated regression coefficients, the White heteroskedasticity test values with their significance level have been estimated to check for heteroskedasticity problem. The estimations have been conducted in four stages. Separate regressions have been carried out for the structural, locational and neighbourhood attributes and also taking all of these three broad attributes combined. All these four estimates have been carried out separately for tenants and owner-occupied respondents.

Also, in order to check for spatial variations in rent across the wards, similar regression for the entire sample units has been conducted by introducing zonal dummies with Ward 1 taken as the control group. In order to know if tenants and owner-occupied households reside in significantly different houses in terms of monthly rent a dummy variable is also used that takes value one for tenants and zero otherwise.

Further, in order to ascertain whether there are significant differences in the monthly rent paid according to community and religion, a Chi-square test has been conducted. This is to understand whether the surveyed respondents have any preference to stay within or near homogeneous religious groups. Here, ward-wise percentage distribution of the sample respondents according to their religion and religion of their neighbours has been tabulated and analyzed. Religion of neighbours has been categorized into three, viz. (1) all neighbours belonging to the respondent's own religion; (2) mix of respondent's religion with other religions, and (3) none of the neighbours belongs to the respondent's religion. Since the housing choice is determined not only by the various housing attributes but also by their capability and preferences, a descriptive statistic of certain important socio-economic and structural characteristics according to their religion has been presented. In order to know how significantly religion and other socio-economic factors impact the demand for housing and its price, linear regression of the type

$$\log P_i = \alpha_1 + \sum_{i=1}^{n} \beta_i \log S_i + \sum_{i=1}^{n} \beta_i R_i + U_i \cdots \ldots \ldots (2.3)$$

has been used where log P_i represents the monthly rent paid by the ith respondent, log S_i and R_i representative variable representing socio-economic characteristics and religion respectively, α_1 represents the constant (intercept), U_i the random disturbance term and β_i represents the impact of a marginal change in the ith explanatory variables. Here, Muslim is taken as the control group.

Also, to know how significantly religion affects housing choice and housing price, a linear regression of the type

$$\log P_i = \alpha_1 + \sum_{i=1}^{n} \beta_i R_i + U_i \qquad \ldots \ldots \ldots (2.4)$$

has been estimated where log P_i represents the monthly rent paid by the ith respondent, R_i represents the ith variable representing religion, α_1 represents the constant (intercept), U_i the random disturbance term and β_i represents the impact of a marginal change in the ith explanatory variables. Here too, Muslim is taken as the control group.

In the same way, in order to check if the surveyed respondents have any preference to stay within or near homogeneous community, community of the respondents and that of their neighbours have been categorized into three categories on the basis of cultural affinity and better adjustability, viz. Naga, Bengali, Assamese, Nepalese and NE Tribes, and Marwari, Bihari and others. Thereafter, a ward-wise percentage distribution of the sample respondents according to their community and community of neighbours in respect of each respondent is computed. Like religion, community of neighbours has been categorized into, (1) all neighbours belonging to the respondent's community; (2) neighbours are mix of respondent's community with other communities, and (3) no one belongs to the respondent's community. To get a better idea about the factors affecting housing choice by the respondents, a descriptive statistics of the socio-economic variables along with the structural characteristics has been analyzed according to their community.

In order to know how significantly community and other socio-economic factors affect housing demand and its price, similar linear regressions of the types are used as is done in case of religion.

Also, in order to check whether the impacts of various locational and neighbourhood attributes vary across socio-economic groups, a simple linear regression of the type

$$P_i = \alpha + \sum_1^k \beta_i Z_i + U_i \quad \text{... (2.5)}$$

has been estimated separately for different groups of each categories. Here P_i represents the monthly rent paid by the ith respondent, Z_i represents the value of ith explanatory variable representing locational or neighbourhood attributes, U_i the random disturbance term and β the impact of a marginal change in ith explanatory variables.

For the purpose, we have considered community, education and status of occupation of the head of household and monthly family income. Community is classified as Naga and Non-Naga while education and family income are classified on the basis of less than or greater than their respective averages. For occupation, we considered private service, business/self-employed and government service as available in plenty in the survey.

Finally, all the results obtained are discussed to interpret how the housing choice is made and how various factors and housing attributes determine the housing price.

REFERENCES

Ahlfeldt, G.M. and Maennig, W. (2011). Arenas, arena architecture and the impact on location desirability: the case of 'Olympic Arenas' in Prenzlauer Berg, Berlin. *Urban Studies*, 46 (7), 1343-1362. DOI: 10.1177/0042098009104569.

Akpon, U.N. (1996). Housing attributes and the cost of private rental buildings in Lagos Nigeria: A hedonic price analysis. *The Review of Regional Studies*, 26 (3), 351-365.

Anderson, R.J. Jr. and Crocker, T.D. (1971). Air pollution and residential property value. *Urban Studies,* 8, 171-180.

Augustina, O. (2015). Housing infrastructural facilities as determinants of rental values of residential properties in Osogbo, Osun State – Nigeria. *Journal of Research in Business, Economics and Management*, 1(1), 7-14.

Bajari, P. and Benkard, C.L. (2005). Demand estimation with heterogeneous consumers and unobserved product characteristics: A hedonic approach. *Journal of Political Economy*, 113(6), 1239-1276.

Bartik, T.J. (1987). The estimation of demand parameters in hedonic price models. *Journal of Political Economy*, 95(1), 81-88.

Brasington, D.M. and Hite, D. (2005). Demand for environmental quality: A spatial hedonic analysis. *Regional Science and Urban Economics*, 35, 57-82.

Brown, J.N. and Rosen, H.S. (1982). On the estimation of structural hedonic price models. *Econometrica*, 50(3), 765-768.

Bello, M.O. and Bello, V.A. (2007). The influence of consumers behaviour on the variables determining residential property values in Lagos, Nigeria. *American Journal of Applied Sciences*, 4(10), 774-778.

Benson, E.D., Hansen, J.L., Schwartz, A.L.Jr. and Smersh, G.T. (1998). Pricing residential amenities: The value of a view. *Journal of Real Estate Finance and Economics*, 16 (1), 55-73.

Black, S.E. (1999). Do better schools matter? Parental valuation of elementary education. *Quarterly Journal of Economics*, 114 (2), 577-599.

Bourassa, S.C. and Peng, V.S. (1999). Hedonic prices and house numbers: The influence of Feng Shui. *International Real Estate Review*, 2(1), 79-93.

Braden, J.B., Feng, X. and Won, D.H. (2011). Waste sites and property values: A meta-analysis. *Environmental and Resource Economics*, 50(2), 175-201.

Carroll, T.M., Clauretie, T.M. and Jensen, J. (1996). Living next to Godliness: Residential property values and churches. *Journal of Real Estate Finance and Economics*, 12(3), 319-330.

Chattopadhyay, S. (1999). Estimating the demand for air quality: New evidence based on the Chicago housing market. *Land Economics*, 75(1), 22-38.

Chau, K.W., Ma, V.S.M. and Ho, D.C.W. (2001). The pricing of 'luckiness' in the apartment market. *Journal of Real Estate Literature*, 9(1), 31-40.

Chau, K.W., Ng, F. F. and Hung, E.C.T. (2001). Developer's goodwill as significant influence on apartment unit prices. *Appraisal Journal*, 69(1), 26-34.

Chau, K.W., Wong, S.K. and Yiu, C.Y. (2004). The value of the provision of a balcony in apartments in Hong Kong. *Property Management*, 22(3), 250-264.

Chay, K.Y. and Greenstone, M. (1998). *Does air quality matter? Evidence from the housing market.* NBER Working Paper 6826. Retrieved from: citeseerx.ist.psu.edu/viewdoc/download?doi= 10.1.1.199.480 &rep=rep1& type=pdf

Clapman, E., Englund, P., Quigley, J.M. and Redfoearn, C. (2006). Revisiting the past and settling the score: Index revision for house price derivatives. *Real Estate Economics*, 34(2), 275-302.

Clauretie, T. M and Neill, H.R. (2000). Year-round school schedules and residential property values. *Journal of Real Estate Finance and Economics*, 20(3), 311-322.

Cohen, J.P. and Coughlin, C.C. (2008). *Changing noise levels and housing prices near the Atlanta Airport.* Working Paper 2005 – 060D. Federal Reserve Bank of St. Louis. Retrieved from: www.http:// research.stlouisfed.org/wp/2005/2005-060.pdf

Colwell, P.F. and Dilmore, G. (1999). Who was first? An examination of an early hedonic study. *Land Economics*, 75(4), 620-626.

Conroy, S., Narwold, A. and Sandy, J. (2013). The value of a floor: Valuing floor level in High-Rise condominiums in San Diego. *International Journal of Housing Markets and Analysis*, 6(2), 197-208.

Corell, M.R., Lillydahl, J.H. and Singell, L.D. (1978). The effects of Greenbelts on residential property values: Some findings on the Political Economy of open space. *Land Economics*, 54(2), 207-217.

Court, A.T. (1939). Hedonic price indexes with automotive examples. *The Dynamics of Automobile demand*, General Motors Company, New York, pp. 99-117.

Court, L.M. (1941). Entrepreneurial and consumer demand theories for commodity spectra. *Econometrica*, 9(2), 135-162.

Cropper, M.L., Deck, L.B. and McConnell, K.E. (1988). On the choice of functional form for hedonic price functions. *The Review of Economics and Statistics*, 70(4), 668-675.

Deaton, B.J. and Hoehn, J.P. (2002). The effect of hazardous waste sites on property values in zones of high industrial activity: a hedonic approach. *Paper submitted for the AAEA 2002 Annual Meeting,* Long Beach, California. Retrieved from: http://ageconsearch.umn.edu/bitstream/19612/1/sp02de01.pdf on 25/1/2014.

Deaton, B.J. and Hoehn, J.P. (2004). Hedonic analysis of hazardous waste sites in the presence of other urban disamenities. *Environmental Science & Policy*, 7, 490-508.

Des Rosiers, F., Lagana, A., Theriault, M. and Beaudoin, M. (1996). Shopping centres and house values: An empirical investigation. *Journal of Property Valuation and Investment*, 14(4), 41-62.

Els, M. and Fintel, D.V. (2008). *Residential property prices in a sub-market of South Africa: Separating real growth from attribute growth.* Stellenbosch Economic Working Paper: 14/08, University of Stellenbosch. Retrieved from: https://ideas.repec.org/p/sza/wpaper/wpapers62.html on 11/4/2015.

Epple, D. (1987). Hedonic prices and implicit markets: Estimating demand and supply functions for differentiated products. *Journal of Political Economy,* 95(1), 59-80.

Espey, M. and Lopez, H. (2000). The impact of airport noise and proximity on residential property values. *Growth and Change*, 31, 408-419.

Fisher, R. A. (1954). Statistical methods for research workers. 12th ed. Oliver and Boyd, Edinburgh; Hafner Publishing Co., Inc., New York.

Fleischer, A. (2011). A room with a view – A valuation of the Mediterranean Sea view. *Tourism Management*, 30, 1-5.

Follain, J.R. and Jimenez, E. (1985). Estimating the demand characteristics: A survey and critique. *Regional Science and Urban Economics*, 15, 77-107.

Follain, J.R. and Calhoun, C.A. (1997). Constructing indices of the price of multifamily properties using the 1991 Residential finance survey. *Journal of Real Estate Finance and Economics*, 14 (1), 235-255. DOI: 10.1023/A:1007748807628. Retrieved from: link.springer.com/article/10.1023/A:1007748807628 on 27/2/2015.

Forrest, D., Glen, J. and Ward, R. (1996). The impact of a Light Rail system on the structure of house prices: A hedonic longitudinal study. *Journal of Transport Economics and Policy*, 30(1), 15-29.

Fortin, N.M., Hill, A.J. and Huang, J. (2013). Superstition in the housing market. IZA Discussion Paper No. 7484, *Paper presented at the Institute for the Study of Labor*, Bonn, Germany. Retrieved from: faculty.arts.ubc.ca/nfortin/Superstition.pdf on 11/2/2014.

Francke, M.K., Vos, G.A. and Janssen, J.E. (2000). Standardised price indices for the regional housing market: A comparison between the Fixed-Sample Index and Hedonic Index. *Paper Presented at the 7th European Real Estate Society Conference*, Bordeaux, 2000.

Freeman, A.M. (1979). Hedonic prices, property values and measuring environmental benefits: A survey of the issues. *The Scandinavian Journal of Economics*, 81(2), 154-174.

Frew, J. and Jud, G.D. (2003). Estimating the value of apartment buildings. *Paper presented at the 2002 American Real Estate Society Annual Meeting.* Retrieved from: aux.zicklin.baruch.cuny.edu/jrer/papers/pdf/past/vol25n01/05.77_86.pdf on 15/6/2014.

Frew, J. and Wilson, B. (2002). Estimating the connection between location and property value. *Journal of Real Estate Practice and Education*, 5 (1), 17-25.

Frischtak, C. & Mandel, B.R. (2012). *Crime, House Prices, and Inequality: The Effect of UPPs in Rio.* Staff Report no. 542, Federal Reserve Bank of New York. Retrieved from https://www.newyorkfed.org/medialibrary/media/research/staff_reports/sr542.pdf on 18/9/2016.

Garrod, G. and Willis, K.G. (1992). Valuing goods' characteristics: An application of the Hedonic Price Method to environmental attributes. *Journal of Environmental Management*, 34(1), 59-76.

Garrod, G. and Willis, K.G. (1999). *Economic Valuation of the Environment: Methods and case studies*, Edward Elgar Publishing Ltd., UK.

Gibler, K.M. and Nelson, S.L. (2003). Consumer behaviour applications to real estate education. *Journal of Real Estate Practice and Education*, 6(1), 63-83.

Goodman, A.C. (1978). Hedonic prices, price indices and housing markets. *Journal of Urban Economics*, 5(4), 471-484.

Goodman, A.C. (1989). Topics in empirical urban housing research. In R. Muth and A. Goodman (eds), *The Economics of Housing Markets*, Harwood Academic, Chur, Switzerland, 49-146.

Government of India, Census of India 2011, New Delhi. Retrieved from: www.census2011.co.in/census/city/183-dimapur.html (on 12th November, 2013).

Griliches, Z. (1961). Hedonic price indices for automobiles: An econometric analysis of quality change, in *The Price Statistics of the Federal Government, General Series No. 73*. 137-196, Columbia University for the National Bureau of Economic Research, New York.

Haas, G.C. (1922). *A statistical analysis of farm sales in Blue Earth County, Minnesota as a basis for farmland appraisal* (Masters Dissertation, the University of Minnesota).

Hansen, J. (2006). *Australian house prices: A comparison of Hedonic and Repeat Sales measures*. Research Discussion Paper: 2006-03, Reserve Bank of Australia. Retrieved from: http://www.rba.gov.au/publications/rdp/2006/pdf/rdp2006-03.pdf on 4/3/2015.

Haurin, D. and Brasington, D. (1996). *The impact of School quality on real house prices: Interjurisdictional effects.* Working Paper 010, Ohio State University. Retrieved from: www.econ.ohio-state.edu/pdf/haurin/haurin.pdf on 11/2/2014.

Ho, J. (2008). *The economics of luckiness: The impact of number superstition on condominium prices in Singapore* (Honours dissertation, Department of Economics, Amherst College, 2008).

Houthakker, H.S. (1952). Compensated changes in quantities and qualities consumed. *Review of Economic Studies*, 19(3), 155-164.

Huh, S. & Kwak, S.J. (1997). The choice of functional form and variables in the hedonic price model in Seoul. *Urban Studies*, 34(7), 989-998.

Kain, J.F. and Quigley, J.M. (1970). Measuring the value of housing quality. *Journal of the American Statistical Association*, 65(5), 532-548.

Ketkar, K. (1992). Hazardous waste sites and property values in the state of New Jersey. *Applied Economics*, 24, 647-659.

Kiel, K.A. (1995). Measuring the impact of the discovery and cleaning of identified hazardous waste sites on house value. *Land Economics*, 71(4), 428-435.

Kockelman, K.M. (1997). The effects of location elements on home purchase prices and rents: Evidence from the San Francisco Bay area. *Transportation Research record No. 1606*, pp. 40-50.

Kruse, S.A. and Ahmann, J. (2009). *The value of Lake adjacency: A hedonic pricing analysis on the Klamath River, California*. Ecotrust Working Paper Series No. 5. Retrieved from: www.ecotrust.org/workingpapers on 18/1/2014.

Lancaster, K.J. (1966). A new approach to consumer theory. *Journal of Political Economy*, 74(2), 132-157.

Lansford, H. Jr. and Jones, L.L. (1995). Marginal price of Lake recreation and aesthetics: An hedonic approach. *Journal of Agricultural and Applied Economics*, 27 (1), 212-223.

Leggett, C.G. and Bockstael, N.E. (2000). Evidence of the effects of water quality on residential land prices. *Journal of Environmental Economics and Management*, 39, 121-144. Retrieved from: http://www.idealibrary.com on 24/11/2013.

Li, M.M. and Brown, H.J. (1980). Micro-neighbourhood externalities and hedonic housing prices. *Land Economics*, 56 (2), 125-141.

Lorenz, D.P. (2006). *The application of Sustainable Development Principles to the theory and practice of property valuation.* (Ph.D. Dissertation), University of Karlsruhe, Germany, 2006.

Maurer, R., Martin P. and Sebastian, S. (2004). Hedonic price indices for the Paris housing market. *All gemeines Statistisches Archiv*, 88 (3), 303-326. Retrieved from: http://papers.ssrn.com/sol3/papers.cfm?abstract_id=691242 on 23/1/2014.

Max, S. (2004). Schools, what is it good for? When it comes to home prices, school matters. Buyers will pay a premium to live near top schools. CNN. com, August 27, 2004. Retrieved from http://money.cnn.com/2004/08/27/real_estate/buying_selling/schools/ on 12/2/2014.

McMillen, D. and McDonald, J.F. (1998). Suburban subcenters and employment density in metropolitan Chicago. *Journal of Urban Economics,* 43(1), 157-180.

McMillan, M.L., Reid, B.G. and Gillen, D.W. (1980). An extension of the hedonic approach for estimating the value of quiet. *Land Economics*, 56 (3), 315-328.

Menger, C. (1871). *Principles of Economics.* Reprinted in 2007 by the Ludwig von Mises Institute, Alabama, USA, 2007.

Millhouse, J.A. (2005). *Assessing the effects of architectural design on real estate values: A qualitative approach.* (Masters Dissertation), Rice University.

Mishra, S.K. and Ngullie, M.L. (2008). Hedonic demand for rented house in Kohima, Nagaland. *Munich Personal RePEc Archive.* MPRA Paper No. 10076. Retrieved from: http://mpra.ub.uni-muenchen.de/10076 on 23/8/2013.

Morancho, A.B. (2003). A hedonic valuation of urban green areas. *Landscape and Urban Planning*, 66, 35-41.

Morris, E.W., Woods, M.E. and Jacobson, A.L. (1972). The measurement of housing quality. *Land Economics*, 48(4), 383-387.

Murty, M.N. and Gulati, S.C. (2004). A generalized method of hedonic prices: Measuring benefits from reduced urban air pollution. *Natural Resources Accounting*, CSO, GOI. Retrieved from: http://www.iegindia.org/workpap/wp254.pdf on 24/11/2013.

Muth, R.F. (1966). Household production and consumer demand functions. *Econometrica*, 34 (6), 699-708.

Nelson, J.P. (1980). Airports and property values: A survey of recent evidence. *Journal of Transport Economics and Policy*, 14(1), 37-52.

Nelson, J.P. (1982). Highway noise and property values: A survey of recent evidence. *Journal of Transport Economics and Policy*, 16(2), 117-138.

Nunns, P., Hitchins, H. and Balderston, K. (2015). *The value of land, floor space and amenities: a hedonic price analysis of property sales in Auckland 2011-2014*. Auckland Council technical report, TR2015/012. Retrieved from: http://knowledgeauckland.org.nz/assets/publications/TR2015-012-Value-of-land-floorspace-and-amenities-Auckland.pdf on 22/8/2016.

Ottensmann, J.R., Payton, S. and Man, J. (2008). Urban location and housing prices within a hedonic model. *The Journal of Regional Analysis and Policy*, 38(1),19-35.

Peng, T.C. & Chiang, Y.H. (2015). The non-linearity of hospitals' proximity on property prices: Experiences from Taipei, Taiwan. *Journal of Property Research*, 3(4), 341-361, DOI: 10.1080/09599916.2015.1089923. Retrieved from http://dx.doi.org/10.1080/09599916.2015.1089923 on 18/9/2016.

Pennington, G., Topham, N. and Ward, R. (1990). Aircraft noise and residential property values adjacent to Manchester International Airport. *Journal of Transport Economics and Policy*, 24(1), 49-59.

Quigley, J.M. (1995). A simple Hybrid Model for estimating real estate Price Indexes. *Journal of Housing Economics*, 4(1), 1-12.

Rahadi, R.A. *et al.* (2012). Relationship between consumer preferences and value propositions: A study of residential product. *Procedia—Social and Behavioral Sciences,* 50, 865-874.

Ridker, R.G. and Henning, J.A. (1967). Determinants of residential property values with special reference to air pollution. *The Review of Economics and Statistics*, 49 (2), 246-257.

Rodriguez, M. and Sirmans, C.T. (1994). Quantifying the value of a view in single-family housing markets. *The Appraisal Journal*, 62, 600-603.

Rohani, M. (2012). *Impact of Hauraki Gulf amenity on the land price of neighbourhood properties*. An empirical Hedonic Pricing Method case study, North Shore, Auckland. Auckland Council Working Paper 2012/001.

Rosen, S. (1974). Hedonic prices and implicit markets: Product differentiation in pure competition. *Journal of Political Economy*, 82(1), 35-55.

Samarasinghe, O. & Sharpe, B. (2010). Flood prone risk and amenity values: A spatial hedonic analysis. *The Australian Journal of Agricultural and Resource Economics*, 54(1), 457-475.

Selim, S. (2008). Determinants of house prices in Turkey: A hedonic regression model. *Dogus University Journal*, 9(1), 65-76.

Shimizu, C. and Nishimura, K.G. (2007). Pricing structure in Tokyo metropolitan land markets and its structural changes: Pre-bubble, bubble, and post-bubble periods. *Journal of Real Estate Finance and Economics*, 35, 475-496.

Sirpal, R. (1994). Empirical modeling of the relative impacts of various sizes of shopping centres on the value of surrounding residential properties. *Journal of Real Estate Research*, 9(4), 487-505.

So, H.M., Tse, R.Y.C. and Ganesan, S. (1997). Estimating the influence of transport on house prices: Evidence from Hong Kong. *Journal of Property Valuation & Investment*, 15(1), 40-47.

Soderberg, B. and Janssen, C. (2001). Estimating distance gradients for apartment properties. *Urban Studies*, 38(1), 61-79.

Srour, I.M., Kockelman, K.M. and Dunn, T.P. (2002). Accessibility indices: A connection to residential land prices and location choices. *Paper Presented at the 81st Annual Meeting of the Transport Research Board,* March-April 2002, Washington. Retrieved from: citeseerx.ist.psu.edu/viewdoc/download?doi=10.1.1.80.7338&rep=rep1&type=pdf on 16/1/2014.

Thaler, R. (1978). A note on the value of crime control: Evidence from the property market. *Journal of Urban Economics*, 5(1), 137-145.

Tse, R.Y.C. (2002). Estimating neighbourhood effects in house prices: Towards a new hedonic model approach. *Urban Studies*, 39(7), 1165-1180.

Tse, R.Y.C. and Love, P.E.D. (2000). Measuring residential property values in Hong Kong. *Property Management*, 18(5), 366-374.

Tyrvainen, L. (1997). The amenity value of the urban forest: An application of the hedonic pricing method. *Landscape and Urban Planning*, 37, 211-222.

Vessali, K.V. (1996). Land use impacts of rapid transit: A review of the empirical literature. *Berkeley Planning Journal*, 11(1), 71-105.

Vor, F.de & Groot, H.L.F.de (2011). The impact of industrial sites on residential property values: A hedonic pricing analysis from the Netherlands. *Regional Studies*, 45(5), 609-623, DOI: 10.1080/00343401003601925.

Waddell, P. (2011). Integrated land use and transport planning and modelling: Addressing challenges in research and practice. *Transport Review*, 31(2), 209-229.

Waugh, F.V. (1928). Quality factors influencing vegetable prices. *Journal of Farm Economics,* 10(2), 185-96.

Welch, T.F. (2010). *Estimating the effects of transportation infrastructure proximity using multiple longitudinal regression methods: The case of Atlanta* (Master's dissertation), Florida State University.

Wooldridge, J.M. (2015). *Introductory econometrics: A modern approach.* Nelson Education.

Zabel, J.E. and Kiel, K.A. (2000). Estimating the demand for air quality in four U.S. cities. *Land Economics*, 76(2), 174-194.

Zou, G. (2015). The effect of Central Business District on house prices in Chengdu Metropolitan area: A hedonic approach. *Paper Presented at the International Conference on Circuits and Systems, August 2015, Paris, France.* Retrieved from: www.atlantis-press.com/php/download_paper.php?id=23016 on 22/8/2016.

3
Trends of Residential Properties, Amenities and Housing Demand in Dimapur

Introduction

The centre of most people's lives is their home where they return after the days' works and spend nights with family. Generally, their residence is the place where they spend maximum time and where they mainly need to get comfort and security. Apart from providing shelter, privacy and storage of possessions, it is also the primary base for family and social activities and a forum for expression of personality and taste. Moreover, it serves as the centre for gratification of leisure activities for many people (Habitat for Humanity, 2015).

In a developing economy, the push of the rural areas and the pull of the town have resulted in significant impact of rapid population growth on housing development (Aluko, 2010). A key determinant of migration is the income differential between rural and urban regions (Michaelsen &Haiskan-DeNew, 2015). Abiodun (1976) asserted that the most outstanding of all the problems of urbanization is that of providing ample housing facilities for the residents. One of life's big decisions for most owner-occupied households is finding a place to live which is suitable, attractive and convenient yet affordable. Once purchased or built, their house is likely to be their most valuable economic asset and the kind of house occupied by a household is an important pointer of its lifestyle and socio-economic status.

Households attempt to maximize well-being by their location decisions (Blomquist, Berger and Hoehn, 1988). The deep connection between urban change and the housing stock is evident in the strong correlation between population sizes and housing units. There is little argument that the less available is land, the more difficult it is to build house. The rise of multi-storeyed buildings to house multiple families in a single building solved the problem of space. The cost per square foot in multi-floor apartments is considerably higher than the cost per square foot to build single-family detached homes, and congestion in a city can increase the difficulty of building in many other ways. However, very limited multi-storeyed buildings are found in Dimapur. Places that are densely built generally are locations where housing demand is relatively high (Glaeser, Gyourko and Saks, 2005). It is thus difficult to empirically separate out the effect of limited housing supply in dense locations from higher housing demand.

The demographic variables used in different analyses have little uniformity, making it difficult for comparison. Studies by Lee (1968), Lee and Kong (1977), and Mayo (1981) found that inclusion of demographic variables in demand equations has significant impact on estimated demand elasticities, while others (Maisel, Burnham and Austin, 1971; and Rosen, 1977) have found little impact. The first empirical results connecting demography and housing prices were given by Mankiw and Weil (1989). Since they found a strong positive association between the aggregate demographic index of housing demand and the average house price, they concluded that demography has been a key cause for house price fluctuations in the U.S. However, Mankiw and Weil's results may suffer from a specification bias as Hendershott (1991) and Swan (1995) both detected that real per capita income was not included in their model. Di Pasquale and Wheaton (1992) found that real per capita income has a significant impact on housing demand. The crucial role of real income has also been emphasized by Holly and Jones (1997).

Fortin and Leclerc (2000), using price movements over the period 1956-1997 in Canada, found that the only demographic constituent that significantly changes the time path of housing prices is the growth rate of population previously. Lee *et al.* (2001) also found statistical basis that increase in adult population (including net migration) in Austria contributed positively to housing demand. However, they called for addressing the other factors like income, subsidy effect, cost of housing finance and cost shifters such as unemployment rate while analysing housing demand. Lindh and Malmberg (2008) also concluded that theoretical considerations and empirical data support a clear effect of demographic change on residential construction even if the price effect may be less clear-cut for various reasons.They found that working age population has a positive effect while increasing population shares in the dependent age groups have a negative effect on residential construction. The growth in income level has a significant positive impact on the quantity of housing demanded. The level of the rental rate for a given housing stock increases with the number of people in high demand age groups, i.e. essentially the working population. Eichholtz and Lindenthal (2014) found the demand for most housing components increase with household size. They also found that human capital is a key driver for housing demand. Income and education (as a proxy for human capital) have positive correlation with the demand for housing. However, they did not find a direct impact of age on housing demand.

Growth of Population, Area and Density of Population

Population growth is a major underlying factor behind the demand for housing and without sufficient new supply of dwellings; it pushes up the prices for both renting and purchasing houses (Karantonis, 2008). The population of Dimapur town has grown rapidly since 1971 as shown in Table 3.1. The exponential growth of population is not only leading to the geographical expansion of the town but they are also becoming more concentrated as is evident from the rising population density per square kilometre. The population which was merely 12,426 in 1971, more than doubled in 1981 to 32,878. Over the next three decades, population of the town increased to 1,22,834 in 2011 (Census of India reports). Density of population has also increased rapidly over the past four decades. The population density was about 781 persons per sq.km. in 1971 and it increased to 1,813.46 in 1981. Thereafter, it increased to 2,238.92 and 3840.88 persons per sq. km. in 1991 and 2001 respectively. According to 2011 Census, the density of population stands at about 4,809 persons per sq. km. Population figure touched 1,31,955 and density to 5,166.59 per sq. km. in 2015. Though the growth rate of population and density has decelerated, absolute growth of population and density is expected to increase parallelly mounting pressure on the housing requirement.

Table 3.1: Growth of Population, Area and Density of Population in Dimapur since 1971 to 2015

Year	Popul-ation	Decadal Growth of Popul-ation (%)	Area (sq. km.)	Density (per sq. km.)	Decadal Growth of Density (%)	Number of Wards
1971	12426	—	15.9	781.51	—	6
1981	32878	164.5	18.13	1813.46	132.05	6
1991	57182	73.9	25.54	2238.92	23.46	15
2001	98096	71.5	25.54	3840.88	71.55	21
2011	122834	25.2	25.54	4809.47	25.22	23
2015	131955	—	25.54	5166.59	—	23

Note: 2015 population is projected.

Source: Census of India, 1971, 1981, 1991, 2001 & 2011.

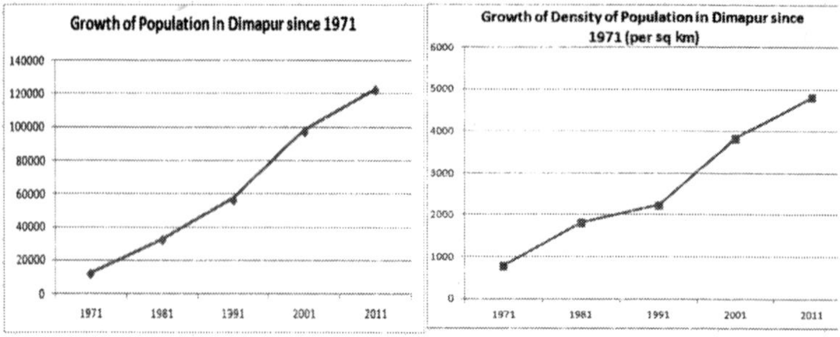

Fig. 3.1: Growth of Population and Density of Population in Dimapur

Source: Census of India Reports.

It is observed that growth of area of Dimapur town has been seized since 1991 but not the population. Of course, pattern of demand for categories of houses may change due to the variation in socio-economic composition of population. Density of housing units is one obvious proxy for the elasticity of housing supply in a city (Glaeser, Gyourko and Saks, 2005). Educational status of individuals, which has also been increasing, may be an important factor affecting the choice of housing of the individuals through changing occupational locations.

The growth of town can, however, be observed from the increasing number of wards too. Till 1981, there were only 6 wards in the town, but it increased to 15 wards in 1991, 21 wards in 2001 and thereafter to presently 23 wards (Census of India Reports 1971, 1981, 1991, 2001 and 2011). However, the number of wards not only increased by bifurcating existing ones and covering new areas but the ward numbers associated with the localities and population were also altered over the period.

Further, the growth of the town can also be viewed in terms of the length of road in the town over time that shows the rising requirement of surface transport road. With the expansion of human settlement over erstwhile uninhibited areas, area coverage of human habitation in the town also enlarged. To connect these new settlements, new roads are being constructed. In 1991, the total length of roads in the town consisted of 144 km of surfaced road and 9 km of unsurfaced road. In 2001, it increased to about 287 km of surfaced road and 96 km of unsurfaced road (NPWD, R & B, Dimapur). As per census Reports 2011, it recorded as 393.7 km and 158.48 km respectively. Even though the area of the town stopped expanding after 1991, whatever expansion of settlement area took place before 1991 was covered by rising road connectivity with rising demand of growing people. Therefore, despite slow spatial expansion with population growth and its composition, requirement and demand for housing is expected to increase at varied locations.

Growth of Residential Properties and Amenities

In all communities, some changes have continuously been taking place whether it is in the domiciles of people or land use pattern. Some of these changes lead to new physical developments in land by public or private agencies, and consequently, changes in the housing sector take place. The most basic physical requirements that a dwelling house provides are shelter, adequate space for all the occupants to live, eat and sleep and a degree of privacy for the household as a whole including its individual members. However, according to recent census reports, as part of the basic minimum housing provisions we also take into account other built-in housing amenities, such as availability of sufficient and good quality water for drinking and cooking, bathing and sanitary facilities, source of lighting and fuel, and availability of other durable household goods. We also expect that the structure and facilities of the dwelling house would be properly maintained and in working order.

The characteristics of house and the dwelling unit of households such as the type of structure, condition of the structure, use of house, status of ownership of the house, number of rooms etc., constitute important aspects of housing condition. Besides, the micro environmental ambience surrounding the house ensured by availability of proper drainage arrangement, garbage disposal system, availability of roads etc., has an impact on the quality of life of the households (GOI-UNDP Project, 2013).

Trend of Residential Properties

Faster economic growth and development have also been observed to be related to the growth of housing sector in Dimapur (Jud and Watts, 1981; and Clauretie and Neill, 2000). Population growth, particularly the growth in the number of households, leads to a growth in housing demand (Mulder, 2006). The progression of households through the life cycle and the changes that take place within households generate diverse needs for housing space at different times (Clark, Deurloo & Dieleman, 2000). It is observed that residential houses have expanded both geographically as well as within a locality in the survey area. The growth of the town over the years has resulted in increased economic activities. This phenomenon is constantly attracting new migrants into the town as evident from the fast increase of population as per census records. Accordingly, it is observed that residential houses and the number of households have been increasing over the years in the survey area, though at a diminishing rate (Table 3.2). But the decadal growth of residential houses was much lower than that of households during 1991 to 2001 though it was marginally higher during 1981-91 and 2001-11.The number of households which was 6627 in 1981 increased to 27,857 during the last thirty years. The phenomenal growth of households has resulted in the sharp increase of residential houses in the town over the years. The number of occupied residential houses (ORH), which was just 6620 in 1981, increased by about 90 per cent to 12,581 in 1991. It further increased by about 60 per cent to 20,198 in 2001. The last decade also witnessed a growth rate of about 37 per cent to 27,640 as per 2011 Census report. Housing supply in Dimapur town is mainly based on informal operations, championed by individuals in the private sector, but at a scale that is not commensurate with the growing housing demand in the town.

Table 3.2: Growth of Occupied Residential Houses and No. of Households in Dimapur during 1981 to 2011

Year	Occupied Residential Houses	Decadal Growth of Residential Houses (%)	No. of Households	Decadal Growth of No. of Households (%)
1981	6620	N.A.	6627	N.A.
1991	12581	90.04	12581	89.84
2001	20198	60.54	20996	66.89
2011	27640	36.84	27857	32.68

Source: Census of India Reports, various issues.

Ownership of urban dwelling is associated with higher standard of living (Ademiluyi, 2010). The share of owner-occupied households increased from 23 per cent in 2001 to about 27 per cent in 2011. The percentage of households living on rented houses has decreased from 74.67 per cent to 68.39 per cent during the same period. The residential houses have, however, shown qualitative improvement during the period (Table 3.3). The number of residential houses is leaning towards categories 'Good' and 'Permanent' during the first decade of the 21st century. In 2011, almost 65 per cent of the total number of households is living in 'good' residential houses in contrast to just 44.56 per cent in 2001. On the other hand, the number of households living under 'Dilapidated' condition has gone down from 10.27 per cent to 2.49 per cent during the same period. The total number of households under 'permanent' and 'semi-permanent'

Table 3.3: Status of Residential Properties in Dimapur Town in 2001 and 2011

Year	No. of House-holds	Ownership status			Condition of Residential Houses			Type of Residential House			
		Owned	Rented	Any other	Good	Liveable	Dilapi-dated	Permanent	Semi-Permanent	Tempo-rary	Unclassi-fiable
2001	20996	4866 (23.18)	15677 (74.67)	453 (2.16)	9001 (44.56)	9123 (45.17)	2074 (10.27)	9764 (48.34)	7062 (34.96)	3372 (16.69)	0 (0.00)
2011	27857	7403 (26.58)	19051 (68.39)	1403 (5.04)	18073 (64.88)	9091 (32.63)	693 (2.49)	14625 (52.50)	11449 (41.10)	1532 (5.50)	251 (0.90)

Note: Figures in the parentheses represent percentage to total.
Source: Census of India Reports 2001 and 2011.

structure of building also increased from 48.34 per cent and 34.96 per cent in 2001 to 52.50 per cent and 41.10 per cent respectively in 2011.

The status of ownership of residential houses in 2001 and 2011 has been depicted in Pie diagrams in Figure 3.2. It is observed that the percentage of households living on rented houses has decreased during the period but the percentage of households living in own and any other houses have increased during the same period.

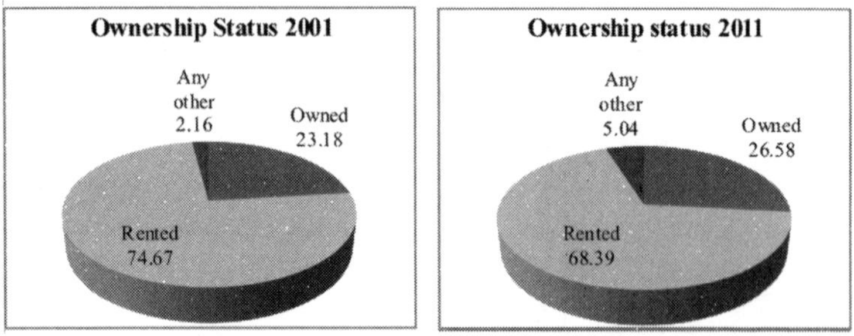

Fig. 3.2: Ownership Status of Residential Houses in Dimapur Town during 2001 and 2011.

Source: Census of India Reports 2001 & 2011.

Growth of Amenities

The increase in population and standard of living necessitates the growth of amenities such as schools, hospitals, banks etc. Over the past four and half decades, these amenities have witnessed rapid growth in absolute terms in Dimapur town (Table 3.4). However, the availability of amenities per thousand populations has decreased in respect of schools, dispensaries and banks over the period.

Dimapur town is becoming an important centre for education with the number of schools, colleges, professional institutes and coaching centres sprouting across the town over the years. The number of schools (all Government schools and private High and Higher Secondary schools) has increased from a mere 16 in 1970 to 78 in 2015 (SSA Report, DEO office, 2015). However, with the rapid increase in population, the availability of schools per thousand populations has decreased from 1.29 in 1971 to only 0.59 in 2015. On the other hand, the number of colleges and its availability per thousand persons have both increased during the same period. The mushrooming of educational centres has also positively impacted the literacy rate of the town.

Table 3.4: Growth of Schools, Colleges, Hospitals and Banks during 1971-2011 in Dimapur Town (Number)

Amenities	1971	2015
Schools	16 (1.29)	78 (0.59)
Colleges	1 (0.08)	14 (0.11)
Hospitals	1 (0.08)	20 (0.15)
Dispensaries	1 (0.08)	7 (0.05)
Banks (Including Branch)	3 (0.24)	30 (0.23)

Note: Figures in the parentheses represent numbers per thousand populations.
Source: Various Government Offices and Field Survey conducted during March-April 2015.

Increase in population also necessitates greater health care facilities (Oluwatoyin, Sunday and Folake, 2013). Dimapur town has also been witnessing a fast growth of health care facilities to cater to its rapidly growing population. During 1971, there was only one Government hospital and dispensary each in the town. Whereas in 2015, there is one Government hospital and Primary Health Centre each, 6 Sub-Centres (Dispensaries) and 19 Private hospitals (CMO office, 2015). Besides, there are a host of Private Clinics catering to out-patients across the town. It is observed that availability of hospital per thousand populations has also increased but that of dispensaries has decreased over the period.

There is no doubt that increase in income is exhibited in higher standard of living and better quality of life (Mishra and Ngullie, 2003). The per capita NSDP of Nagaland at constant prices has increased over time. At 2004-05 prices, it increased from Rs. 16,314 in 1980-81 to Rs. 23,689 in 1990-91. It stood at Rs. 27,673 and Rs. 43,992 in 2000-01 and 2010-11 respectively. This growth in the per capita income is also likely to be associated with the growth of banks and banking activities in Dimapur town. Comprehensive data on the establishment of banks in the study area is not available and so the data on the year of establishment of each bank has been collected through field survey. At the time of statehood in 1963, there was only 1 bank in the town. In 1971, it increased to 3 banks and then rapidly increased to 10 by 1981. There has been a strong positive growth over the next 3 decades and the number of bank branches grew to 14, 15 and further to 25 in 1991, 2001 and 2011 respectively. As on 31st March 2015, there are 30 bank branches operating in the town. However, the availability of banks per thousand populations has remained almost constant over the same period (Table 3.4). As per the Census reports, there were 6,726 households availing banking facilities in the town in 2001,

Table 3.5: Status of Sanitary, Lighting and Cooking Fuel used by the Households in Dimapur Town in 2001 & 2011

Year	Bathroom within Premises	Latrine within Premises	Drainage System		Source of Lighting at Home			Type of Cooking Fuel Used			
			Closed	Open	Electricity	Kerosene	Others	Firewood	LPG	Kerosene	Others
2001	12029 (57.29)	19721 (93.93)	2571 (12.25)	11346 (81.53)	18596 (88.57)	2110 (10.05)	290 (1.38)	7939 (37.81)	9496 (45.23)	2561 (12.20)	1000 (4.76)
2011	26559 (95.34)	26769 (96.09)	4715 (16.93)	18218 (79.44)	27232 (97.76)	577 (2.07)	48 (0.17)	5995 (21.52)	20469 (73.48)	700 (2.51)	693 (2.49)

Note: Figures in the parentheses represent percentage to total.
Source: Census of India Reports 2001 & 2011.

which almost tripled to 18,090 households in 2011. In terms of percentage, it is 32.03 per cent and 64.94 per cent of total households respectively in 2001 and 2011.

The status of the amenities associated with the dwelling units determines the quality of life to a great extent. Availability of bathroom and latrine within premises increased from 57.29 per cent and 93.93 per cent in 2001 to 95.34 per cent and 96.09 per cent respectively in 2011 (Table 3.5). The percentage of total households having closed drainage facilities also increased during the period from 12.24 per cent in 2001 to 16.93 per cent in 2011. 81.53 per cent of households had open drainage facilities in 2001, and it marginally decreased to 79.44 per cent in 2011. Use of electricity as the main source of lighting and use of LPG as the principal source for cooking is the reflection of higher standard of living. The percentage of households using electricity as the major source of lighting has increased from about 89 per cent in 2001 to about 98 per cent in 2011 (Fig. 3.3). The percentage of total households using LPG as the main source for cooking has also increased from 45.23 per cent in 2001 to 73.48 per cent in 2011. It has, however, been observed that the share of Kerosene and other sources of lighting have decreased during the same period.

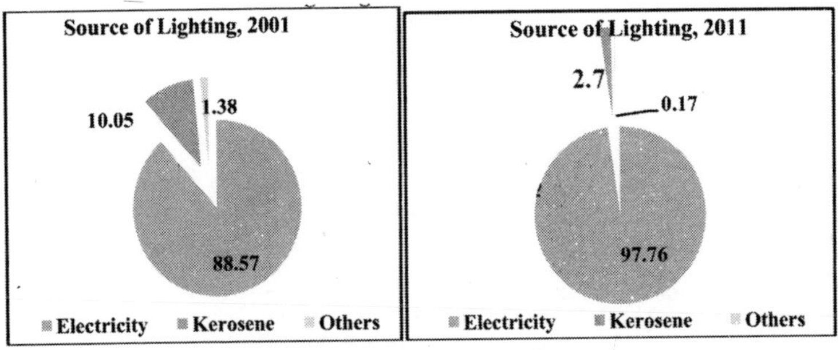

Fig. 3.3: Percentage Distribution of Households on the basis of Sources of Lighting in 2001 and 2011.

Source: Census of India Reports 2001 & 2011.

The main sources of drinking water in Dimapur town are the private sources (Table 3.6). The percentage of Government sources (tap), however, increased slowly from 9.73 per cent in 2001 to 16.14 per cent in 2011. People depend heavily on private sources for the collection of drinking water because of poor public water supply and also because it is relatively easy to get underground water as exploited by the individuals. This is evident from the wide availability of wells and tube/bore wells in

Table 3.6: Percentage Distribution of Households on the basis of Source and Location of Drinking Water used in 2001 & 2011

Year	Sources of Drinking Water				Location of Drinking Water		
	Tap	Tube/Bore	Well	Others	Within Premises	Outside Premises	Away
2001	2043 (9.73)	1540 (7.33)	12155 (57.89)	5258 (25.04)	13664 (67.98)	4881 (24.28)	1554 (7.73)
2011	4496 (16.14)	9089 (32.63)	10216 (36.67)	4056 (14.56)	24519 (88.02)	3958 (14.21)	1380 (4.95)

Note: Figures in the parentheses represent percentage to total.
Source: Census of India Reports 2001 & 2011.

the town owned by private individuals. It is observed that percentage of people who use tube/bore well as source of drinking water has increased rapidly from about 7 per cent in 2001 to almost 33 per cent in 2011, while the share of well and other sources has declined during the same period. Availability of drinking water within premises also enhances the quality of life. The percentage of households having the source of drinking water within their premises also increased from 67.98 per cent in 2001 to 88.02 per cent in 2011.

The percentage distribution of the sources of drinking water in 2001 and 2011 are depicted in Fig. 3.4. The percentage of households using Government tap water and tube/bore has increased from 9.73 per cent and 7.33 per cent to 16.14 per cent and 32.63 per cent respectively over the decade. In contrast, the share of well and other sources of drinking water has decreased during the same period.

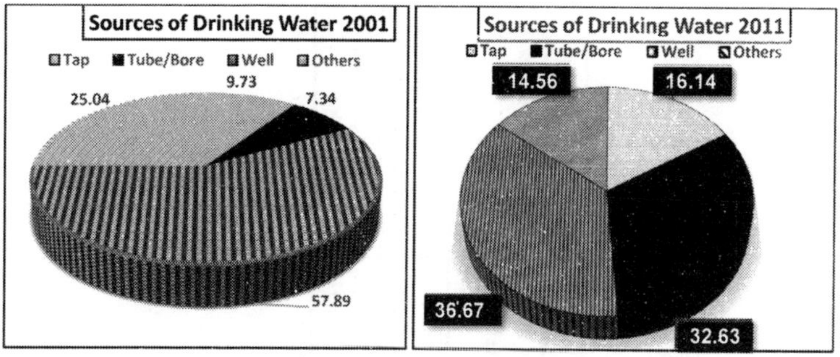

Fig. 3.4: Percentage Distribution of Households using Sources of Drinking Water in 2001 and 2011

Source: Census of India Reports 2001 & 2011.

The type of materials used for constructing a house determines the type and quality of the house. It is observed that cement is the most commonly used material for flooring while CGI/Asbestos is the most common material used for roof in Dimapur (Table 3.7). With respect to material of wall, it is observed that wall made of bricks or cement increased from 55.82 per cent in 2001 to 63.46 per cent in 2011 of the total houses.

The percentage of census houses using cement for floor also increased from 65.67 per cent in 2001 to 78.95 per cent in 2011 (Fig. 3.5). The share of houses with Mosaic or Tiles floor also increased but marginally, whereas the percentage of houses with mud floor has decreased more rapidly from 29.43 to 14.03 per cent during the same period.

Table 3.7: Distribution of Houses in terms of Material of Floor, Roof and Wall in 2001 & 2011

Year	No. of Census Houses	Material of Floor				Material of Roof				Material of Wall			
		Cement	Mosaic or Tiles	Mud	Others	CGI or Asbestos	Concrete	Thatch	Others	Grass or Bamboo	Bricks or Cement	Plastic or Poly-thene	Others
2001	30419	19976 (65.67)	850 (2.79)	8951 (29.43)	642 (2.11)	18743 (61.62)	7188 (23.63)	3846 (12.64)	642 (2.11)	11101 (36.49)	16981 (55.82)	201 (0.66)	2136 (7.02)
2011	38749	30592 (78.95)	1628 (4.20)	5436 (14.03)	1093 (3.08)	21551 (55.62)	12605 (32.53)	1832 (4.73)	2761 (7.13)	11742 (30.30)	24591 (63.46)	259 (0.67)	2157 (5.57)

Note: Figures in the parentheses represent percentage to total.
Source: Census of India Reports 2001 & 2011.

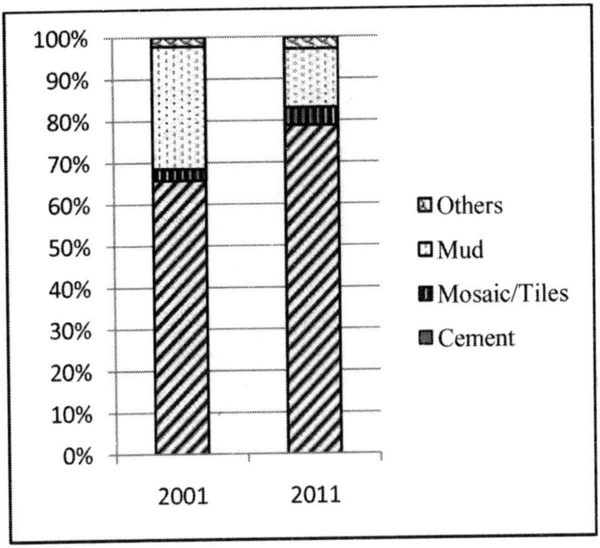

Fig. 3.5: Percentage distribution of Houses on the basis of Material of Floor in 2001 and 2011.

Source: Census of India Reports, 2001 & 2011.

Having concrete roof indicates that there is an upward growth in double or multi-storied buildings in the town over the years. The percentage of total census houses with concrete roof rose from 23.63 per cent to 32.53 per cent, whereas the percentage of houses with CGI/ Asbestos and thatch has decreased during 2001 to 2011 (Fig. 3.6).

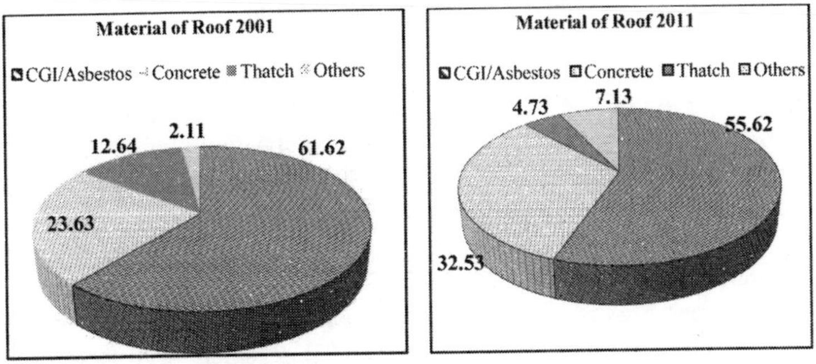

Fig. 3.6: Percentage distribution of Houses in terms of Material of Roof in 2001 and 2011.

Source: Census of India Reports, 2001 & 2011.

Growth of Housing Price in Dimapur since 2000

Though Dimapur town is growing very fast over the past few decades, the real estate sector is still not developed. Apartment or flat system is not yet in existence. Most houses are detached and so it is very difficult to segregate house prices from land prices. But, considering the small geographical spread of the town, it is assumed that similar structural buildings constructed during a given period have identical cost of construction and so variations in the price per unit area of housing is reflected in different land prices. Thus, the price of land would go up with an increased demand for housing since land and housing are complementary goods in this case. However, due to lack of any Government Administered prices in Dimapur town, the land prices may also vary depending on the bargaining power of the sellers and buyers.

Owing to rapid urbanisation, access to land for housing development has become an almost insurmountable challenge for many people in Dimapur. In recent years, the price of land has risen exponentially, making it unaffordable to many low and middle-income earners. However, as stated earlier since the number of wards have not only changed several times through expansion in area as well as bifurcation of existing ones but also changes in the ward number associated with the same locality; it is difficult to study the characteristics of respective wards overtime. Moreover, there are no secondary data available with regard to the actual land prices for the town. Therefore, to overcome this problem, direct verbal interviews were conducted across the present 23 wards with former Councillors, Gaon Buras (G.Bs.), Colony Chairmen and prominent citizens of the localities to ascertain the trend of land prices in the respective colonies/wards during 2000 to 2015. It may be noted that most land transactions are carried out with the G.Bs. and Chairmen of colonies as witnesses and so they have a sound knowledge of the different rates in their localities. Information on current land/house prices are also collected from newspaper advertisements given by potential sellers in the study area. It is observed that land prices and its growth rates vary substantially across various categories of area during the period 2000-2015.

The spatial variation in land prices has been viewed on the basis of land use which has been categorized into six categories as adopted by the Land Records and Survey Department, Dimapur, viz. Special Commercial, Commercial A, Commercial B, Residential A, Residential B, and Homestead/Barren/Agricultural land. An analysis of the temporal land prices shows substantial differences in land prices across the wards and also its growth rates during 2000-2015 (Table 3.8). For the town as

Table 3.8: Temporal Land Prices Category-wise at Current Prices, Constant Prices and Average Annual Growth Rates at Constant Prices (per sq. ft.)

Category	Land Prices at Current Prices			Land Prices at Constant Prices (2004-05 prices)			Average Annual Growth Rates at Constant Prices		
	2000	**2010**	**2015**	**2000**	**2010**	**2015**	**2000-10**	**2010-15**	**2000-15**
Special Commercial	2000	4500	5500	2405.91	3139.72	3035.18	3.05	-0.66	1.74
Commercial A	1200	2300	3500	1443.54	1604.74	1931.48	1.12	4.07	2.25
Commercial B	500	1250	2000	601.48	872.14	1103.70	4.50	5.31	5.57
Residential A	300	900	1500	360.89	627.94	827.78	7.40	6.36	8.62
Residential B	150	500	800	180.44	348.86	441.48	9.33	5.31	9.64
Homestead/ Barren	60	200	350	72.18	139.54	193.15	9.33	7.68	11.17
Average	701.67	1608.33	2275.00	844.07	1122.16	1255.46	5.79	4.68	6.50

Source: Field Survey conducted during March-April 2015.

a whole, the average land prices at current prices in 2000 is found to be Rs. 701.67 per square feet and it increased to Rs. 1,608.33 per square feet in 2010 and that increased further to Rs. 2,275 per square feet in 2015. At constant prices (2004-2005 prices), the land prices are found to be Rs. 844.07, Rs. 1,122.06 and Rs. 1255.46 per square feet respectively, 2000, 2010 and 2015. In 2015, the price per square feet at 2004-05 prices has been estimated to be Rs. 3,035.18 in respect of special commercial land while it is merely Rs. 193.15 in case of homestead/barren/agricultural land. Wide variations in the average annual growth rates at constant prices in respect of the various categories are also observed during the period. During 2010-2015, it is observed that, at constant prices, the average annual growth of special commercial land prices has been negative. On the whole, during 2000-2015 all categories of land recorded positive growth in prices with homestead/barren/agricultural land recording the highest growth rate of 11.17 per cent, while the overall growth in land prices during the period is found to be 6.50 per cent.

At constant prices the average annual growth rate varies from 1.74 per cent to 11.17 per cent during 2000-2015. Growth of price of homestead is the highest because the price per unit of area was relatively low while special commercial recorded the lowest growth rate because its price has already reached saturation level. Also, due to very low price and after rising scarcity in the commercial areas, the demand for the outskirt barren areas has increased significantly.

Table 3.9: Periodic Growth Rate of Land Prices at 2004-05 Prices

Category	2000-10	2010-15	2000-15
Special Commercial	30.50	-3.33	26.16
Commercial A	11.17	20.36	33.80
Commercial B	45.00	26.55	83.50
Residential A	74.00	31.82	129.37
Residential B	93.33	26.55	144.66
Homestead/ Barren	93.33	38.41	167.60
Average	57.89	23.39	97.52

Source: Field Survey conducted during March-April 2015.

The periodic growth rate of land prices at 2004-05 prices as displayed in Table 3.9 reveals substantial variations within a category across periods and across categories over different periods.

During 2000-2010, growth of land prices varied from 11.17 per cent to 93.33 per cent with an average of 57.89 per cent. From 2010 to 2015, however, land prices witnessed an overall growth of 23.39 per cent but special commercial land prices experienced a negative growth (-3.33). During 2000 to 2015, land prices increased substantially in the range of 26.16 per cent to 167.60 per cent with an overall growth rate of 97.52 per cent.

Land Records and Survey Office, Dimapur classifies land into six categories, viz. Commercial Special, Commercial-A & B, Residential-A & B, Homestead and Barren/Agricultural. Commercial Special land covers the main market area (CBD) which is under the marked area of W-19 in Fig. 3.7.

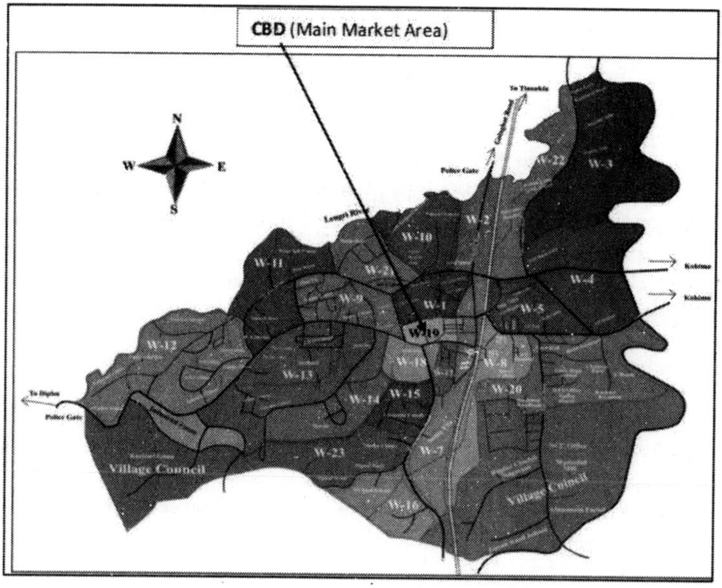

Fig. 3.7: Categories of Land Use.

Source: Field Survey conducted during March-April 2015.

Conclusion

Dimapur town is considered as the economic gateway of Nagaland state and is one of the fastest growing towns in the North-Eastern region of India. The progress of the town in economic and educational fields has been attracting new entrants continuously. Over the past few decades, there has been an exponential growth of population with people flocking the town not only from different parts of Nagaland and various other states of India, but also from neighbouring countries. Increasing population brings along more number of households who require housing facilities. It is quite natural that with rising economic activities, growth of labour force and urbanisation, population and required housing sector also grow in any town. This phenomenon led to rise in pressure exerted on the housing sector in the town like Dimapur. Due to lack of proper planning and spatial expansion, it has resulted in congestion and overcrowding of people and buildings in certain parts of the town. With the continued increase in population and households, the demand for housing is ever rising. This pressure is most visible in the rapidly growing land prices in the town. Spatial variation in land prices and population density also exhibits people's preference of location of residence.

REFERENCES

Abiodun, J.O. (1976). Housing problems in Nigerian cities. *The Town Planning Review*, 47(4), 339-347.

Ademiluyi, I.A. (2010). Public housing delivery strategies in Nigeria: A historical perspective of policies and programmes. *Journal of Sustainable Development in Africa,* 12(6), 153-161.

Aluko, O.E. (2010). The impact of urbanization on housing development: The Lagos experience, Nigeria. *Ethiopian Journal of Environmental Studies and Management*, 3(3), 64-74.

Blomquist, G.C., Berger, M.C. and Hoehn, J.P. (1988). New estimates of quality of life in urban areas. *The American Economic Review*, 78(1), 89-107.

Clark, W.A.V., Deurloo, M.C. and Dieleman, F.M. (2000). Housing consumption and residential crowding in U.S. housing markets. *Journal of Urban Affairs*, 22(1), 49-63.

Clauretie, T.M. and Neill, H.R. (2000). Year-round school schedules and residential property values. *Journal of Real Estate Finance and Economics*, 20(3), 311-322.

Di Pasquale, D. and Wheaton, W.C. (1992). The markets for real estate assets and space: A conceptual framework. *Journal of the American Real Estate and Urban Economics Association*, 20(1), 181-197.

DMC official website – dmcnagaland.nic.in/SSL/login.aspx

Eichholtz, P. and Lindenthal, T. (2014). Demographics, human capital and the demand for housing. *Journal of Housing Economics*, 26, 19-32.

Fortin, M. and Leclerc, A. (2000). *Demographic changes and real housing prices in Canada.* Working Paper No. 00-06. University of Sherbrooke. Retrieved from http://citeseerx.ist.psu.edu/viewdoc/download?doi=10.1.1.198.9803&rep=rep1&type=pdf on 23/5/2015.

Glaeser, E.L., Gyourko, J. and Saks, R.E. (2005). *Urban Growth and Housing Supply*. Discussion Paper No. 2062, Harvard Institute of Economic Research. Retrieved from: http://post.economics.harvard.edu/hier/2005list.html on 22/5/2015.

Government of India, Census of India, 1961, 1971, 1981, 1991, 2001 and 2011. Retrieved from: censusindia.gov.in

GoI-UNDP Project (2013). *District Human Development Report, Dimapur, Nagaland*. Government of Nagaland, Department of Planning and Coordination, Nagaland.

Habitat for Humanity, Ireland. (2015). *The importance of housing*. Retrieved from www.habitatireland.ie/2015/01/importance-housing/ on 22/11/2016.

Hendershott, P.H. (1991). *Are real house prices likely to decline by 47 per cent?* NBER Working Paper No. 3880. DOI: 10.3386/w3880. Retrieved from: http://www.nber.org/papers/w3880.pdf on 8/6/2015.

Holly, S. and Jones, N. (1997). House prices since the 1940s: Cointegration, demography and asymmetries. *Economic Modelling*, 14, 549-565.

Jud, G.D. and Watts, J.M. (1981). Schools and housing value. *Land Economics*, 57(3), 459-470.

Karantonis, A. (2008). *Population growth and housing affordability in the modern city–Sydney, a case study*. University of Technology, Sydney. Retrieved from: http://www.prres.net/papers/Karantonis_Population_Growth_and_Housing_Affordability.pdf on 22/5/2015.

Lee, G.S., Dengler, P.S., Felderer, B. and Helmenstein, C. (2001). Austrian demography and housing demand: Is there a connection. *Empirica*, 28, 259-276.

Lee, T.H. (1968). Housing and permanent income: Tests based on a three-year reinterview survey. *The Review of Economics and Statistics*, 50 (4), 480-490. Retrieved from: http://www.jstor.org/stable/1926817 on 8/6/2015.

Lee, T.H. and Kong, C.M. (1977). Elasticities of housing demand. *Southern Economic Journal*, 44(2), 298-305.

Lindh, T. and Malmberg, B. (2008). Demography and housing demand—What can we learn from residential construction data? *Journal of Population Economics*, 21, 521-539.

Maisel, S.J., Burnham, J.B. and Austin, J.S. (1971). The demand for housing: A comment. *The Review of Economics and Statistics*, 53(4), 410-413.

Mankiw, N.G. and Weil, D.N. (1989). The baby boom, the baby bust, and the housing market. *Regional Science and Urban Economics*, 19, 235-258.

Mayo, S.K. (1981). Theory and estimation in the economics of housing demand. *Journal of Urban Economics*, 10, 95-116.

Michaelsen, M.M. and Haisken-DeNew, J.P. (2015). Migration magnet: The role of work experience in rural–urban wage differentials. *IZA Journal of Migration*, 4 (21). DOI 10.1186/s40176-015-0046-7. Retrieved from: https://izajom.springeropen.com/articles/10.1186/s40176-015-0046-7 on 23/5/2015.

Mishra, S.K. and Ngullie, M.L. (2003). Quality of life in Dimapur Nagaland (India). *SSRN Electronic Journal*. Retrieved from: https//www.researchgate.net/publication/249960907 on 8/6/2015.

Mulder, C.H. (2006). Population and housing: A two-sided relationship. *Demographic Research*, 15(13), 401-412. DOI: 10.4054/DemRes.2006.15.13. Retrieved from http:www.demographic-reseach.org/Volumes/Vol15/13 on 22/05/2015.

Oluwatoyin, O.J., Sunday, S.K. and Folake, A. (2013). Population growth and health facilitiesin Nigeria (A case study of Ondo State). *International Journal of Scientific and Technology Research*, 2(8), 108-113.

Rosen, S. (1977). *Labour quality, the demand for skill, and market selection*. NBER Working Paper no. 162, Center for economic Analysis of Human Behaviour. Retrieved from: http://www.nber.org/papers/w0162.pdf on 26/5/2015.

Swan, C. (1995). Demography and the demand for housing: a reinterpretation of the Mankiw-Weil demand variable. *Regional Science and Urban Economics*, 25, 41-58.

4
Socio-Economic and Demographic Characteristics of the City Dwellers

Introduction

Socio-economic factors play important roles in housing decision-making through which demand for housing types and residential neighbourhood are made (Akinyode *et al.*, 2015). Social and economic factors like family size and age profile of the households, their gender and marital status, nature of employment and level of income are expected to significantly affect the nature of housing units sought by them. Family size, gender and age distribution of the family members and marital status determine the requirement of housing for a normal livelihood, whereas income and employment affect the capability and desire for standard of housing with various facilities, which is expected to rise with better job-opportunities and more income. With less income even a larger family is found to manage in a relatively smaller house with limited facilities. Also, livelihood pattern varies across communities due to their very inherent nature and thus the pattern of housing preferred by them. Further, education of individual and that of the neighbours through demonstration effect and due to awareness change the facilities urged by the individuals. Therefore, a detailed examination of the socio-economic characteristics of the sample households living in Dimapur town is worth to understand the nature of demand for housing and its variation across different socio-economic groups in the town; which in turn can guide in the development of proper housing policy with respect to the 'needs' of the households living there.

Socio-Economic and Demographic Status of the Sample Respondents

Among the social characteristics, the following quantifiable factors have been considered in the present study: Marital Status, religion, nature of domicile, community, level of education and family size. With regard to economic characteristics, nature of employment and income of the head of household as well as of the family have been considered. Personal assets like possession of vehicle and employment of domestic servant, which signify the economic status of a household, are also taken into account. Besides these characteristics, personal details of the households like duration of stay in Dimapur town, number of families living in the same building, time taken for arranging accommodation first time and their preference for further change in accommodation are also taken into consideration. Changes in time taken to find the first accommodation by the individuals with different length of years of stay by the individuals help us in understanding the variation in demand for housing and thus changes in difficulty in getting accommodation over time.

Out of the 490 surveyed respondents, 414 respondents are found to be tenants and 76 respondents are house-owners living in their own houses. Since there are certain basic differences between tenant households and owner households, especially in respect of their mobility and preference for various housing attributes, a comparative picture of the two cases is also presented.

Distribution of Surveyed Households as per the Family Size across Wards

Family size, other things remaining identical, affects the requirement of house space for a household. Thus, it may be one of the important variables determining the demand for housing. A poor household with big family size, however, may manage with less space while a rich but small family may enjoy the luxury of a big house space.

It is revealed that the average family size of owner households (5.19) is larger than that of the tenant households (4.15) (Table 4.1). Overall, it is also observed that 43.24 per cent of tenant households and 67.11 per cent of owner households have more than four members in the family. In respect of the tenants, Ward 12 recorded the highest average family size (5.22), whereas Ward 2 recorded the lowest average family size. With regard to the owners, Ward 17 recorded the highest (6.33) and Ward 14 recorded the lowest (3) average family size respectively. On the other hand, it may be noted that the average number of rooms have been found to be 2.60 and 4.83 for tenants and owners respectively. This implies that the surveyed tenants are living in comparatively more congested housing units as compared to the sample owners.

Table 4.1: Ward-wise Distribution of Respondents According to their Family Size

Ward	Tenant Households				Owner Households			
	2 and less	3-4	More than 4	Avg.	2 and less	3-4	More than 4	Avg.
Ward 1	2 (11.76)	8 (47.06)	7 (41.18)	3.94	0 (0)	1 (33.33)	2 (66.67)	4.67
Ward 2	3 (16.67)	11 (61.11)	4 (22.22)	3.44	0 (0)	1 (33.33)	2 (66.67)	4.67
Ward 3	2 (11.76)	8 (47.06)	7 (41.18)	3.88	0 (0)	1 (33.33)	2 (66.67)	5
Ward 4	4 (22.22)	8 (44.44)	6 (33.33)	3.72	0 (0)	2 (50)	2 (50)	5
Ward 5	4 (25)	6 (37.5)	6 (37.5)	3.69	0 (0)	0 (0)	4 (100)	5.5
Ward 6	3 (15.79)	6 (31.58)	10 (52.63)	4.32	0 (0)	1 (33.33)	2 (66.67)	4.67
Ward 7	2 (10.53)	7 (36.84)	10 (52.63)	4.21	0 (0)	2 (50)	2 (50)	4.5
Ward 8	3 (16.67)	11 (61.11)	4 (22.22)	3.61	0 (0)	1 (33.33)	2 (66.67)	5.67
Ward 9	3 (17.65)	6 (35.29)	8 (47.06)	4.47	0 (0)	0 (0)	3 (100)	7
Ward 10	3 (15.79)	5 (26.32)	11 (57.89)	4.63	0 (0)	1 (33.33)	2 (66.67)	5
Ward 11	5 (26.32)	6 (31.58)	8 (42.11)	4.47	0 (0)	1 (33.33)	2 (66.67)	6
Ward 12	3 (16.67)	4 (22.22)	11 (61.11)	5.22	0 (0)	0 (0)	4 (100)	5.5
Ward 13	4 (22.22)	5 (27.78)	9 (50)	4.39	0 (0)	2 (50)	2 (50)	4.75
Ward 14	5 (26.32)	6 (31.58)	8 (42.11)	3.95	1(33.33)	1(33.33)	1 (33.33)	3
Ward 15	3 (16.67)	6 (33.33)	9 (50)	4.5	0 (0)	1 (33.33)	2 (66.67)	5.67

(Contd.)

Ward	Tenant Households				Owner Households			
	2 and less	3-4	More than 4	Avg.	2 and less	3-4	More than 4	Avg.
Ward 16	4 (23.53)	3 (17.65)	10 (58.82)	4	0 (0)	1 (25)	3 (75)	5.75
Ward 17	1 (5.56)	12 (66.67)	5 (27.78)	4.22	0 (0)	1 (33.33)	2 (66.67)	6.33
Ward 18	3 (16.67)	6 (33.33)	9 (50)	4.17	0 (0)	2 (66.67)	1 (33.33)	5.67
Ward 19	1 (5.26)	13 (68.42)	5 (26.32)	4.26	0 (0)	1 (33.33)	2 (66.67)	5
Ward 20	3 (16.67)	7 (38.89)	8 (44.44)	4.22	0 (0)	2 (66.67)	1 (33.33)	4
Ward 21	0 (0)	11 (57.89)	8 (42.11)	4.21	0 (0)	0 (0)	3 (100)	6
Ward 22	3 (16.67)	5 (27.78)	10 (55.56)	4.28	0 (0)	1 (33.33)	2 (66.67)	5.33
Ward 23	3 (17.65)	8 (47.06)	6 (35.29)	3.76	0 (0)	1 (25)	3 (75)	4.75
Total	**67 (16.18)**	**168 (40.58)**	**179 (43.24)**	**4.15**	**1 (1.32)**	**24 (31.58)**	**51 (67.11)**	**5.19**

Source: Field Survey by the researcher during 2015-16.

Note: Figures in the parentheses represent percentage to total.

Table 4.2: Ward-wise Distribution of Respondents According to their Marital Status

Ward	Tenant Households					Owner Households				
	Married	Un-married	Widowed	Divor-ced	Sub-Total	Married	Unmarried	Wido-wed	Divor-ced	Sub-Total
Ward 1	15 (88.23)	2 (11.76	0 (0)	0 (0)	17	3 (100)	0 (0)	None	None	3
Ward 2	16 (88.89)	2 (11.11)	0 (0)	0 (0)	18	3 (100)	0 (0)			3
Ward 3	11 (64.71)	6 (35.29)	0 (0)	0 (0)	17	2 (66.67)	1(33.33)			3
Ward 4	12 (66.67)	6 (33.33)	0 (0)	0 (0)	18	4 (100)	0 (0)			4
Ward 5	12 (75)	4 (25)	0 (0)	0 (0)	16	4 (100)	0 (0)			4
Ward 6	16 (84.21)	3 (15.79)	0 (0)	0 (0)	19	3 (100)	0 (0)			3
Ward 7	16 (84.21)	3 (15.79)	0 (0)	0 (0)	19	4 (100)	0 (0)			4
Ward 8	16 (88.89)	2 (11.11)	0 (0)	0 (0)	18	3 (100)	0 (0)			3
Ward 9	14 (82.35)	3 (17.65)	0 (0)	0 (0)	17	3 (100)	0 (0)			3
Ward 10	12 (63.16)	3 (15.79)	3 (15.79)	1(5.26)	19	3 (100)	0 (0)			3
Ward 11	12 (63.16)	7 (36.84)	0 (0)	0 (0)	19	3 (100)	0 (0)			3
Ward 12	12 (66.67)	4 (22.22)	1 (5.55)	1 (5.55)	18	4 (100)	0 (0)			4

(Contd.)

Ward	Tenant Households					Owner Households				
	Married	Un-married	Widowed	Divor-ced	Sub-Total	Married	Unmarried	Wido-wed	Divor-ced	Sub-Total
Ward 13	13 (72.22)	5 (27.78)	0 (0)	0 (0)	18	3 (75)	1 (25)	None	None	4
Ward 14	12 (63.16)	7 (36.84)	0 (0)	0 (0)	19	2 (66.67)	1 (33.33)			3
Ward 15	14 (77.78)	4 (22.22)	0 (0)	0 (0)	18	3 (100)	0 (0)			3
Ward 16	13 (76.47)	4 (23.53)	0 (0)	0 (0)	17	4 (100)	0 (0)			4
Ward 17	18 (100)	0 (0)	0 (0)	0 (0)	18	3 (100)	0 (0)			3
Ward 18	15 (83.33)	3 (16.67)	0 (0)	0 (0)	18	3(100)	0 (0)			3
Ward 19	19 (100)	0 (0)	0 (0)	0 (0)	19	3 (100)	0 (0)			3
Ward 20	13 (72.22)	5 (27.78)	0 (0)	0 (0)	18	3 (100)	0 (0)			3
Ward 21	17 (89.47)	2 (10.53)	0 (0)	0 (0)	19	2 (66.67)	1 (33.33)			3
Ward 22	13 (72.22)	5 (27.78)	0 (0)	0 (0)	18	3 (100)	0 (0)			3
Ward 23	15 (88.23)	2 (11.76)	0 (0)	0 (0)	17	4 (100)	0 (0)			4
Total	**320 (79.29)**	**88 (21.26)**	**4 (0.97)**	**2 (0.48)**	**414**	**72 (94.74)**	**4 (5.26)**			**76**

Source: Field Survey by the researcher during 2015-16.
Note: Figures in the parentheses represent percentage to total.

Distribution of Surveyed Respondents by Marital Status and Religion

The residential choice by an individual, apart from other factors, may be influenced by his/her marital status. The ward-wise distribution of marital status of respondents is displayed in Table 4.2.

It is observed that across the 23 wards of the town, 100 per cent respondents in Ward 17 and Ward 19 are married. In case of tenant households, percentage of married respondents is found to be very high ranging from about 63 to 100 per cent across the wards. Wards 17 and 19 have all tenant respondents married, while Wards 11 and 14 have the highest percentage of unmarried tenant respondents (36.84%). A few widowed (4) and divorced (2) tenant respondents are also found in Wards 10 and 12 respectively. Among the owner households, proportion of married respondents is found to be much higher than that of tenants.

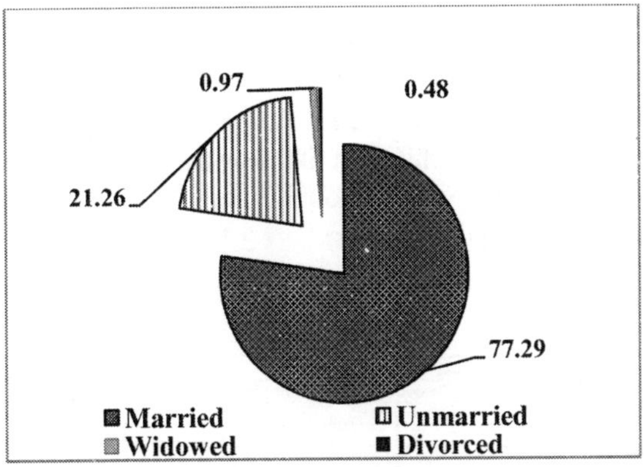

Fig. 4.1a: Distribution of Tenant Respondents According to Marital Status

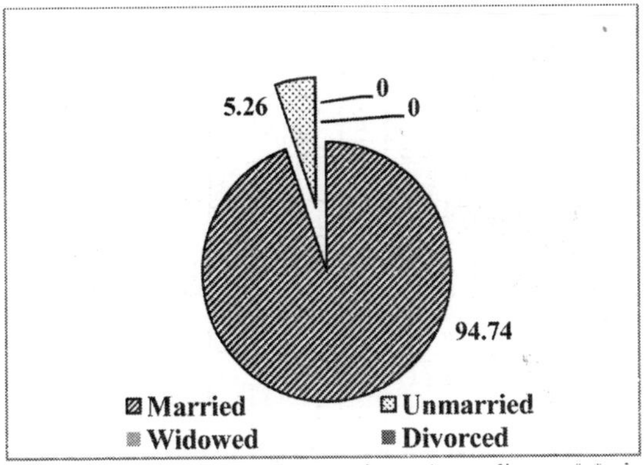

Fig. 4.1b: Distribution of Owner Respondents According to Marital Status

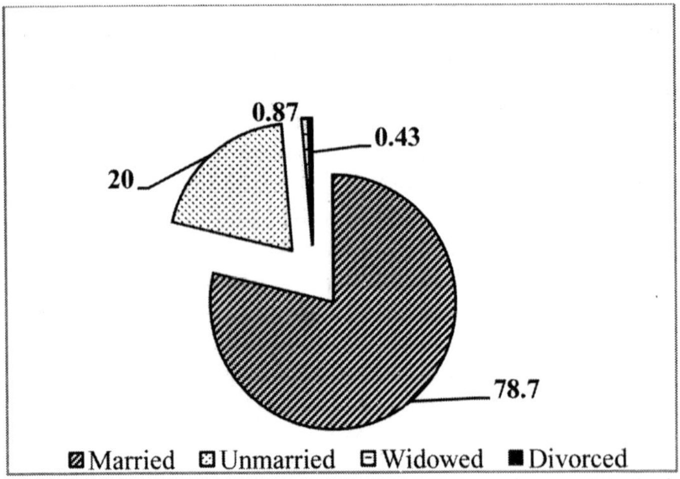

Fig. 4.1c: Distribution of All Respondents According to Marital Status.

Fig. 4.1a shows that overall, 77.29 per cent (320) of the tenant respondents are married while that of the owner respondents is 94.74 per cent (72) (Fig. 4.1b). Overall, about 80 per cent (392) of the surveyed respondents are married (Fig. 4.1c).

Table 4.3: Ward-wise Distribution of the Surveyed Households according to their Religion

Ward	Christians		Hindu		Muslim		Jain		Sikh		Buddhist	
	Tenants	Owners	Tenants	Owners	Tenants	Owners	Tenants	Owners	Tenants	Owners	Tenants	Owners
Ward 1	8 (47.06)	3 (100)	7 (41.18)	0 (0)	0 (0)		1 (5.88)	0 (0)	1 (5.88)		0 (0)	
Ward 2	7 (38.89)	3 (100)	10 (55.55)	0 (0)	1 (5.55)		0 (0)	0 (0)	0 (0)		0 (0)	
Ward 3	10 (58.82)	3 (100)	4 (23.53)	0 (0)	3 (17.65)		0 (0)	0 (0)	0 (0)		0 (0)	
Ward 4	11 (61.11)	4 (100)	5 (27.78)	0 (0)	2 (11.11)		0 (0)	0 (0)	0 (0)		0 (0)	
Ward 5	10 (62.50)	4 (100)	5 (31.25)	0 (0)	0 (0)		0 (0)	0 (0)	1 (6.25)		0 (0)	
Ward 6	2 (10.53)	2 (66.67)	7 (36.84)	0 (0)	4 (21.05)		2 (10.53)	1 (33.33)	2 (10.53)		2 (10.53)	
Ward 7	3 (15.79)	4 (100)	14 (73.68)	0 (0)	2 (10.52)		0 (0)	0 (0)	0 (0)		0 (0)	
Ward 8	7 (38.89)	3 (100)	9 (50)	0 (0)	1 (5.55)		0 (0)	0 (0)	0 (0)		1 (5.55)	
Ward 9	9 (52.94)	2 (66.67)	8 (47.06)	0 (0)	0 (0)		0 (0)	1 (33.33)	0 (0)		0 (0)	
Ward 10	14 (73.68)	3 (100)	3 (15.79)	0 (0)	2 (10.53)		0 (0)	0 (0)	0 (0)		0 (0)	
Ward 11	17 (89.47)	3 (100)	2 (10.53)	0 (0)	0 (0)		0 (0)	0 (0)	0 (0)		0 (0)	
Ward 12	18 (100)	4 (100)	0 (0)	0 (0)	0 (0)	NIL	0 (0)	0 (0)	0 (0)	NIL	0 (0)	NIL
Ward 13	14 (77.78)	4 (100)	4 (22.22)	0 (0)	0 (0)		0 (0)	0 (0)	0 (0)		0 (0)	
Ward 14	16 (84.21)	3 (100)	1 (5.26)	0 (0)	2 (10.53)		0 (0)	0 (0)	0 (0)		0 (0)	
Ward 15	2 (11.11)	2 (66.67)	13 (72.22)	1(33.33)	3 (16.67)		0 (0)	0 (0)	0 (0)		0 (0)	
Ward 16	10 (58.82)	4 (100)	6 (35.29)	0 (0)	1 (5.88)		0 (0)	0 (0)	0 (0)		0 (0)	
Ward 17	0 (0)	0 (0)	6 (33.33)	1(33.33)	1 (5.55)		11 (61.11)	2 (66.67)	0 (0)		0 (0)	
Ward 18	5 (27.78)	2 (66.67)	9 (50)	0 (0)	1 (5.55)		3 (16.67)	1 (33.33)	0 (0)		0 (0)	
Ward 19	2 (10.53)	3 (100)	9 (47.37)	0 (0)	6 (31.58)		1 (5.26)	0 (0)	1 (5.26)		0 (0)	
Ward 20	14 (77.78)	3 (100)	3 (16.67)	0 (0)	1 (5.55)		0 (0)	0 (0)	0 (0)		0 (0)	
Ward 21	11 (57.89)	3 (100)	5 (26.31)	0 (0)	1 (5.26)		2 (9.52)	0 (0)	0 (0)		0 (0)	
Ward 22	9 (50)	3 (100)	5 (27.78)	0 (0)	4 (22.22)		0 (0)	0 (0)	0 (0)		0 (0)	
Ward 23	6 (35.29)	4 (100)	10 (58.82)	0 (0)	1 (5.88)		0 (0)	0 (0)	0 (0)		0 (0)	
Total	205(49.52)	69(90.79)	145(35.02)	2 (2.63)	36 (8.69)		20 (4.83)	5 (6.58)	5 (1.21)		3 (0.72)	

Source: Field Survey by the Author during 2015-16.
Note: Figures in the parentheses represent percentage to total.

Religion is one element of life that has connected the races and societies of the world for centuries. For most people, religion is considered to be dear and provides them a sense of purpose and order. In the housing market too it has been observed that individuals or households desire to live among people of the same faith resulting in some sort of clustering in residential areas. This trend is also observed from the data collected in the study area. The respondents are found to belong to only 6 different religions, namely Christianity, Hinduism, Islam, Jainism, Sikhism and Buddhism (Table 4.3).

In most of the wards, however, concentration of one religion is recorded. Tenant respondents belonging to Christianity are in clear majority constituting 50 per cent or more of the surveyed households in 13 wards, with Ward 12 having 100 per cent of Christians. The field survey also reveals that in 6 wards, tenant respondents belonging to Hinduism are in clear majority with 50 per cent or more of the surveyed tenant respondents. It is also observed that people belonging to Jainism are mostly clustered in Ward 13 with 61.11 per cent of the tenant respondents.

In case of owner households, the survey showed a highly skewed distribution in favour of Christianity. This is due to the fact that most house owners are Nagas who are Christians by faith. From Table 4.3, it is observed that 100 per cent owner respondents in 18 wards are Christians. It is about two-third in Wards 6, 9, 15 and 18. Surprisingly, no Christian owner respondent is found in Ward 17. Owner respondents belonging to Hinduism are very few in Ward 15 and 17. However some Jain owner respondents are found in Wards 17, 6, 9 and 18.

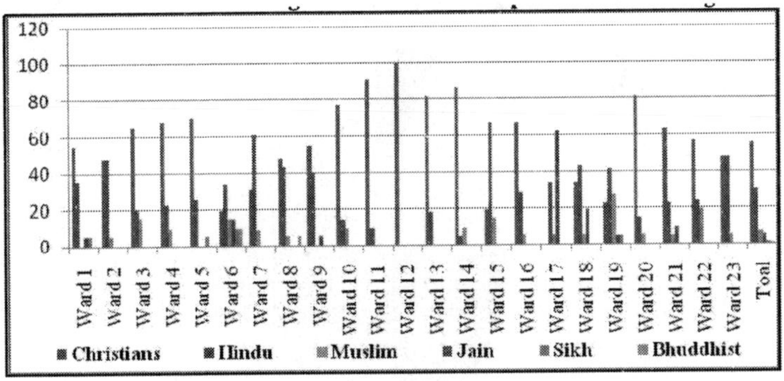

Fig. 4.2: Ward-wise Percentage Distribution of Respondents According to Religion.

Fig. 4.2 also displays the ward-wise percentage distribution of all the surveyed respondents according to their religion. Also, the overall religious distribution of the surveyed respondents according to their religion is displayed in 3 Pie charts. Fig. 4.3a shows that Christians constitute 49.52 per cent of the tenant respondents which is followed by Hindus (about 35%). The other 4 religions comprising Muslims, Jains, Sikhs and Buddhists constitute barely 15 per cent of the total surveyed tenant respondents. Owner respondents, however, belong to only 3 religions. The Christian owners are in clear majority (90.79%) while Jains account for only 6.58 per cent. Hindu owner respondents constitute merely 2.63 per cent of the sample (Fig. 4.3b). Among all the respondents, however, 55.92 per cent are Christians, followed by Hindus (30%), Muslims (7.35%) and then Jains (5.10%) (Fig. 4.3c).

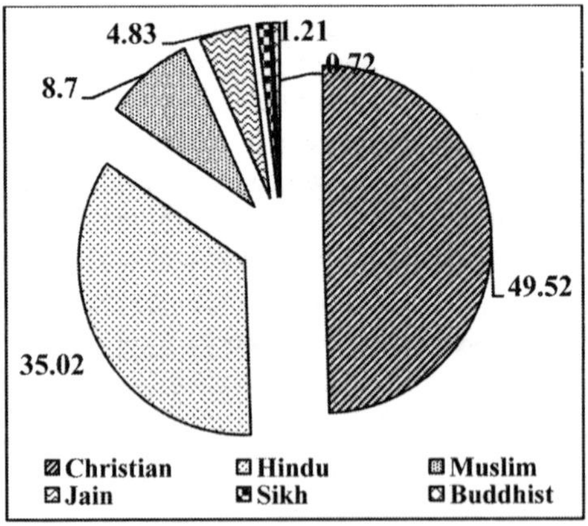

Fig. 4.3a: Distribution of Tenant Households According to Religion

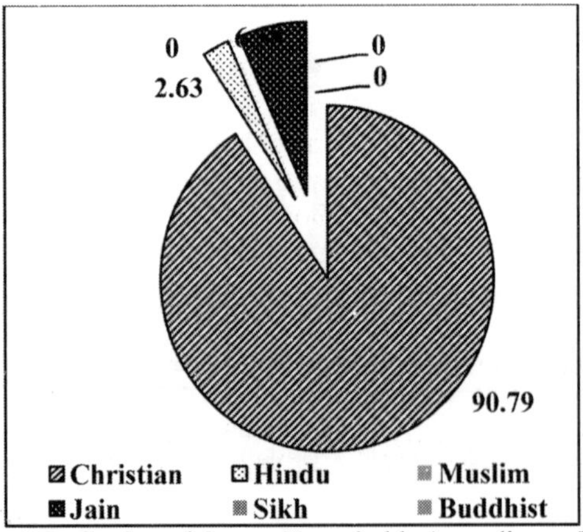

Fig. 4.3b: Distribution of Owner Households According to Religion

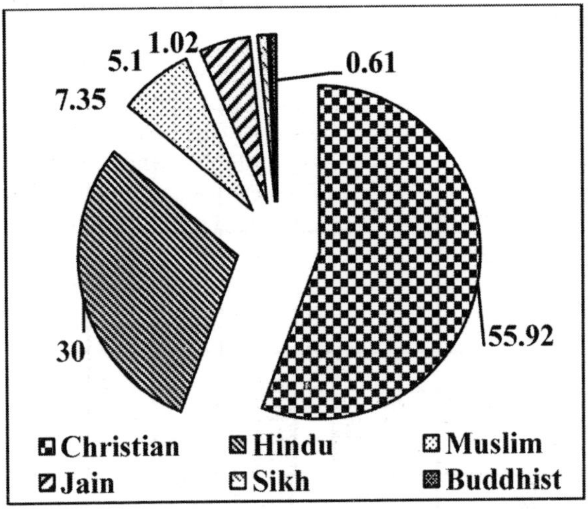

Fig. 4.3c: Distribution of All Households According to Religion

Distribution of Surveyed Respondents by Community and Status of Domicile

People belonging to the same race and culture have been found to have a strong attachment with each other and is considered to be a key determinant for location of residential choice. Most people are strongly bonded towards their community and feel a greater sense of security living among members of their own community. For the same reason, they are even ready to pay some more rent to occupy a house in their cluster. The field survey revealed similar trend in Dimapur Town which is displayed in Table 4.4.

The respondents are broadly classified into three categories – Naga, Non-Naga and non-Indian. The "Naga" category includes all Naga tribes from the state of Nagaland and the neighbouring states. The "Non-Naga" category includes all respondents who are not Naga but are Indians. The "non-Indian" category refers to those who are not Indians. This third category has only three respondents who are from Tibet. It is observed from the table that there is a clear concentration of a particular community in most of the wards.

In respect of tenant respondents, Nagas are found to be in majority in 9 wards, and Non-Nagas are more in 13 wards with Ward 17 witnessing 100 per cent in the survey. Two major communities are equally placed in Ward 22 constituting 50 per cent each. The "non-Indian" category is found only in Ward 6 and Ward 8 of the town constituting 10.53 per cent and 5.55 per cent of the tenant respondents respectively. They are basically traders in Hong Kong market and prefer to reside in close proximity to their workplace.

Table 4.4: Ward-wise Distribution of Respondents According to their Community and Domicile Status

Ward	Community						Domicile Status			
	Tenant Respondents			Owner Respondents			Tenant Respondents		Owner Respondents	
	Naga	Non-Naga	Non-Indian	Naga	Non-Naga	Non-Indian	Migrated	Domicile	Migrated	Domicile
Ward 1	7 (41.18)	10 (58.82)	0 (0)	3 (100)	0 (0)	None	15 (88.23)	2 (11.76)	2 (66.67)	1 (33.33)
Ward 2	6 (33.33)	12 (66.67)	0 (0)	3 (100)	0 (0)		18 (100)	0 (0)	1 (33.33)	2 (66.67)
Ward 3	10 (58.82)	7 (41.18)	0 (0)	3 (100)	0 (0)		15 (88.23)	2 (11.76)	1 (33.33)	2 (66.67)
Ward 4	11 (61.11)	7 (38.89)	0 (0)	4 (100)	0 (0)		18 (100)	0 (0)	2 (50)	2 (50)
Ward 5	9 (56.25)	7 (43.75)	0 (0)	4 (100)	0 (0)		16 (100)	0 (0)	2 (50)	2 (50)
Ward 6	2 (10.53)	15 (78.95)	2 (10.53)	2 (66.67)	1 (33.33)		19 (100)	0 (0)	0 (0)	3 (100)
Ward 7	2 (10.53)	17 (89.47)	0 (0)	4 (100)	0 (0)		18 (94.74)	1 (5.26)	3 (75)	1 (25)
Ward 8	5 (27.78)	12 (66.67)	1 (5.55)	3 (100)	0 (0)		16 (88.89)	2 (11.11)	2 (66.67)	1 (33.33)
Ward 9	6 (35.29)	11 (64.71)	0 (0)	2 (66.67)	1 (33.33)		17 (100)	0 (0)	2 (66.67)	1 (33.33)
Ward 10	13 (68.42)	6 (31.58)	0 (0)	3 (100)	0 (0)		19 (100)	0 (0)	2 (66.67)	1 (33.33)

(*Contd.*)

Ward	Community						Domicile Status			
	Tenant Respondents			Owner Respondents			Tenant Respondents		Owner Respondents	
	Naga	Non-Naga	Non-Indian	Naga	Non-Naga	Non-Indian	Migrated	Domicile	Migrated	Domicile
Ward 11	17 (89.47)	2 (10.53)	0 (0)	3 (100)	0 (0)		19 (100)	0 (0)	1 (33.33)	2 (66.67)
Ward 12	17 (94.44)	1 (5.55)	0 (0)	4 (100)	0 (0)		17 (94.44)	1 (5.55)	3 (75)	1 (25)
Ward 13	12 (66.67)	6 (33.33)	0 (0)	4 (100)	0 (0)		16 (88.89)	2 (11.11)	3 (75)	1 (25)
Ward 14	15 (78.95)	4 (21.05)	0 (0)	3 (100)	0 (0)		19 (100)	0 (0)	2 (66.67)	1 (33.33)
Ward 15	2 (11.11)	16 (88.89)	0 (0)	2 (66.67)	1 (33.33)		15 (83.33)	3 (16.67)	2 (66.67)	1 (33.33)
Ward 16	8 (47.06)	9 (52.94)	0 (0)	4 (100)	0 (0)		16 (94.12)	1 (5.88)	2 (50)	2 (50)
Ward 17	0 (0)	18 (100)	0 (0)	0 (0)	3 (100)		14 (77.78)	4 (22.22)	1 (33.33)	2 (66.67)
Ward 18	5 (27.78)	13 (72.22)	0 (0)	2 (66.67)	1 (33.33)		18 (100)	0 (0)	2 (66.67)	1 (33.33)

(Contd.)

Ward	Community						Domicile Status			
	Tenant Respondents			Owner Respondents			Tenant Respondents		Owner Respondents	
	Naga	Non-Naga	Non-Indian	Naga	Non-Naga	Non-Indian	Migrated	Domicile	Migrated	Domicile
Ward 19	2 (10.53)	17 (89.47)	0 (0)	3 (100)	0 (0)	None	16 (84.21)	3 (15.79)	1 (33.33)	2 (66.67)
Ward 20	12 (66.67)	6 (33.33)	0 (0)	3 (100)	0 (0)		18 (100)	0 (0)	2 (66.67)	1 (33.33)
Ward 21	8 (42.10)	11 (57.89)	0 (0)	3 (100)	0 (0)		14 (73.68)	5 (26.32)	1 (33.33)	2 (66.67)
Ward 22	9 (50)	9 (50)	0 (0)	3 (100)	0 (0)		16 (88.89)	2 (11.11)	2 (66.67)	1 (33.33)
Ward 23	6 (35.29)	11 (64.71)	0 (0)	4 (100)	0 (0)		15 (88.23)	2 (11.76)	4 (100)	0 (0)
Total	**184 (44.44)**	**227 (54.83)**	**3 (0.72)**	**69 (90.79)**	**7 (9.21)**		**384 (92.75**	**30 (7.25)**	**43 (56.58)**	**33 (43.42)**

Source: Field Survey by the researcher during 2015-16.
Note: Figures in the parentheses represent percentage to total.

In case of owner households, it is observed that Nagas constitute a clear majority with 100 per cent share in 18 wards of the town. The Non-Naga owner respondents are found in 5 wards where it is 100 per cent in Ward 17. It shares 33.33 per cent of the owner respondents in Wards 6, 9, 15 and 18 of the town.

Fig. 4.4a displays the percentage distribution of surveyed tenant respondents according to their community. Among the 414 tenant respondents surveyed, it is observed that 44.44 per cent are Naga and a meagre 0.72 per cent belong to "non-Indian" category. For the town as a whole, it is recorded that Non-Naga community constitutes 54.83 per cent of the tenant respondents. Significantly, houses in Dimapur town are owned by the Nagas. House owners belonging to Naga community constitute about 90 per cent and the rest is owned by Non-Nagas (Fig. 4.4b). For the overall surveyed respondents, 51.36 per cent belongs to Naga community and 47.76 per cent belong to Non-Naga community. This distribution of the population reveals the cosmopolitan characteristics of the town.

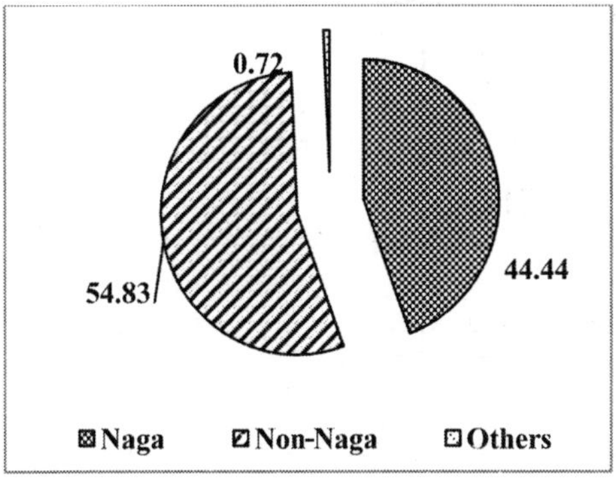

Fig. 4.4a: Distribution of Tenant Households According to their Community

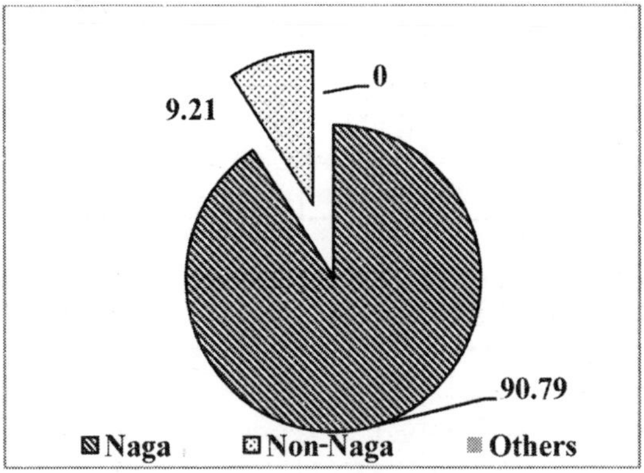

Fig. 4.4b: Distribution of Owner Households According to their Community

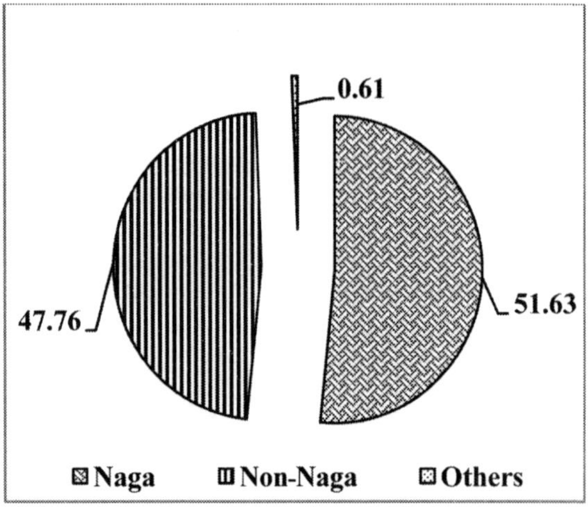

Fig. 4.4c: Distribution of All Households According to their Community

Fig. 4.5 displays the ward-wise percentage distribution of all the surveyed respondents according to their community. Ward 17 of the town recorded the presence of only non-Nagas. Fig. 4.5 also shows highly skewed distribution of respondents towards Naga community in more than half of the wards. A close look at the distribution reveals that except Ward 1, concentration of Non-Nagas is more towards highly commercialised areas and Nagas are more concentrated in wards farther from highly commercialised areas. The "non-Indian" category community is also found to be located near the highly commercialised areas of the town. This distribution of the communities may be explained by the fact that 61.70 per cent and 100 per cent of non-Nagas and non-Indians are self-employed and run their own businesses, whereas only 32.67 per cent of Nagas are into business and majority of them (44.22%) are Government employees.

Dimapur town has been growing rapidly both as a commercial centre as well as educational centre over past few decades. And migration is a consequential effect of urbanisation. This is evident in Table 4.4 which shows the ward-wise distribution of the respondents according to their status of domicile. Migration according to the Census of India is of two types – Migration by Birth place and Migration by place of last residence. When a person is enumerated in Census at a place, i.e. village or town, different from her/his place of birth, she/he would be considered a migrant by place of birth. A person would be considered a migrant by place of last residence, if she/he had last resided at a place other than her/his place of enumeration. In this study, we adopted the first definition of migration and all the respondents who have taken up residence after moving into the town from a different place after birth is considered.With regard to domicile category, all respondents who had been living in Dimapur town (parents migrated and stayed there) since birth are considered.

The percentage of tenant respondents who migrated to the town is very high in all the 23 wards of the town. It is observed that there are 10 wards in the town where all the tenant respondents have migrated to the town from elsewhere. This may be because some of the tenant residents may already have a house or a piece of land in their respective place of domicile and may not need (or be interested) in ownership housing in Dimapur and looked for affordable rental accommodation. On the other hand, very few tenant respondents have been found to be domiciles of the town. Interactions with most of the respondents who have moved to the town (migrants) revealed that several of them first came as singles or unmarried for either studies or employment and they ultimately got married and settled down. Besides, some respondents who were already married and first came without their families brought their families after getting a secured employment for their children's education. This may be one of the reasons for the high incidence of changing locations by several respondents across the wards.

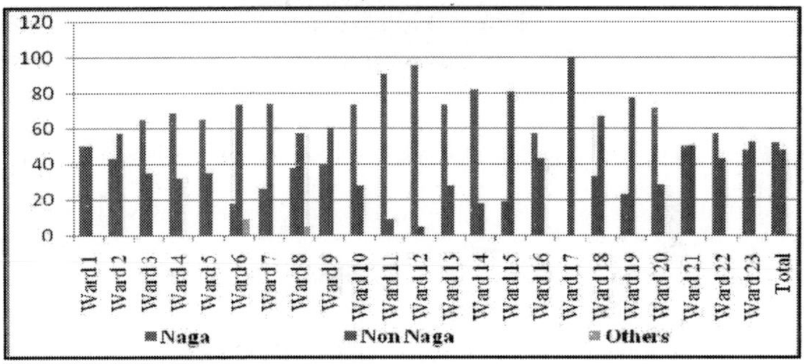

Fig. 4.5: Ward-wise Percentage Distribution of Respondents According to their Community.

Among the owner respondents surveyed, it is found that majority of the respondents have also migrated to the town. However, the proportion of domiciles with regard to owner respondents is much higher as compared to the tenant respondents. It is recorded that in Ward 6, percentage of domicile is 100 per cent. In 6 wards, the percentage of domicile of owner respondents is 66.67 and in 3 other wards it is 50 per cent.

For the town as a whole, the survey shows that 92.75 per cent of the tenant respondents have migrated to the town at different points of time, while only 7.25 per cent of the tenant respondents had settled in the town since their birth (Fig. 4.6a). In Fig. 4.6b, it is observed that 56.58 per cent of the owner respondents are migrants and 43.42 per cent are domiciles. For all the surveyed respondents, it is observed that 87.14 per cent of the respondents have migrated to the town, whereas only 12.86 per cent of the respondents are domiciles of the town.

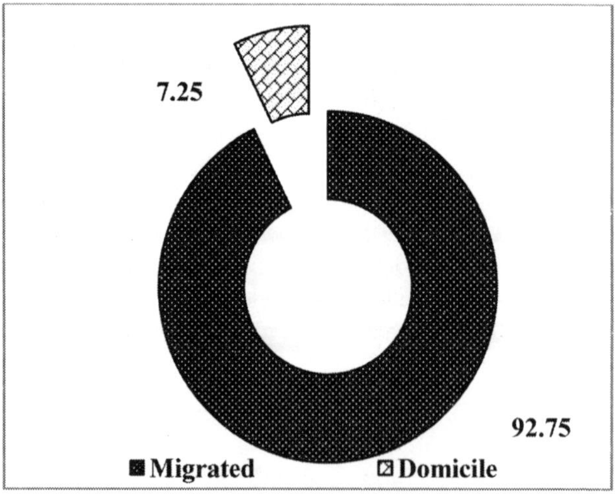

Fig. 4.6a: Distribution of Tenant Households According to Status of Domicile

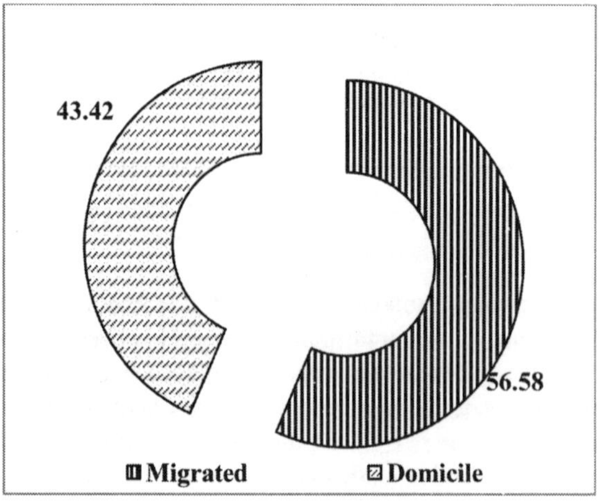

Fig. 4.6b: Distribution of Owner Households According to Status of Domicile

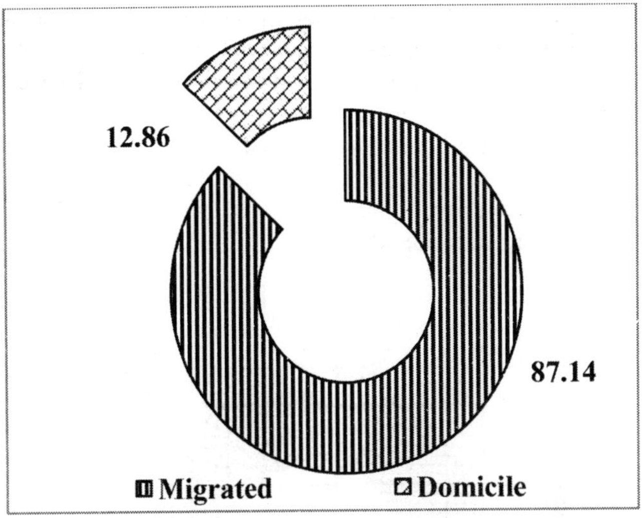

Fig. 4.6c: Distribution of All Households According to Status of Domicile.

Distribution of Surveyed Household Heads and their Spouses According to their Educational Level

The level of educational attainment plays very significant role in an individual's activity patterns and earnings and thereby perceptions, evaluations, preferences and demands of their residential environment (Fields, 1980). Thus, level of educational attainment affects people's standard of living and their residential choice.

Educational level of the respondent heads and spouses are classified into 5 categories and presented in Table 4.5. It is observed that merely 0.72 per cent of the head of tenant households is illiterate and is located in wards 2, 5 and 21. It is also evident that most of the tenant household heads are graduates accounting for 41.06 per cent of the surveyed households. Ward-wise distribution reveals that Ward 13 has the highest percentage of graduates (83.33%) while Ward 6 has the lowest percentage (5.26%). About half the respondents of Ward 15 are literate but only 5.55 per cent of Ward 18 are literates. Ward 6 recorded 47.37 per cent of respondents having HS level of education. Among the owner households, none of the head is found illiterate. Over half of them are at least graduates. The survey also revealed that there are 6 wards where all heads of owner households are graduates. Moreover, heads of owner households with HS level was found in 13 wards, those with secondary level in 7 wards and those who are just literate is present only in 4 wards.

Table 4.5: Ward-wise Distribution of Surveyed Head of Tenant and Owner Households According to their Educational Level

Ward	Illiterate		Literate		Secondary		HS		Graduate & Above	
	Tenant	Owner	Tenant	Owner	Tenant	Owner	Tenant	Owner	Tenant	Owner
Ward 1	0 (0)	NIL	2 (11.76)	0 (0)	2 (11.76)	0 (0)	6 (35.29)	1 (33.33)	7 (41.18)	2 (66.67)
Ward 2	1 (5.56)		6 (33.33)	0 (0)	3 (16.67)	0 (0)	1 (5.55)	1 (33.33)	7 (38.89)	2 (66.67)
Ward 3	0 (0)		3 (17.65)	0 (0)	4 (23.53)	0 (0)	7 (41.18)	0 (0)	3 (17.65)	3 (100)
Ward 4	0 (0)		3 (16.67)	1 (25)	2 (11.11)	1 (25)	4 (22.22)	0 (0)	9 (50)	2 (50)
Ward 5	1 (6.25)		2 (12.5)	1 (25)	1 (6.25)	0 (0)	3 (18.75)	1 (25)	9 (56.25)	2 (50)
Ward 6	0 (0)		5 (26.32)	0 (0)	4 (21.05)	0 (0)	9 (47.37)	0 (0)	1 (5.26)	3 (100)
Ward 7	0 (0)		3 (15.79)	0 (0)	4 (21.05)	1 (25)	5 (26.32)	2 (50)	7 (36.84)	1 (25)
Ward 8	0 (0)		5 (27.78)	0 (0)	2 (11.11)	1 (33.33)	6 (33.33)	1 (33.33)	5 (27.78)	1 (33.33)
Ward 9	0 (0)		4 (23.53)	1 (33.33)	1 (5.88)	0 (0)	5 (29.41)	0 (0)	7 (41.18)	2 (66.67)
Ward 10	0 (0)		7 (36.84)	0 (0)	2 (10.53)	1 (33.33)	3 (15.79)	0 (0)	7 (36.84)	2 (66.67)
Ward 11	0 (0)		4 (21.05)	0 (0)	0 (0)	0 (0)	3 (15.79)	0 (0)	12 (63.16)	3 (100)
Ward 12	0 (0)		0 (0)	0 (0)	0 (0)	0 (0)	4 (22.22)	0 (0)	14 (77.78)	4 (100)
Ward 13	0 (0)		2 (11.11)	0 (0)	1 (5.55)	0 (0)	0 (0)	0 (0)	15 (83.33)	4 (100)
Ward 14	0 (0)		4 (21.05)	0 (0)	3 (15.79)	0 (0)	2 (10.53)	0 (0)	10 (52.63)	3 (100)
Ward 15	0 (0)		9 (50)	1 (33.33)	3 (16.67)	0 (0)	2 (11.11)	2 (66.67)	4 (22.22)	0 (0)
Ward 16	0 (0)		5 (29.41)	0 (0)	4 (23.53)	1 (25)	4 (23.53)	1 (25)	4 (23.53)	2 (50)

(*Contd.*)

Ward	Illiterate		Literate		Secondary		HS		Graduate & Above	
	Tenant	Owner	Tenant	Owner	Tenant	Owner	Tenant	Owner	Tenant	Owner
Ward 17	0 (0)		2 (11.11)	0 (0)	4 (22.22)	1 (33.33)	3 (16.67)	1 (33.33)	9 (50)	1 (33.33)
Ward 18	0 (0)		1 (5.55)	0 (0)	2 (11.11)	0 (0)	6 (33.33)	2 (66.67)	9 (50)	1 (33.33)
Ward 19	0 (0)		4 (21.05)	0 (0)	3 (15.79)	0 (0)	7 (36.84)	2 (66.67)	5 (26.32)	1 (33.33)
Ward 20	0 (0)		6 (33.33)	0 (0)	2 (11.11)	0 (0)	4 (22.22)	2 (66.67)	6 (33.33)	1 (33.33)
Ward 21	1(5.26)		5 (26.32)	0 (0)	3 (15.79)	0 (0)	2 (10.53)	0 (0)	8 (42.10)	3 (100)
Ward 22	0 (0)		7 (38.89)	0 (0)	2 (11.11)	0 (0)	3 (16.67)	2 (66.67)	6 (33.33)	1 (33.33)
Ward 23	0 (0)		3 (17.65)	0 (0)	7 (41.18)	1 (25)	1 (5.88)	1 (25)	6 (35.29)	2 (50)
Total	**3 (0.72)**		**92 (22.22)**	**4 (5.26)**	**59 (14.25)**	**7 (9.21)**	**90 (21.74)**	**19 (25)**	**170 (41.06)**	**46 (60.53)**

Source: Field Survey by the researcher during 2015-16.
Note: Figures in the parentheses represent the number of Head of owner households.

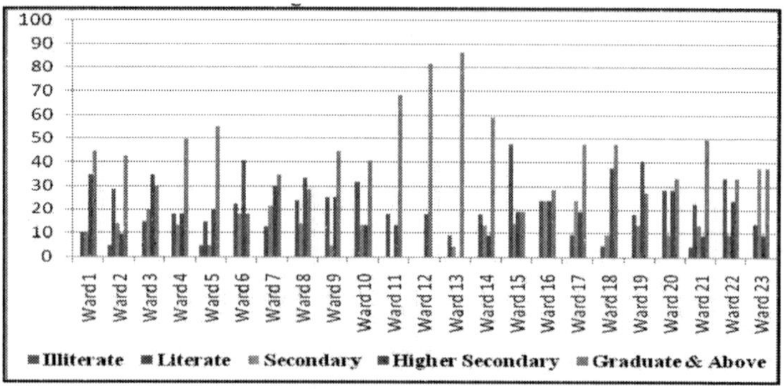

Fig. 4.7: Ward-wise Percentage Distribution of All Surveyed Head of Households According to their Level of Education.

The ward-wise percentage distribution of all heads of households surveyed according to the level of their educational attainment is displayed in Fig. 4.7. It is observed that graduate and above is more than any other single category in 13 numbers of wards of the town. The highest number of graduates and above is found in Ward 13 that accounts for 86.36 per cent. On the other hand, illiterate heads of households are found only in 3 wards of the town. Interestingly, it is also observed that Ward 12 has heads of households that are all HS and above.

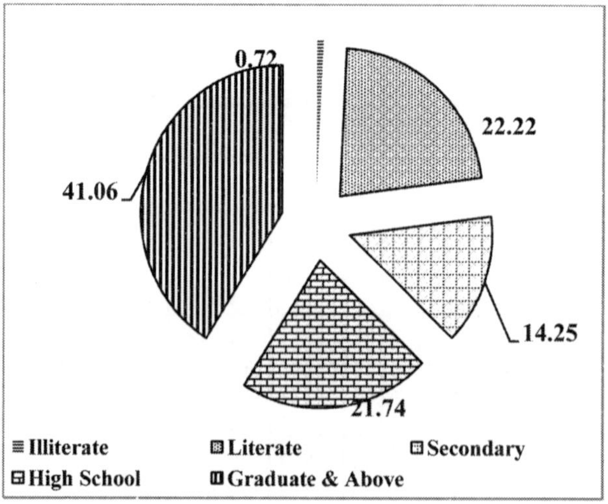

Fig. 4.8a: Distribution of Head of Tenant Households According to Education Level

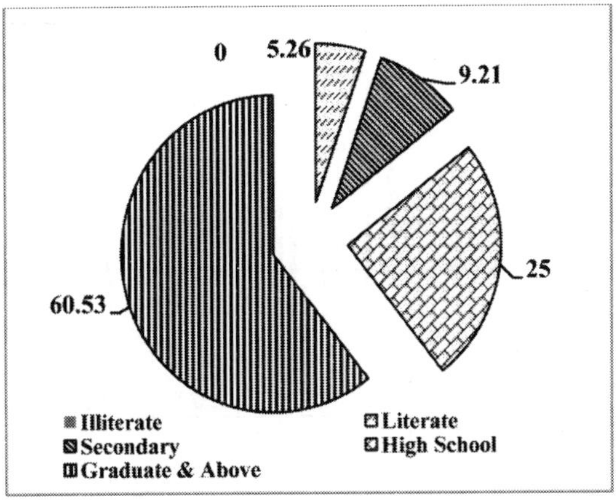

Fig. 4.8b: Distribution of Head of Owner Households According to Education Level

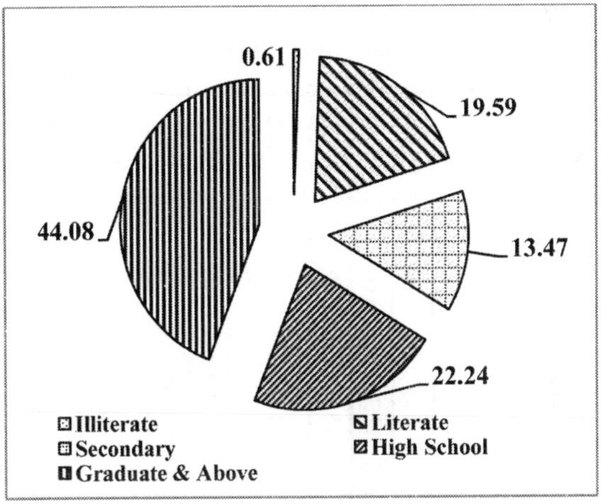

Fig. 4.8c: Distribution of Head of All Households According to Education Level

Fig. 4.8a shows that 22.22 per cent of the heads of tenant households are just literate, while 21.74 and 41.06 per cent of them are higher secondary and graduate respectively. Among the owner respondents surveyed, 60.53 per cent are found to be graduate and above and 25 per cent have HS level of education (Fig. 4.8b). The proportion of secondary and below among the owner households is found to be about 14 per cent and none is illiterate. Overall, it is observed that majority of the head of households are graduate and above accounting for 44.08 per cent (Fig. 4.8c).

Table 4.6: Ward-wise Distribution of Surveyed Spouse of Tenant and Owner Households According to Their Level of Education

Ward	Illiterate		Literate		Secondary		HS		Graduate& Above	
	Tenant	Owner	Tenant	Owner	Tenant	Owner	Tenant	Owner	Tenant	Owner
Ward 1	1 (6.67)	0 (0)	3 (20)	0 (0)	4 (26.67)	0 (0)	1 (6.67)	1 (33.33)	6 (40)	2 (66.67)
Ward 2	3 (18.75)	0 (0)	7 (43.75)	0 (0)	1 (6.25)	1 (33.33)	1 (6.25)	1 (33.33)	4 (25)	1 (33.33)
Ward 3	2 (15.38)	0 (0)	2 (15.38)	0 (0)	1 (7.69)	0 (0)	4 (30.77)	2 (66.67)	4 (30.77)	1 (33.33)
Ward 4	1 (7.69)	0 (0)	4 (30.77)	1 (25)	3 (23.08)	0 (0)	1 (7.69)	1 (25)	4 (30.77)	2 (50)
Ward 5	0 (0)	0 (0)	3 (25)	0 (0)	1 (8.33)	0 (0)	5 (41.67)	2 (50)	3 (25)	2 (50)
Ward 6	2 (12.5)	0 (0)	5 (31.25)	0 (0)	3 (18.75)	0 (0)	2 (12.5)	1 (33.33)	4 (25)	2 (66.67)
Ward 7	0 (0)	0 (0)	4 (25)	0 (0)	5 (31.25)	0 (0)	4 (25)	3 (75)	3 (18.75)	1 (25)
Ward 8	1 (6.25)	0 (0)	4 (25)	2 (66.67)	3 (18.75)	0 (0)	3 (18.75)	1 (33.33)	5 (31.25)	0 (0)
Ward 9	1 (7.14)	1 (33.33)	5 (35.71)	0 (0)	3 (21.43)	0 (0)	1 (7.14)	1 (33.33)	4 (28.57)	1 (33.33)
Ward 10	1 (8.33)	0 (0)	4 (33.33)	0 (0)	2 (16.67)	1 (33.33)	2 (16.67)	0 (0)	3 (25)	2 (66.67)
Ward 11	0 (0)	0 (0)	4 (26.67)	0 (0)	3 (20)	0 (0)	3 (20)	0 (0)	5 (33.33)	3 (100)
Ward 12	0 (0)	0 (0)	3 (18.75)	1 (25)	1 (6.25)	0 (0)	4 (25)	1 (25)	8 (50)	2 (50)
Ward 13	1 (7.14)	0 (0)	2 (14.28)	0 (0)	0 (0)	0 (0)	3 (21.43)	1 (33.33)	8 (57.14)	2 (66.67)
Ward 14	4 (28.57)	0 (0)	6 (42.86)	0 (0)	3 (21.43)	0 (0)	0 (0)	0 (0)	3 (21.43)	2 (100)
Ward 15	1 (7.14)	0 (0)	8 (57.14)	1 (33.33)	2 (14.28)	0 (0)	0 (0)	0 (0)	3 (21.43)	2 (66.67)

(Contd.)

Ward	Illiterate		Literate		Secondary		HS		Graduate& Above	
	Tenant	**Owner**	**Tenant**	**Owner**	**Tenant**	**Owner**	**Tenant**	**Owner**	**Tenant**	**Owner**
Ward 16	0 (0)	1 (25)	6 (46.15)	0 (0)	2 (15.38)	0 (0)	3 (23.08)	1 (25)	2 (15.38)	2 (50)
Ward 17	0 (0)	0 (0)	8 (44.44)	2 (66.67)	2 (11.11)	0 (0)	5 (27.78)	0 (0)	3 (16.67)	1 (33.33)
Ward 18	0 (0)	0 (0)	2 (13.33)	0 (0)	3 (20)	2 (66.67)	3 (20)	0 (0)	7 (46.67)	1 (33.33)
Ward 19	3 (15.79)	0 (0)	7 (36.84)	1 (33.33)	1 (5.26)	0 (0)	6 (31.58)	1 (33.33)	2 (10.53)	1 (33.33)
Ward 20	2 (13.33)	0 (0)	4 (26.67)	0 (0)	4 (26.67)	0 (0)	3 (20)	2 (66.67)	2 (13.33)	1 (33.33)
Ward 21	4 (22.22)	0 (0)	2 (11.11)	0 (0)	4 (22.22)	0 (0)	4 (22.22)	1 (33.33)	4 (22.22)	2 (66.67)
Ward 22	2 (13.33)	0 (0)	6 (40)	0 (0)	2 (13.33)	0 (0)	2 (13.33)	0 (0)	3 (20)	3 (100)
Ward 23	0 (0)	0 (0)	5 (33.33)	1 (25)	2 (13.33)	1 (25)	3 (20)	0 (0)	5 (33.33)	2 (50)
Total	**27 (7.85)**	**2 (2.70)**	**104 (30.23)**	**9 (12.16)**	**55 (15.99)**	**5 (6.76)**	**63 (18.31)**	**20 (27.03)**	**94 (27.32)**	**38 (51.35)**

Source: Field Survey by the researcher during 2015-16.
Note: Figures in the parentheses represent percentage to total.

The ward-wise distribution of the spouses of tenant and owner households according to their educational attainment is displayed in Table 5.6. Out of 344 spouses of tenant households, literates are in majority in 11 wards of the town while graduates and above are more in 6 wards. It is also observed that HS and secondary levels of education are more in Wards 5 and 7 respectively. Among 74 spouses of the owner households, graduates are in majority in 13 wards, while very few are illiterate and most of the spouses are of HS level educated and above.

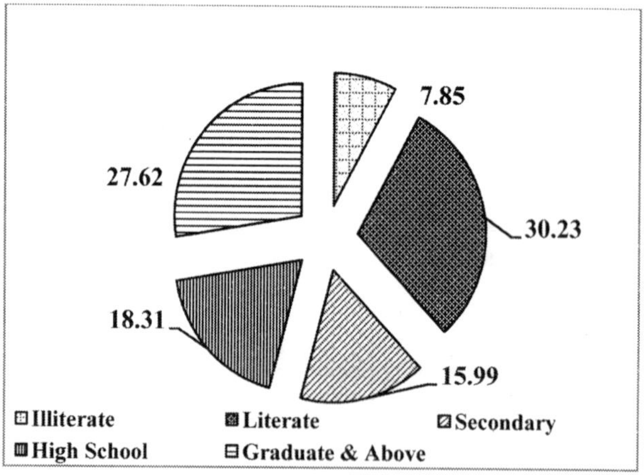

Fig. 4.9a: Distribution of Spouses of Tenant Households According to Education Level

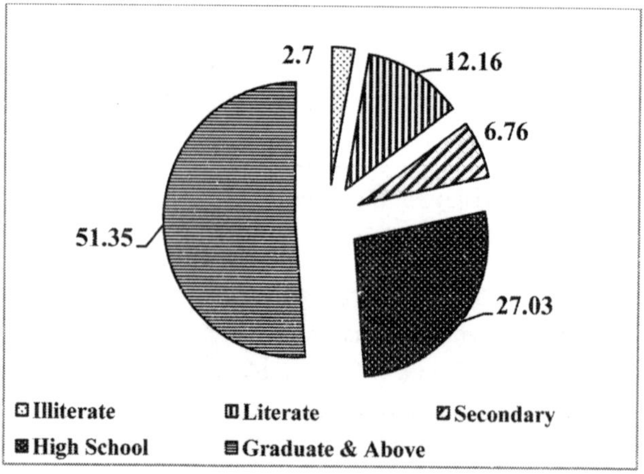

Fig. 4.9b: Distribution of Spouses of Owner Households According to Education Level

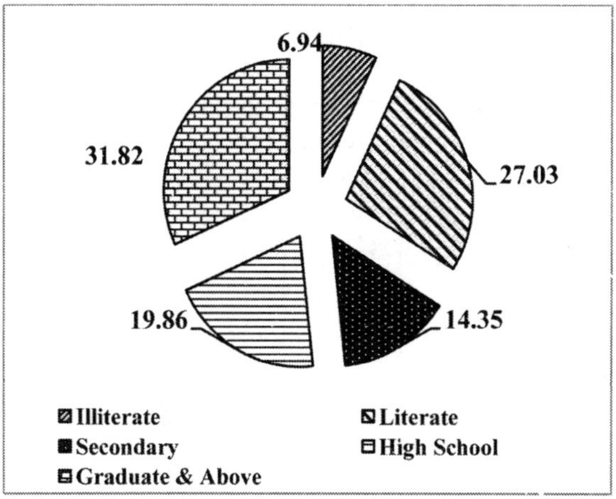

Fig. 4.9c: Distribution of Spouses of All Households According to Education Level

Overall, 30.23 per cent of tenant housewives are literate and 27.33 per cent are graduate and above (Fig. 4.9a). About 34 per cent of them have school level education. Among the spouses of owner households, 51.35 per cent are found to be at least graduates while 27.03 per cent have school level education (Fig. 4.9b). The tenants and their wives who mostly belong to non-local groups are there either for job or business and mostly educated unlike that of the many locals who are mostly in informal activities (as found in the next sub-section). With regard to all the surveyed spouses, it is observed that 31.58 per cent are graduates and over one-fourth are just literate (Fig. 4.9c). Literate and school level of education constitutes about 61 per cent of them.

Distribution of Surveyed Households According to Nature of Employment of the Head and Spouse

The nature and status of employment is an important indicator of the economic position of an individual. Most of the tenant household heads across the wards are found in 3 types of employment, namely self-employed/business, private or government services (Table 4.7). The self-employed or businessmen are found to be in majority in 14 wards of the town with Ward 19 recording the highest (94.74%) while those in government services is in majority in 4 wards (Ward 12 being the highest

Table 4.7: Ward-wise Distribution of Head of Surveyed Tenant and Owner Households by Nature of Employment

Ward	Unemployed		Daily Wage		Self Empl./Business		Private		Govt.		Others	
	Tenant	Owner	Tenant	Owner	Tenant	Owner	Tenant	Owner	Tenant	Owner	Tenant	Owner
Ward 1	NIL	NIL	0 (0)	NIL	10 (58.82)	1 (33.33)	4 (23.53)	0 (0)	3 (17.65)	2 (66.67)	0 (0)	0 (0)
Ward 2			3(16.67)		6 (33.33)	1 (33.33)	5 (27.78)	0 (0)	4 (22.22)	1 (33.33)	0 (0)	1 (33.33)
Ward 3			2(11.76)		7 (41.18)	1 (33.33)	3 (17.65)	0 (0)	4 (23.53)	2 (66.67)	1 (5.88)	0 (0)
Ward 4			1 (5.56)		6 (33.33)	1 (25)	9 (50)	1 (25)	2 (11.11)	2 (50)	0 (0)	0 (0)
Ward 5			0 (0)		7 (43.75)	2 (50)	5 (31.25)	0 (0)	4 (25)	2 (50)	0 (0)	0 (0)
Ward 6			0 (0)		14 (73.68)	3 (100)	5 (26.32)	0 (0)	0 (0)	0 (0)	0 (0)	0 (0)
Ward 7			0 (0)		9 (47.37)	2 (50)	9 (47.37)	0 (0)	1 (5.26)	2 (50)	0 (0)	0 (0)
Ward 8			0 (0)		8 (44.44)	2 (66.67)	5 (27.78)	1(33.33)	4 (22.22)	0 (0)	1 (5.56)	0 (0)
Ward 9			0 (0)		8 (47.06)	2 (66.67)	3 (17.65)	0 (0)	6 (35.29)	1 (33.33)	0 (0)	0 (0)
Ward 10			1 (5.26)		9 (47.37)	2 (66.67)	5 (26.32)	0 (0)	4 (21.05)	1 (33.33)	0 (0)	0 (0)
Ward 11			0 (0)		3 (15.79)	1 (33.33)	8 (42.10)	0 (0)	8 (42.10)	2 (66.67)	0 (0)	0 (0)
Ward 12			0 (0)		3 (16.67)	1 (25)	3 (16.67)	0 (0)	12 (66.67)	3 (75)	0 (0)	0 (0)
Ward 13			0 (0)		2 (11.11)	1 (25)	9 (50)	0 (0)	6 (33.33)	3 (75)	1 (5.56)	0 (0)
Ward 14			0 (0)		6 (31.58)	1 (33.33)	4 (21.05)	0 (0)	9 (47.37)	2 (66.67)	0 (0)	0 (0)
Ward 15			0 (0)		13 (72.22)	3 (100)	4 (22.22)	0 (0)	1 (5.56)	0 (0)	0 (0)	0 (0)
Ward 16			0 (0)		8 (47.06)	2 (50)	6 (35.29)	0 (0)	3 (17.65)	2 (50)	0 (0)	0 (0)

(*Contd.*)

Ward	Unemployed		Daily Wage		SelfEmpl./Business		Private		Govt		Others	
	Ten-ant	Ow-ner	Tenant	Ow-ner	Tenant	Owner	Tenant	Owner	Tenant	Owner	Tenant	Owner
Ward 17	NIL	NIL	0 (0)		17 (94.44)	3 (100)	1 (5.56)	0 (0)	0 (0)	0 (0)	0 (0)	0 (0)
Ward 18			0 (0)		10 (55.56)	2 (66.67)	7 (38.89)	0 (0)	1 (5.56)	1 (33.33)	0 (0)	0 (0)
Ward 19			1 (5.26)		18 (94.74)	3 (100)	0 (0)	0 (0)	0 (0)	0 (0)	0 (0)	0 (0)
Ward 20			0 (0)		3 (16.67)	2 (66.67)	7 (38.89)	0 (0)	8 (44.44)	1 (33.33)	0 (0)	0 (0)
Ward 21			1 (5.26)		6 (31.58)	2 (66.67)	4 (21.05)	0 (0)	8 (42.10)	1 (33.33)	0 (0)	0 (0)
Ward 22			1 (5.56)		9 (50)	2 (66.67)	4 (22.22)	0 (0)	4 (22.22)	1 (33.33)	0 (0)	0 (0)
Ward 23			0 (0)		4 (23.53)	4 (100)	9 (52.94)	0 (0)	4 (23.53)	0 (0)	0 (0)	0 (0)
Total			**10 (2.41)**		**186 (44.93)**	**44 (57.89)**	**119 (28.74)**	**2 (2.63)**	**96 (23.19)**	**29 (38.16)**	**3 (0.72)**	**1 (1.32)**

Source: Field Survey by the researcher during 2015-16.

Note: Figures in the parentheses represent percentage to total.

with 66.67%). It is also observed that those in private service are more in 3 wards. There are 3 respondents who had retired from government service and are in the others category.

On the other hand, most of the owner household heads are found to be self-employed/businessmen or government servants. The self-employed/ businessmen are found to be in majority in 12 wards of the town, whereas those in government service are more in 7 wards. 100 per cent heads of owner households are recorded to be self-employed/businessmen in 5 wards. There is no unemployed or daily wage earner in respect of heads of owner households.

It is further observed that 44.93 per cent (186 in number) of overall tenant household heads are self-employed/businessmen and 119 respondents (28.74%) are in private service, followed by 96 respondents (23.19%) in government services (Fig. 4.10a). Among the heads of owner households, 44 respondents (57.89%) are self-employed/businessmen, which is followed by the group of government service holders (29 in number i.e., 38.16%) (Fig. 4.10b). In the overall sample 46.94 per cent (230) are, however, self-employed and followed by government service (25.51%) (125) and private employees and daily wage earners constitute 24.69 per cent.

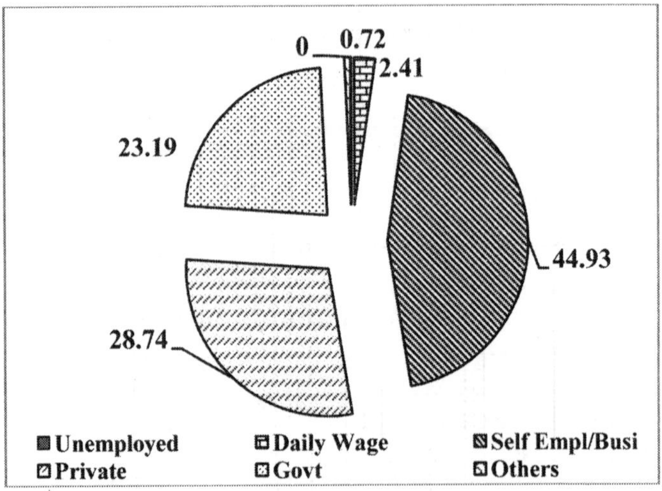

Fig. 4.10a: Distribution of Heads of Tenant Households According to their Employment

Table 4.8: Ward-wise Distribution of Spouse of Respondents by Nature of Employment

Ward	Unemployed		Daily Wage		Self Empl/Business		Private		Government		Others	
	Tenant	Owner	Tenant	Own-er	Tenant	Owner	Tenant	Owner	Tenant	Owner	Tenant	Ow-ner
Ward 1	8(53.33)	0(0)	0(0)	NIL	2(13.33)	1(33.33)	5(33.33)	0(0)	0(0)	2(66.67)	0(0)	NIL
Ward 2	5(31.25)	1(33.33)	4(25)		0(0)	1(33.33)	5(31.25)	0(0)	1(6.25)	1(33.33)	1(6.25)	
Ward 3	6(46.15)	1(33.33)	1(7.69)		0(0)	0(0)	5(38.46)	0(0)	1(7.69)	2(66.67)	0(0)	
Ward 4	6(46.15)	0(0)	0(0)		3(23.08)	0(0)	4(30.77)	3(75)	0(0)	1(25)	0(0)	
Ward 5	4(33.33)	2(50)	1(8.33)		4(33.33)	1(25)	2(16.67)	0(0)	1(8.33)	1(25)	0(0)	
Ward 6	11(68.75)	1(33.33)	0(0)		3(18.75)	1(33.33)	1(6.25)	1(33.33)	1(6.25)	0(0)	0(0)	
Ward 7	13(81.25)	2(50)	0(0)		3(18.75)	1(25)	0(0)	0(0)	0(0)	1(25)	0(0)	
Ward 8	9(56.25)	2(66.67)	0(0)		2(12.5)	1(33.33)	3(18.75)	0(0)	2(12.5)	0(0)	0(0)	
Ward 9	7(50)	2(66.67)	0(0)		4(28.57)	1(33.33)	3(21.43)	0(0)	0(0)	0(0)	0(0)	
Ward 10	9(75)	1(33.33)	0(0)		1(8.33)	1(33.33)	2(16.67)	0(0)	0(0)	1(33.33)	0(0)	
Ward 11	7(46.67)	0(0)	0(0)		1(6.67)	1(33.33)	3(20)	1(33.33)	4(26.67)	1(33.33)	0(0)	
Ward 12	5(31.25)	2(50)	0(0)		3(18.75)	0(0)	5(31.25)	0(0)	3(18.75)	2(50)	0(0)	
Ward 13	8(57.14)	1(33.33)	0(0)		1(7.14)	0(0)	5(35.71)	0(0)	0(0)	2(66.67)	0(0)	
Ward 14	11(78.57)	1(50)	0(0)		1(7.14)	0(0)	1(7.14)	0(0)	1(7.14)	1(50)	0(0)	
Ward 15	10(71.43)	2(66.67)	0(0)		2(14.29)	0(0)	2(14.29)	0(0)	0(0)	1(33.33)	0(0)	

(Contd.)

Ward	Unemployed		Daily Wage		Self Empl/Business		Private		Government		Others	
	Tenant	Owner	Tenant	Own-er	Tenant	Owner	Tenant	Owner	Tenant	Owner	Tenant	Ow-ner
Ward 16	10(76.92)	2(50)	0(0)	NIL	1(7.69)	1(25)	2(15.38)	0(0)	0(0)	1(25)	0(0)	NIL
Ward 17	17(94.44)	2(66.67)	0(0)		0(0)	1(33.33)	1(5.55)	0(0)	0(0)	0(0)	0(0)	
Ward 18	9(60)	0(0)	0(0)		1(6.67)	2(66.67)	4(26.67)	1(33.33)	0(0)	0(0)	1(6.67)	
Ward 19	16(84.21)	2(66.67)	0(0)		2(10.53)	0(0)	0(0)	0(0)	0(0)	1(33.33)	1(5.26)	
Ward 20	7(46.67)	2(66.67)	0(0)		4(26.67)	0(0)	1(6.67)	0(0)	3(20)	1(33.33)	0(0)	
Ward 21	13(72.22)	2(66.67)	0(0)		1(5.55)	0(0)	2(11.11)	1(33.33)	2(11.11)	0(0)	0(0)	
Ward 22	8(53.33)	1(33.33)	3(20)		1(6.67)	0(0)	3(20)	2(66.67)	0(0)	0(0)	0(0)	
Ward 23	10(66.67)	2(50)	0(0)		1(6.67)	0(0)	4(26.67)	0(0)	0(0)	2(50)	0(0)	
Total	**209(60.76)**	**31(41.89)**	**9(2.62)**		**41(11.92)**	**13(17.57)**	**63(18.31)**	**9(12.16)**	**19(5.52)**	**21(28.38)**	**3(0.87)**	

Source: Field Survey by the researcher during 2015-16.

Note: Figures in the parentheses represent percentage to total.

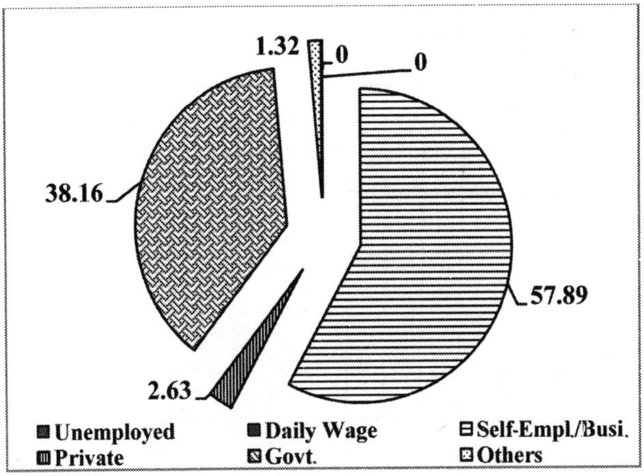

Fig. 4.10b: Distribution of Head of Owner Households According to their Employment

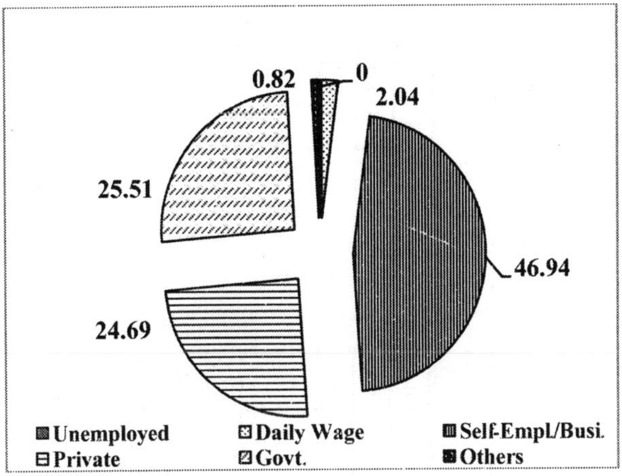

Fig. 4.10c: Distribution of Head of All Households According to their Employment

The ward-wise distribution of spouses of the surveyed households according to their type of employment is shown in Table 4.8. Majority of the spouses of the tenant respondents (60.76%) are unemployed, while the figure is about 42 per cent in case of owner respondents (Figs. 4.11a and 4.11b). Incidence of unemployment among the wives of tenant respondents is the highest in Ward 17 (94.44%) in Ward 17. 18.31 per cent of spouses of tenant respondents are in private services, largely teachers in private schools across 21 wards, whereas some are also self-employed or into Business and very few are in government services as well as daily wage earners. Among the wives of respondent owners, however, about 28 per cent are in government services and about 18 per cent are in self-businesses and a very few are in private jobs. The status and percentage distributions vary significantly across the 23 wards.

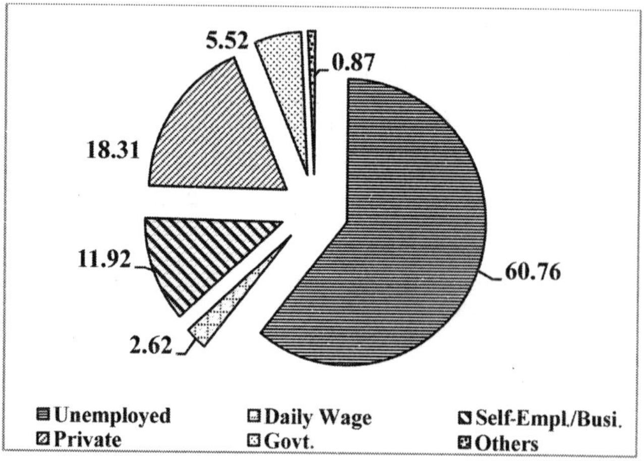

Fig. 4.11a: Distribution of Spouse of Tenant Households According to their Employment

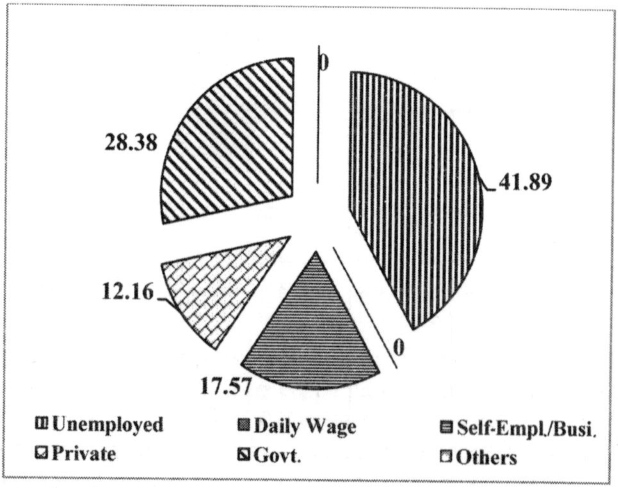

Fig. 4.11b: Distribution of Spouses of Owner Households According to their Employment

Table 4.9: Ward-wise Distribution of Tenant and Owner Households by Monthly Per Capita Family Income (Rs.)

Ward	0 - 5000		5001 - 10000		10001 - 15000		15001 & above		Tenant		Owner	
	Tenant	Owner	Tenant	Owner	Tenant	Owner	Tenant	Owner	Average	CV	Average	CV
Ward 1	5(29.41)	0(0)	7(41.18)	1(33.33)	5(29.41)	2(66.67)	0(0)	0(0)	8250	49.58	11583.33	27.33
Ward 2	8(44.44)	0(0)	3(16.67)	1(33.33)	2(11.11)	2(66.67)	5(27.78)	0(0)	11263.89	109.45	11583.33	21.18
Ward 3	10(58.82)	1(33.33)	4(23.53)	0(0)	1(5.88)	2(66.67)	2(11.76)	0(0)	6838.23	70.36	9861.11	57.68
Ward 4	7(38.89)	0(0)	6(33.33)	3(75)	3(16.67)	1(25)	2(11.11)	0(0)	8408.07	84.56	9166.67	28.02
Ward 5	4(25)	0(0)	5(31.25)	1(25)	3(18.75)	3(75)	4(25)	0(0)	13008.93	117.59	13071.43	20.61
Ward 6	11(57.89)	0(0)	5(26.32)	2(66.67)	3(15.79)	1(33.33)	0(0)	0(0)	6206.77	49.29	10250	23.27
Ward 7	9(47.37)	1(25)	9(47.37)	1(25)	1(5.26)	1(25)	0(0)	1(25)	5846.49	39.22	11312.5	62.91
Ward 8	7(38.89)	1(33.33)	8(44.44)	0(0)	2(11.11)	1(33.33)	1(5.55)	1(33.33)	7513.89	60.54	10376.98	58.29
Ward 9	7(41.18)	0(0)	4(23.53)	2(66.67)	1(5.88)	1(33.33)	5(29.41)	0(0)	9937.21	79.90	11250	28.87
Ward 10	11(57.89)	0(0)	6(31.58)	1(33.33)	1(5.26)	1(33.33)	1(5.26)	1(33.33)	7107.46	101.35	13194.44	50.36
Ward 11	6(31.58)	0(0)	6(31.58)	1(33.33)	7(38.84)	1(33.33)	0(0)	1(33.33)	8375.94	50.22	13194.44	32.26
Ward 12	6(33.33)	0(0)	3(16.67)	1(25)	5(27.78)	3(75)	4(22.22)	0(0)	15116.73	117.91	12916.67	21.40
Ward 13	3(16.67)	1(25)	5(27.78)	0(0)	9(50)	2(50)	1(5.55)	1(25)	10315.15	51.93	14330.36	61.15
Ward 14	5(26.32)	0(0)	8(42.10)	0(0)	4(21.05)	1(33.33)	2(10.53)	2(66.67)	9273.81	66.44	31666.67	65.74
Ward 15	13(72.22)	1(33.33)	3(16.67)	1(33.33)	1(5.55)	1(33.33)	1(5.55)	0(0)	5881.06	96.62	7208.33	65.95
Ward 16	10(58.82)	1(25)	2(11.76)	1(25)	4(23.53)	1(25)	1(5.88)	1(25)	8014.71	106.59	11160.71	87.96
Ward 17	6(33.33)	1(33.33)	6(33.33)	1(33.33)	5(27.78)	0(0)	1(5.55)	1(33.33)	8375	53.38	10327.38	72.61

(Contd.)

Ward	0 - 5000		5001 - 10000		10001 - 15000		15001 & above		Tenant		Owner	
	Tenant	Owner	Tenant	Owner	Tenant	Owner	Tenant	Owner	Average	CV	Average	CV
Ward 18	9(50)	0(0)	8(44.44)	2(66.67)	1(5.55)	1(33.33)	0(0)	0(0)	6115.74	52.21	8611.11	29.17
Ward 19	9(47.37)	0(0)	7(38.84)	1(33.33)	3(15.79)	2(66.67)	0(0)	0(0)	6288.85	58.06	11250	33.33
Ward 20	5(27.78)	0(0)	7(38.89)	1(33.33)	4(22.22)	1(33.33)	2(11.11)	1(33.33)	9786.38	84.12	15916.67	51.63
Ward 21	7(38.84)	1(33.33)	7(38.84)	0(0)	3(15.79)	2(66.67)	2(10.53)	0(0)	8666.67	68.20	10375	61.28
Ward 22	11(61.11)	0(0)	3(16.67)	1(33.33)	3(16.67)	1(33.33)	1(5.55)	1(33.33)	6347.22	93.39	13202.38	41.27
Ward 23	9(52.94)	0(0)	2(11.76)	2(50)	6(35.29)	2(50)	0(0)	0(0)	7504.9	61.82	10187.5	36.25
Total	**178(42.99)**	**8(10.53)**	**124(29.95)**	**24(31.58)**	**77(18.60)**	**33(43.42)**	**35(8.45)**	**11(14.47)**	**8418.31***	**91.26****	**12212.33***	**59.01****

Source: Field Survey by the researcher during 2015-16.

Note: (i) Figures in the parentheses represent percentage to (ii). * and ** represent the mean and CV across all the ward srespectively.

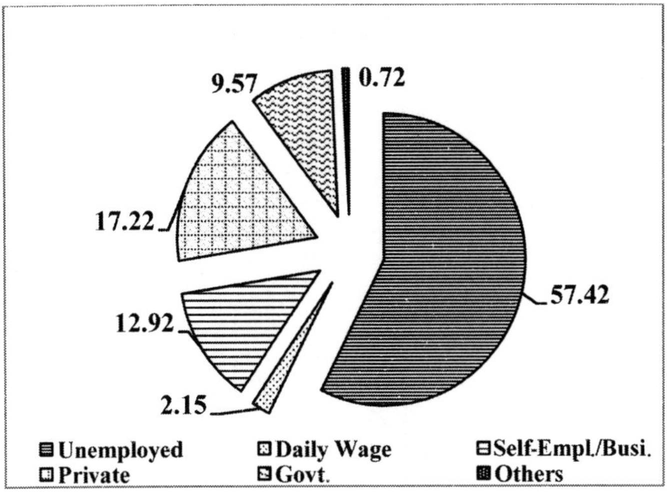

Fig. 4.11c: Distribution of Spouses of All Households According to their Employment

With regard to the overall surveyed spouses 57.42 per cent are found to be unemployed while 17.22 per cent are in private service and followed by 12.92 per cent of them who are self-employed or do some business of their own. Only 9.57 per cent of them are government employees (Fig. 4.11c).

Ward-wise Distribution of Respondents as per Per Capita Family Income

Economic factor plays an important role in housing decision making through which demand for housing types and residential neighbourhood are made. Among other factors, the choice of residence by any individual or household is constrained by income that provides entitlement to select various features of their residences.

A ward-wise comparison of tenant households in Table 4.9 shows that Ward 15 has the majority of respondents with the lowest monthly per capita income (Rs.0-5000) constituting of 72.22 per cent, while Ward 13 has the least (16.67%) of such category. Ward 8 and Ward 18 share the greatest number of tenant households with monthly per capita income between Rs.5,001-10,000 (44.44%) and Ward 16 and Ward 23 have the minimum number of households with such per capita income. On the other hand, Ward 9 has the highest concentration of households who get Rs.15,001 and above (29.41%) while there are 7 wards without any such household having monthly per capita income over Rs. 15,000.

With regard to owner households, it is observed that 43.42 per cent of them earn monthly per capita income between Rs.10,001-15,000 across 22 wards and out of which 8 wards have the highest concentration of households with such income. There are 4 wards where majority of them earn between Rs. 5,001-10,000 while Ward 14 has a greater share of households earning of Rs.15,001 and above.

The percentage distribution of the households according to their monthly per capita income is depicted in the 3 Pie diagrams. Among the tenant households, 43 per cent have a monthly per capita income of Rs. 5,000 or less, while 29.95 per cent of them earn between Rs. 5,001-10,000 (Fig. 4.12a). It is also observed that 18.60 per cent and 8.45 per cent of them earn Rs.10,001-15,000 and over Rs.15,001 respectively.

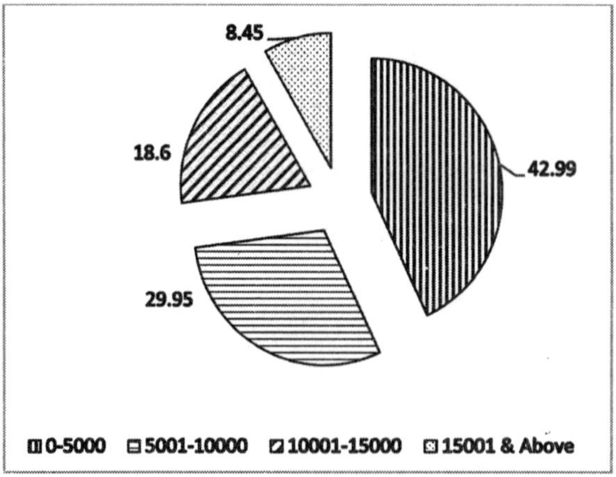

Fig. 4.12a: Distribution of Tenant Households by Monthly Per Capita Income

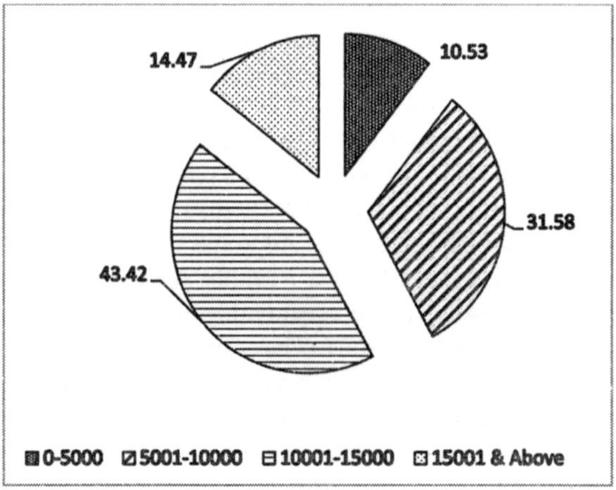

Fig. 4.12b: Distribution of Owner Households by Monthly Per Capita Income

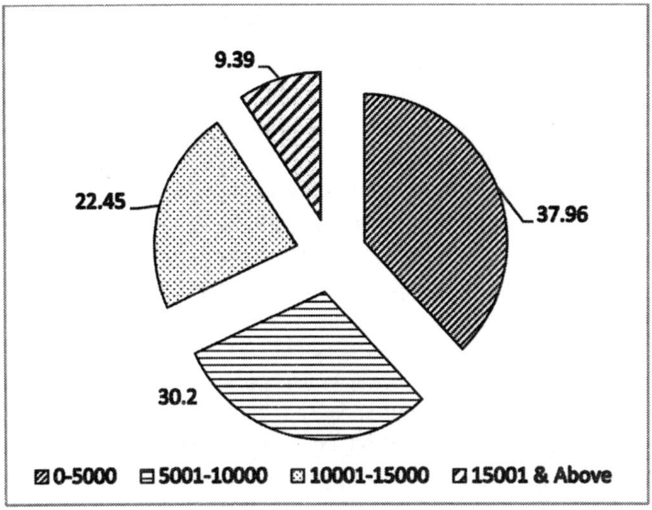

Fig. 4.12c: Distribution of All Households by Monthly Per Capita Income

With regard to owner households, Fig. 4.12b depicts that the largest proportion of them constituting 43.42 per cent earn a sum of Rs.10,001-15,000 per capita per month, which is followed by 31.58 per cent with earning ranges Rs. 5,001-10,000. The owner households who get above Rs.15,000 constitute 14.47 per cent whereas those who get between Rs. 0-5,000 constitute 10.53 per cent.

In respect of all surveyed households, Fig. 4.12c shows that the highest number of the households earn a monthly per capita income below Rs. 5,000 accounting for 37.96 per cent. The second largest group constituting 30.20 per cent earn between Rs. 5,001-10,000 per capita and followed by 22.45 per cent of the samples who earn between Rs.10,001-15,000 per capita per month. The smallest group of households (9.39%) earn the highest monthly per capita income of more than Rs. 15,000.

From Table 4.9, it is also observed that in the case of tenant households, Ward 12 registered the highest average monthly per capita income of Rs. 15,116.73 and Ward 7 has the lowest monthly per capita income of Rs. 5,846.49. The average monthly per capita income of all 414 tenant households is Rs. 8,418.31. Thus, the table reveals that there are 9 wards with monthly per capita income above the overall average of the tenant households and that of other 14 wards is less than that average.

With regard to owner households, it is observed that there is greater income disparity among this group across the wards. The highest ward-wise average monthly per capita income is located in ward 14 amounting to Rs. 31,666.67 and the lowest with Rs. 7,208.33 in ward 15. Overall, the average monthly per capita income is found to be Rs. 12,212.33. It is observed that there are 8 wards with monthly per capita income greater than the overall average and 15 wards with lesser monthly per capita income than the average of the group.

Between the two groups, it is observed that the average monthly per capita income of owner households is significantly greater than that of the tenant households. The coefficient of variation of the average ward-wise monthly per capita incomes, however, shows greater disparity in case of the tenant households. Among the tenant households, the coefficient of variation is the highest in Ward 12 (117.91%) and the lowest in Ward 7 (39.22%). In case of the owner households, the highest coefficient of variation of average per capita income is recorded in Ward 16 (87.96%) and the lowest in Ward 5 (20.61%). Overall, the coefficients of variation of the monthly per capita income for tenant and owner households are found to be 91.26 per cent and 59.01 per cent respectively, which indicates that across the individuals the variability is high across the individual tenants than that of owner households.

Overall, though average per capita income of tenants is much lower than that of owners, inequality in income is much higher in case of tenants than that of owners. Not only that there is significant positive correlation between per capita income across the wards with the coefficient of variation in case tenants ($r = 0.545^{**}$ and $t_{21} = 3.55$). But such correlation is insignificant in case of owner households ($r = 0.166$ and $t_{21} = 0.784$). Of course, the value could change if the sample size of owner households were increased, which was relatively less in the overall distribution of total sample.

In order to get an idea of the spatial income distribution, the ward-wise percentage distribution of monthly family income of all surveyed households is depicted in Fig. 5.13. It is observed that in 11 wards, the number of households with monthly family income of Rs.10,000-Rs. 20,000 is in majority with Ward 7 having the highest concentration accounting for 39.13 per cent. In Ward 2, the households with monthly family income of less than Rs. 10,000 are found to be more. In Wards 4 and 19, families who earn Rs. 20,000-Rs. 30,000 per month recorded higher frequency. In Wards 14 and 17, households with monthly family income of Rs. 30,000-Rs. 40,000 are in majority while in Ward 12 households with monthly family income of Rs. 70,000 and above are found to be more.

Generally, the head of the family is the main earner of the family. Even if other members of the family supplement to the total family income, the

Table 4.10: Ward-wise Distribution of Tenant and Owner Households According to Monthly Income of the Head

Ward	Rs. 0-10000		Rs. 10000-20000		Rs. 20000-30000		Rs. 30000-40000		Rs. 40000-50000		Rs. 50000-60000		Rs. 60000 & Above	
	Tenant	Owner	Tenant	Owner	Tenant	Owner	Tenant	Owner	Tenant	Owner	Tenant	Owner	Tenant	Owner
Ward 1	2 (11.76)	0 (0)	5 (29.41)	0 (0)	3 (17.65)	2 (66.67)	5 (29.41)	0 (0)	1 (5.88)	0 (0)	1 (5.88)	0 (0)	0 (0)	1 (33.33)
Ward 2	6 (33.33)	0 (0)	3 (16.67)	0 (0)	4 (22.22)	1 (33.33)	2 (11.11)	1 (33.33)	1 (5.55)	0 (0)	1 (5.55)	0 (0)	1 (5.55)	1 (33.33)
Ward 3	6 (35.29)	0 (0)	4 (23.53)	1 (33.33)	3 (17.65)	0 (0)	2 (11.76)	1 (33.33)	1 (5.88)	0 (0)	1 (5.88)	0 (0)	0 (0)	1 (33.33)
Ward 4	3 (16.67)	1 (25)	7 (38.89)	0 (0)	6 (33.33)	1 (25)	0 (0)	1 (25)	2 (11.11)	0 (0)	0 (0)	1 (25)	0 (0)	0 (0)
Ward 5	1 (6.25)	0 (0)	8 (50)	0 (0)	3 (18.75)	1 (25)	2 (12.5)	0 (0)	0 (0)	0 (0)	1 (6.25)	0 (0)	1 (6.25)	3 (75)
Ward 6	2 (10.53)	0 (0)	10 (52.63)	0 (0)	5 (26.32)	1 (33.33)	2 (10.53)	1 (33.33)	0 (0)	0 (0)	0 (0)	0 (0)	0 (0)	1 (33.33)
Ward 7	1 (5.26)	0 (0)	10 (52.63)	1 (25)	4 (21.05)	0 (0)	4 (21.05)	1 (25)	0 (0)	1 (25)	0 (0)	0 (0)	0 (0)	1 (25)
Ward 8	2 (11.11)	0 (0)	11 (61.11)	1 (33.33)	2 (11.11)	0 (0)	1 (5.55)	1 (33.33)	1 (5.55)	1 (33.33)	0 (0)	0 (0)	1 (5.55)	0 (0)
Ward 9	2 (11.76)	0 (0)	4 (23.53)	1 (33.33)	5 (29.41)	0 (0)	1 (5.88)	0 (0)	3 (17.65)	0 (0)	0 (0)	0 (0)	2 (11.76)	2 (66.67)
Ward 10	3 (15.79)	1 (33.33)	8 (42.10)	0 (0)	4 (21.05)	0 (0)	2 (10.53)	1 (33.33)	0 (0)	0 (0)	2 (10.53)	0 (0)	0 (0)	1 (33.33)

(Contd.)

Ward	Rs. 0-10000		Rs. 10000-20000		Rs. 20000-30000		Rs. 30000-40000		Rs. 40000-50000		Rs. 50000-60000		Rs. 60000 & Above	
	Tenant	Owner	Tenant	Owner	Tenant	Owner	Tenant	Owner	Tenant	Owner	Tenant	Owner	Tenant	Owner
Ward 11	4 (21.05)	0 (0)	4 (21.05)	0 (0)	6 (31.58)	0 (0)	1 (5.26)	0 (0)	1 (5.26)	2 (66.67)	0 (0)	0 (0)	3 (15.79)	1 (33.33)
Ward 12	0 (0)	0 (0)	5 (27.78)	0 (0)	0 (0)	0 (,0)	5 (27.78)	1 (25)	1 (5.55)	0 (0)	1 (5.55)	0 (0)	6 (33.33)	3 (75)
Ward 13	1 (5.55)	1 (25)	4 (22.22)	0 (0)	6 (33.33)	0 (0)	3 (16.67)	0 (0)	3 (16.67)	0 (0)	0 (0)	1 (25)	1 (5.55)	2 (50)
Ward 14	3 (15.79)	0 (0)	6 (31.58)	0 (0)	3 (15.79)	0 (0)	3 (15.79)	0 (0)	2 (10.53)	1 (33.33)	1 (5.26)	1 (33.33)	1 (5.26)	1 (33.33)
Ward 15	6 (33.33)	1 (33.33)	7 (38.89)	1 (33.33)	5 (27.78)	0 (0)	0 (0)	1 (33.33)	0 (0)	0 (0)	0 (0)	0 (0)	0 (0)	0 (0)
Ward 16	5 (29.41)	0 (0)	6 (35.29)	1 (25)	1 (5.88)	1 (25)	2 (11.76)	0 (0)	2 (11.76)	0 (0)	0 (0)	0 (0)	1 (5.88)	2 (50)
Ward 17	0 (0)	0 (0)	6 (33.33)	1 (33.33)	3 (16.67)	1 (33.33)	4 (22.22)	0 (0)	4 (22.22)	0 (0)	1 (5.55)	0 (0)	0 (0)	1 (33.33)
Ward 18	3 (16.67)	0 (0)	8 (42.10)	1 (33.33)	2 (11.11)	1 (33.33)	3 (16.67)	1 (33.33)	1 (5.55)	0 (0)	0 (0)	0 (0)	1 (5.55)	0 (0)
Ward 19	3 (15.79)	0 (0)	6 (31.58)	0 (0)	5 (26.32)	0 (0)	3 (15.79)	1 (33.33)	2 (10.53)	2 (66.67)	0 (0)	0 (0)	0 (0)	0 (0)
Ward 20	4 (22.22)	0 (0)	4 (22.22)	0 (0)	6 (33.33)	0 (0)	3 (16.67)	0 (0)	1 (5.55)	2 (66.67)	0 (0)	1 (33.33)	0 (0)	0 (0)

(Contd.)

Ward	Rs. 0-10000		Rs. 10000-20000		Rs. 20000-30000		Rs. 30000-40000		Rs. 40000-50000		Rs. 50000-60000		Rs. 60000 & Above	
	Tenant	Owner	Tenant	Owner	Tenant	Owner	Tenant	Owner	Tenant	Owner	Tenant	Owner	Tenant	Owner
Ward 21	4 (21.05)	0 (0)	3 (15.79)	1 (33.33)	5 (26.32)	0 (0)	3 (15.79)	0 (0)	1 (5.26)	1 (33.33)	2 (10.53)	0 (0)	1 (5.26)	1 (33.33)
Ward 22	6 (33.33)	0 (0)	4 (22.22)	0 (0)	5 (27.78)	0 (0)	3 (16.67)	1 (33.33)	0 (0)	1 (33.33)	0 (0)	0 (0)	0 (0)	1 (33.33)
Ward 23	2 (11.76)	0 (0)	8 (47.06)	0 (0)	3 (17.65)	1 (25)	0 (0)	3 (75)	3 (17.65)	0 (0)	1 (5.88)	0 (0)	0 (0)	0 (0)
Total	**69 (16.67)**	**4 (5.26)**	**141 (34.06)**	**9 (11.84)**	**89 (21.50)**	**10 (13.16)**	**54 (13.04)**	**15 (19.74)**	**30 (7.25)**	**11 (14.47)**	**12 (2.90)**	**4 (5.26)**	**19 (4.59)**	**23 (30.26)**

Source: Field Survey by the researcher during 2015-16.

Note: Figures in the parentheses represent percentage to total.

earning of head usually contributes the bulk of the family earnings. The Ward-wise distribution of the monthly income of the head of households is given in Table 4.10. Among the heads of tenant households, a vast majority earn in the range of Rs. 10,000-Rs. 20,000 per month and they are in majority in 13 wards. The heads of tenant households earning Rs. 20,000-Rs. 30,000 per month is more in Wards 11, 13, 20 and 21 while in Wards 2, 3 and 22 majority of them earn less than or equal to Rs. 10,000. Only in Ward 12 we find significant heads of tenant households earn over Rs. 60,000 per month.

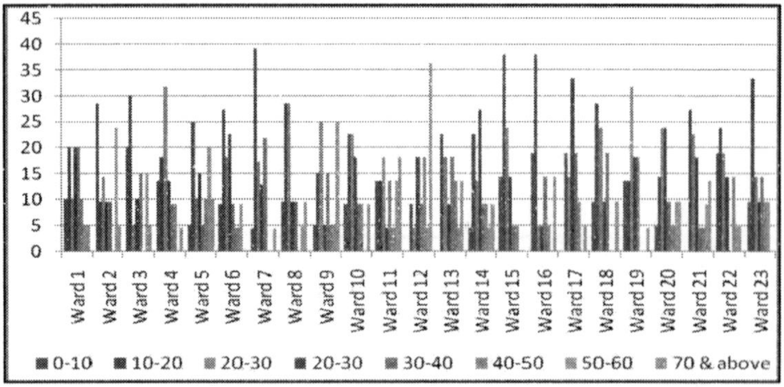

Fig. 4.13: Ward-wise Percentage Distribution of Monthly Family Income of All Surveyed Households (in Thousand Rupees).

Monthly income of the head of owner households is relatively better than the heads of tenant households as a larger proportion of them earn over Rs. 60,000 per month. From Table 4.10, it is revealed that heads of owner households earning over Rs. 60,000 per month is in majority in 16 wards and out of which they are relatively more in percentage in 5 wards than the tenant class. It is also observed that Ward 23 has the most number of those earning between Rs. 30,000-Rs. 40,000 while Wards 11, 19 and 20 have more household heads earning Rs. 40,000-Rs. 50,000.

The ward-wise distribution of all the surveyed households according to the monthly income of the head is also presented in Figure 4.14. The frequency distribution across increme groups vary significantly across the wards. Monthly income of the head ranging from Rs. 10,000-Rs. 20,000 is more in 12 wards where it accounts for nearly 60 per cent in Ward 8. Overall, majority of respondents belong to this group. Only in Ward 12 we find that majority of the heads earning Rs. 60,000 or more per month.

Table 4.11: Ward-wise Distribution of Tenant and Owner Households According to Possession of Vehicle and type of Vehicle

Ward	Vehicle		2-Wheeler		3-Wheeler		Car	
	Tenant	Owner	Tenant	Owner	Tenant	Owner	Tenant	Owner
Ward 1	10 (58.82)	3 (100)	5 (50)	0 (0)	1 (10)	NIL	4 (40)	3 (100)
Ward 2	9 (50)	3 (100)	5 (55.56)	0 (0)	1 (10)		4 (44.44)	3 (100)
Ward 3	6 (35.29)	3 (100)	0 (0)	1 (33.33)	2 (33.33)		4 (66.67)	2 (66.67)
Ward 4	10 (55.56)	4 (100)	5 (50)	1 (25)	1 (10)		4 (40)	3 (75)
Ward 5	11 (68.75)	4 (100)	4 (36.36)	0 (0)	0 (0)		7 (63.64)	4 (100)
Ward 6	8 (42.11)	3 (100)	4 (50)	1 (33.33)	0 (0)		4 (50)	2 (66.67)
Ward 7	15 (78.95)	3 (75)	12 (80)	1 (33.33)	1 (6.67)		2 (13.37)	2 (66.67)
Ward 8	11 (61.11)	2 (66.67)	7 (63.64)	0 (0)	0 (0)		4 (36.36)	2 (100)
Ward 9	12 (70.59)	3 (100)	7 (58.33)	0 (0)	0 (0)		5 (41.67)	3 (100)
Ward 10	10 (52.63)	3 (100)	4 (40)	1 (33.33)	0 (0)		6 (60)	2 (66.67)
Ward 11	9 (47.37)	3 (100)	1 (11.11)	0 (0)	0 (0)		8 (88.89)	3 (100)
Ward 12	12 (66.67)	4 (100)	2 (16.67)	0 (0)	0 (0)		10 (83.33)	4 (100)
Ward 13	11 (61.11)	3 (75)	7 (63.64)	0 (0)	0 (0)		4 (36.36)	3 (100)
Ward 14	6 (31.58)	3 (100)	2 (33.33)	0 (0)	0 (0)		4 (66.67)	3 (100)
Ward 15	10 (55.56)	1 (33.33)	6 (60)	0 (0)	1 (10)		3 (30)	1 (100)
Ward 16	7 (41.18)	4 (100)	1 (14.29)	1 (25)	1 (14.29)		5 (71.43)	3 (75)

(Contd.)

Ward	Vehicle		2-Wheeler		3-Wheeler		Car	
	Tenant	Owner	Tenant	Owner	Tenant	Owner	Tenant	Owner
Ward 17	13 (72.22)	3 (100)	8 (61.54)	1 (33.33)	0 (0)	NIL	5 (38.46)	2 (66.67)
Ward 18	8 (44.44)	2 (66.67)	7 (87.5)	1 (50)	0 (0)		1 (12.5)	1 (50)
Ward 19	10 (52.63)	2 (66.67)	6 (60)	1 (50)	0 (0)		6 (60)	1 (50)
Ward 20	5 (27.78)	3 (100)	0 (0)	0 (0)	0 (0)		5 (100)	3 (100)
Ward 21	12 (63.16)	3 (100)	4 (33.33)	1 (33.33)	3 (25)		5 (41.67)	2 (66.67)
Ward 22	3 (16.67)	3 (100)	1 (33.33)	0 (0)	1 (33.33)		1 (33.33)	3 (100)
Ward 23	13 (76.47)	3 (75)	6 (46.15)	0 (0)	4 (30.77)		3 (23.08)	3 (100)
Total	**221(53.38)**	**68(89.47)**	**104(47.1)**	**10 (14.71)**	**15(6.79)**		**102(46.15)**	**58(85.29)**

Source: Field Survey by the Researcher during 2015-16.
Note: Figures in the parentheses represent percentage to total.

Table 4.12: Ward-wise Distribution of Tenant and Owner Households by Employment of Domestic Servant

Ward	Tenant Households		Owner Households		Total Households	
	Having Domestic Servant	No Domestic Servant	Having Domestic Servant	No Domestic Servant	Having Domestic Servant	No Domestic Servant
Ward 1	2 (11.76)	15 (88.23)	2 (66.67)	1 (33.33)	4 (20)	16 (80)
Ward 2	2 (11.11)	16 (88.89)	3 (100)	0 (0)	5 (23.81)	16 (76.19)
Ward 3	1 (5.88)	16 (94.12)	1 (33.33)	2 (66.67)	2 (10)	18 (90)
Ward 4	2 (11.11)	16 (88.89)	2 (50)	2 (50)	4 (18.18)	18 (90)
Ward 5	2 (12.5)	14 (87.5)	2 (50)	2 (50)	4 (20)	16 (80)
Ward 6	1 (5.26)	18 (94.74)	2 (66.67)	1 (33.33)	3 (13.64)	19 (86.36)
Ward 7	1 (5.26)	18 (94.74)	2 (50)	2 (50)	3 (13.04)	20 (86.96)
Ward 8	2 (11.11)	16 (88.89)	1 (33.33)	2 (66.67)	3 (14.28)	18 (85.71)
Ward 9	5 (29.41)	12 (70.59)	2 (66.67)	1 (33.33)	7 (35)	13 (65)
Ward 10	5 (26.32)	14 (73.68)	2 (66.67)	1 (33.33)	7 (31.82)	15 (68.18)
Ward 11	3 (15.79)	16 (84.21)	2 (66.67)	1 (33.33)	5 (22.73)	17 (77.27)
Ward 12	3 (16.67)	15 (83.33)	1 (25)	3 (75)	4 (18.18)	18 (90)
Ward 13	1 (5.55)	17 (94.44)	2 (50)	2 (50)	3 (13.64)	19 (86.36)
Ward 14	0 (0)	19 (100)	2 (66.67)	1 (33.33)	2 (9.09)	20 (90.91)

(Contd.)

Ward	Tenant Households		Owner Households		Total Households	
	Having Domestic Servant	No Domestic Servant	Having Domestic Servant	No Domestic Servant	Having Domestic Servant	No Domestic Servant
Ward 15	1 (5.55)	17 (94.44)	1 (33.33)	2 (66.67)	2 (9.52)	19 (90.48)
Ward 16	1 (5.88)	16 (94.12)	2 (50)	2 (50)	3 (14.28)	18 (85.71)
Ward 17	5 (27.78)	13 (72.22)	2 (66.67)	1 (33.33)	7 (33.33)	14 (66.67)
Ward 18	3 (16.67)	15 (83.33)	1 (33.33)	2 (66.67)	4 (19.05)	17 (80.95)
Ward 19	2 (10.53)	17 (89.47)	1 (33.33)	2 (66.67)	3 (13.64)	19 (86.36)
Ward 20	3 (16.67)	15 (83.33)	1 (33.33)	2 (66.67)	4 (19.05)	17 (80.95)
Ward 21	4 (21.05)	15 (78.95)	1 (33.33)	2 (66.67)	5 (22.73)	17 (77.27)
Ward 22	1 (5.55)	17 (94.44)	2 (66.67)	1 (33.33)	3 (14.28)	18 (85.71)
Ward 23	3 (17.65)	14 (82.35)	2 (50)	2 (50)	5 (23.81)	16 (76.19)
Total	**53 (12.80)**	**361 (87.20)**	**39 (51.32)**	**37 (48.68)**	**92 (18.78)**	**398 (81.22)**

Source: Field Survey by the researcher during 2015-16.

Note: Figures in the parentheses represent percentage to total.

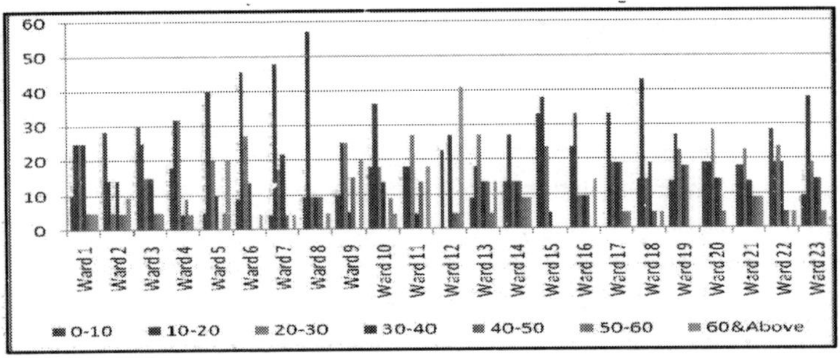

Fig. 4.14: Ward-wise Percentage Distribution of All Households According to the Monthly Income of the Head (in Thousand Rupees).

Distribution of Surveyed Households According to Possession of Personal Vehicle and Employment of Domestic Servant

The possession of personal vehicles and/or employing domestic servants is a good indicator of the economic status of a household. Ward-wise distribution of households according to possession of personal vehicle as well as type of vehicle owned is displayed in Table 4.11. Among the tenant households, it is observed that 53.38 per cent own personal vehicle and the proportion of tenants own vehicle varies significantly across the wards. The percentage is more than half in 14 wards and it is the highest in Ward 7 (78.95%) and the lowest in Ward 22 (16.67%). On the other hand, 89.47 per cent of the sample owner households own a personal vehicle and in 16 wards all of them are found to have personal vehicle. In contrast, Wards 15 recorded that about one-third of them are vehicle owners.

With regard to type of vehicle owned, it is observed that out of the 221 tenant households who own a personal vehicle, 47.1 per cent of them own a 2-Wheeler with Wards 8 and 13 accounting for 63.64 per cent each. Also, 46.15 per cent of them own a car. In Ward 20 all the respondent tenants own a car. The lowest percentage of tenant car owners is found in Ward 18 (12.50%). Among the 68 owner households who possess a personal vehicle, a great majority of them is found to own a car and in 13 wards it is 100 per cent. On the other hand, least percentage of car owners is found in Wards 18 and 19 accounting for 50 per cent. It is also observed that in 10 wards, owner households own a 2-Wheeler.

The ward-wise distribution of households according to employment of domestic servant is provided in the Table 4.12. Among the tenant households, it is observed that a very small proportion of them (53 households) employ domestic servants and the employment of domestic servant is found in all the wards except Ward 14. Ward 9 recorded the highest percentage of employment of domestic servant with 29.41 per cent. Among the owner households, a relatively larger proportion employ domestic servants and the employment of domestic servant is witnessed in all the wards. Ward 2 recorded 100 per cent of domestic servant employment by the owner households.

Fig. 4.15a reveals that 87.20 per cent of tenant households do not employ domestic servants and only 12.80 per cent of them are employing domestic servants. Among the owner households, 51.32 per cent employ domestic servants (Fig. 4.15b). Overall, 81.22 per cent of the surveyed households do not have domestic servants while 18.78 per cent of them employ domestic servant (Fig. 4.15c).

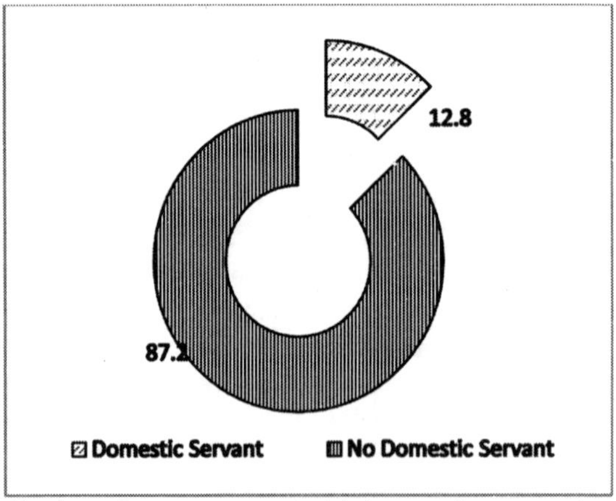

Fig. 4.15a: Distribution of Tenant Households by Employment of Domestic Servant

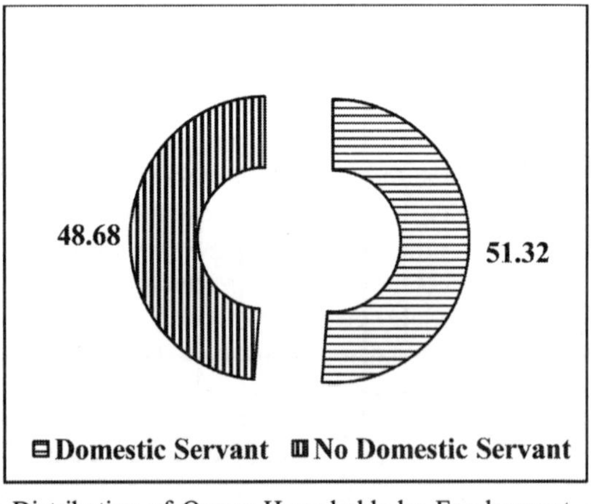

Fig. 4.15b: Distribution of Owner Households by Employment of Domestic Servant

Table 4.13: Ward-wise distribution of Tenant and Owner Households According to Average Number of Families Living in Same Building, Duration of Stay and Time required for arrangement of First Accommodation (Months) by the Tenants

Ward	Average No. of Families in the Building		Average Carpet Area per Capita (Sq. Ft)		Average Period of Stay (Year)		Average Time (Month) for First Accommodation
	Tenant	Owner	Tenant	Owner	Tenant	Owner	Tenant
Ward 1	4.06	2.67	141.41	310	20.7	41	1.35
Ward 2	3.39	1.67	138.88	376	12.5	45.67	1.83
Ward 3	2.18	1	123.57	500	15.94	27.67	1.18
Ward 4	3.28	1.25	123.24	181.88	12.89	30	1.5
Ward 5	3.37	3.25	175.69	326.43	15.12	35	1.75
Ward 6	5.47	4	106.89	205.33	18.26	45	1.74
Ward 7	3.37	1	99.92	252.67	17.63	26	1.58
Ward 8	3.11	2.33	141.27	211.90	18.78	30.33	1.72
Ward 9	6.88	3.33	141.76	371.67	17.29	33	1.65
Ward 10	3.21	2	159.01	218.22	16.79	25.67	1.74
Ward 11	3.63	1	135.31	194.37	9.16	40	2.21
Ward 12	3	1	223.54	322.50	11.67	34.25	1.72
Ward 13	4.72	1.25	172.14	355.36	13.17	30.5	1.61

(Contd.)

Ward	Average No. of Families in the Building		Average Carpet Area per Capita (Sq. Ft)		Average Period of Stay (Year)		Average Time (Month) for First Accommodation
	Tenant	Owner	Tenant	Owner	Tenant	Owner	Tenant
Ward 14	5.05	2	175.36	711.11	11.68	24.67	1.84
Ward 15	5.5	3.67	135.72	180.67	26	35.33	1
Ward 16	3.41	1	158.71	255.36	16.71	25.25	1.12
Ward 17	8.39	4.67	159.10	184.17	32	52.33	0.56
Ward 18	5.78	1.67	113.87	207.78	15.17	39.33	1.56
Ward 19	6.42	3.33	144.41	170.44	26.53	43.67	1.16
Ward 20	3.5	1.67	141.99	342.44	12	22.33	1.78
Ward 21	5.79	4.67	151.96	176.33	22.68	29.67	1.63
Ward 22	2.44	1	122.91	227.14	17.39	39.67	1.5
Ward 23	2.65	1.5	134.75	367	12.35	30.5	1.59
Overall Average	4.28	2.21	144.41	289.08	17.06	34.21	1.53

Source: Field Survey by the researcher during 2015-16.

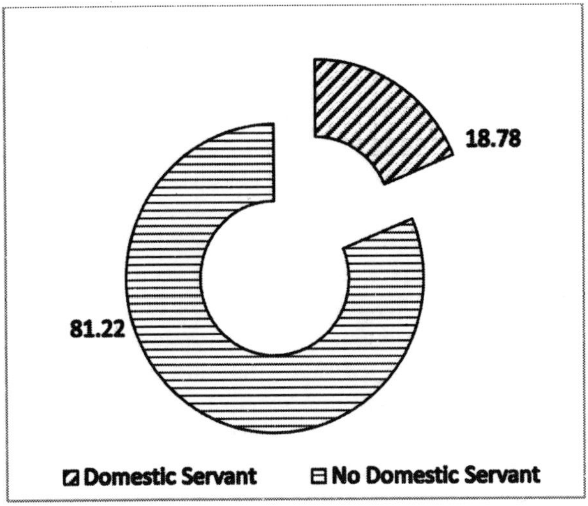

Fig. 4.15c: Distribution of All Households by Employment of Domestic Servant

Distribution of Surveyed Households According to Number of Families in the Same Building and Duration of Stay in Dimapur Town

Table 4.13 provides information on the number of families live in a single building and changes in timing necessitated for arranging accommodation in their initial year of stay, that throws some light on the living conditions of households. It, therefore, offors some insights about the changing living conditions of households in Dimapur town. From the average number of families living in the same building, we can get an idea of the size of building in which a household is residing. Generally, a higher average number of families imply a larger house.

From Table 4.13, it is also observed that in the case of tenant households, Ward 17 has the highest average number of families living in the same building. This imply that there are more double or multi-storied buildings in the ward. On the other hand, Ward 3 has the lowest average number of families in the same building which implies that there are more independent and detached houses in the ward. The average number of families for all the 23 wards is found to be 4.28 families in a building. It thus reflects that bigger house are centrally located in business and administrative area where development took place earlier. On the other hand, relatively less number of families stay in a house with small in size are prevalent in the remote, outskirt areas of town.But the average area occupied by a family member may be opposite due to the availability of space. It is reflected that in the outskirt Wards per capita area occupied is relatively more than that of a building in centrally located ward.

In respect of the owner households, Wards 17 and 21 share the largest average number of families (4.67 families). It is observed that in 6 wards, the average number of families is 1 indicating that the owner households in these wards live with only their own families and do not rent out rooms to tenants. The average number of families in the same building for all the wards is 2.21. Thus, it is observed that there are 14 wards with lesser number of families than the total average and 9 wards with greater average number of families than the total average of the town.

The Ward-wise distribution of average duration of stay in Dimapur town (in years) and the average time taken for getting the first accommodation (in months) in respect of tenant respondents is also provided in Table 4.13. The average duration of stay is 17.06 years in case of tenant respondents and 34.21 years in case of owner respondents. Individually, the longest period of residence among the tenant respondents is 68 years and the average duration of stay is the highest in Ward 17 with 32 years whereas the lowest average is 9.16 years found in Ward 11. Among the owner respondents also the highest average duration of stay is in Ward 17, which is 52.33 years and the lowest is in Ward 20 with 22.33 years.

In regard to the time taken for first accommodation (in months), we take into consideration only the tenant households. The average time taken for first rented accommodation for all the 414 tenant respondents is found to be 1.53 months. It is observed that in Ward 11, the tenants recorded the longest average time with 2.21 months, most of whom came in recent past years. The tenants in all the other wards took an average time ranging between 1 to 2 months except Ward 17 which recorded the shortest time with 0.56 month (about half month), where people gathered long 4 to 5 decades back in the initial stage of development of the township.

In order to see whether housing is becoming scarce and more time is required to find rented accommodations in Dimapur town, the duration of stay (year) in Dimapur of the tenants is compared with the time required to get their first rented house (month). It is observed that for the 145 tenants who have come to Dimapur town in the previous decade (within last 0-9 years), they required an average time of 2.25 months to get their first accommodation. Whereas, the other 110 tenants who came during 10-19 years before, they needed 1.74 months to get their first rented house. 78 of the sample tenants who have been staying for 20-29 years and the other 61 tenants who have been living for 30-39 years, average time required for being able to arrange accommodation the first time on their arrival was

0.96 and 0.52 months respectively. Finally, 20 tenants living for 40 years and more, average time required to get accommodation the first time was merely 0.15 months. It is also observed that larger numbers of people have been coming to Dimapur town during the recent past decades than the earlier decades (Table 4.14 and Fig. 4.16).

Table 4.14: Distribution of Tenants According to Duration of Stay (Years) and Time Taken for First Accommodation (Months)

	0-9 Yrs	10-19 Yrs	20-29 Yrs	30-39 Yrs	40 & Above
Average Time (month)	2.25	1.74	0.96	0.52	0.15
No. of Households	145 (35.02)	110 (26.17)	78 (18.84)	61 (14.73)	20 (4.83)

Source: Field Survey by the researcher during 2015-16.
Note: Figures in the parentheses represent percentage to total.

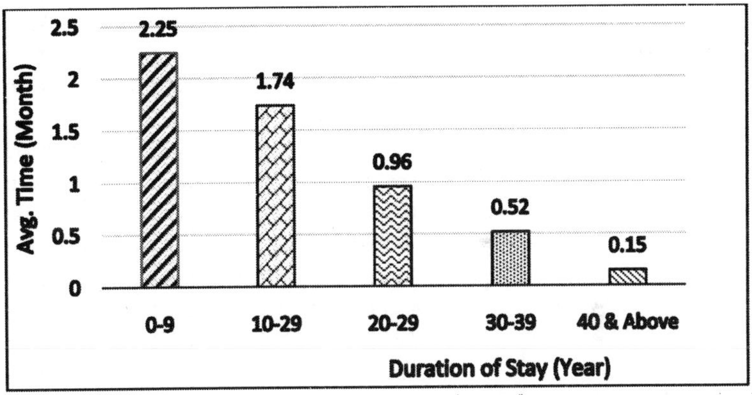

Fig. 4.16: Distribution of Tenants According to Duration of Stay (Years) and Time Taken for First Accommodation (Months)

From Table 4.14 and Fig. 4.16, it is observed that housing is becoming scarcer over the decades and it is requiring more time for the tenants to get a house to stay. This may be due to the fact that supply of housing is not able to keep pace with the growing demand for housing as evidenced by the greater numbers of people coming to settle in the town over the decades.

The correlation between the duration of stay and the time required to arrange accommodation for the first time is found to be -0.63 which is significant at 5 per cent level of significance by two-tailed. The regression equation can be written as,

Table 4.15: Ward-wise Distribution of Tenant Households According to Desire for Accommodation Change and Its Reasons

	Want Accommodation Change	No Accommodation Change	Reasons for Desire to Change				
			Own House	Better House	Better Locality	Family/ Own People	Others
Ward 1	1 (5.88)	16 (94.12)	0 (0)	1 (100)	0 (0)	0 (0)	0 (0)
Ward 2	0 (0)	18 (100)	0 (0)	0 (0)	0 (0)	0 (0)	0 (0)
Ward 3	0 (0)	17 (100)	0 (0)	0 (0)	0 (0)	0 (0)	0 (0)
Ward 4	2 (11.11)	16 (88.89)	1 (50)	0 (0)	0 (0)	0 (0)	1 (50)
Ward 5	1 (6.25)	15 (93.75)	0 (0)	1 (100)	0 (0)	0 (0)	0 (0)
Ward 6	1 (5.26)	18 (94.74)	0 (0)	1 (100)	0 (0)	0 (0)	0 (0)
Ward 7	2 (10.53)	17 (89.47)	0 (0)	1 (50)	1 (50)	0 (0)	0 (0)
Ward 8	4 (22.22)	14 (77.78)	1 (25)	2 (50)	1 (25)	0 (0)	0 (0)
Ward 9	3 (17.65)	14 (82.35)	0 (0)	3 (100)	0 (0)	0 (0)	0 (0)
Ward 10	1 (5.26)	18 (94.74)	0 (0)	1 (100)	0 (0)	0 (0)	0 (0)
Ward 11	1 (5.26)	18 (94.74)	0 (0)	1 (100)	0 (0)	0 (0)	0 (0)
Ward 12	3 (16.67)	15 (83.33)	2 (66.6)	1 (33.3)	0 (0)	0 (0)	0 (0)
Ward 13	2 (11.11)	16 (88.89)	1 (50)	1 (50)	0 (0)	0 (0)	0 (0)
Ward 14	2 (10.53)	17 (89.47)	0 (0)	1 (50)	0 (0)	0 (0)	1 (50)

(Contd.)

	Want Accommodation Change	No Accommodation Change	Reasons for Desire to Change				
			Own House	Better House	Better Locality	Family/ Own People	Others
Ward 15	0 (0)	18 (100)	0 (0)	0 (0)	0 (0)	0 (0)	0 (0)
Ward 16	3 (17.65)	14 (82.35)	2 (66.6)	0 (0)	0 (0)	1 (33.3)	0 (0)
Ward 17	1 (5.56)	17 (94.44)	0 (0)	1 (100)	0 (0)	0 (0)	0 (0)
Ward 18	4 (22.22)	14 (77.78)	0 (0)	2 (50)	2 (50)	0 (0)	0 (0)
Ward 19	0 (0)	19 (100)	0 (0)	0 (0)	0 (0)	0 (0)	0 (0)
Ward 20	2 (11.11)	16 (88.89)	1 (50)	1 (50)	0 (0)	0 (0)	0 (0)
Ward 21	3 (15.79)	16 (84.21)	1 (33.3)	1 (33.3)	0 (0)	0 (0)	1 (33.3)
Ward 22	4 (22.22)	14 (77.78)	1 (25)	3 (75)	0 (0)	0 (0)	0 (0)
Ward 23	2 (11.76)	15 (88.24)	1 (50)	0 (0)	0 (0)	0 (0)	1 (50)
Total	**42 (10.14)**	**372 (89.85)**	**11 (26.19)**	**22 (52.38)**	**4 (9.52)**	**1 (2.38)**	**4 (9.52)**

Source: Field Survey by the researcher during 2015-16.
Note: Figures in the parentheses represent percentage to total.\

$$Y = 2.510\ (33.58)^{***} - 0.058X\ (-16.33)^{***};\ R^2=0.393,\ \text{Adj. } R^2 = 0.391,\ F = 266.567^{***}$$

where, Y = Number of months to find first rented accommodation of stay (when they first came),

X = Total number of years of stay in Dimapur. Figures in the parentheses indicate the t-value and

*** here indicates that the coefficient is significant at one per cent level of significance by two-tailed test. The inverse relation between the two is reflected.

Interactions with several tenants reveal that they are compelled to move into the first available house since they are left with very little or no choice in getting their first accommodation. This may be the reason why several tenants are not satisfied with their present house and expressed their desire to shift their residence even with higher rent. The following sub-section tries to address the desire of the tenants to change their accommodation if any and also to describe the reasons behind it.

Distribution of Surveyed Households According to Desire for Accommodation Change and Its Reasons

The ward-wise distribution of the tenant households according to their desire for accommodation change and the reasons for such desire is provided in Table 4.15. It is found that in most of the wards (19 wards) there are some tenants who desire to change their house. In Wards 8, 18 and 22, 22.22 per cent of the tenants wanted to change accommodation. 22 tenants opined to shift to a better house while 11 tenants wanted to construct their own houses (in or outside the town) and would shift there in near future. 4 tenants who are either living in unhygienic, congested or flood-prone areas have expressed their desire to shift to a better locality. There are also 4 tenants who cited other reasons for such desire while 1 tenant wants to move to a locality to be nearer to family members.

The percentage distribution of the 414 tenant households according to their desire for accommodation change and the reasons for such desire by the 42 tenant households is displayed in the 2 Pie diagrams. Fig. 4.17a, reveals that 80.68 per cent of the tenant households (372) do not want to change accommodation whereas 10.14 per cent (42) want accommodation change. However, during the interactions, most of the 372 tenant households who do not want a change of accommodation also revealed that their stay in the present houses is purely at the will of the house owner. Thus, they can continue to stay so long as the house owners allow them.

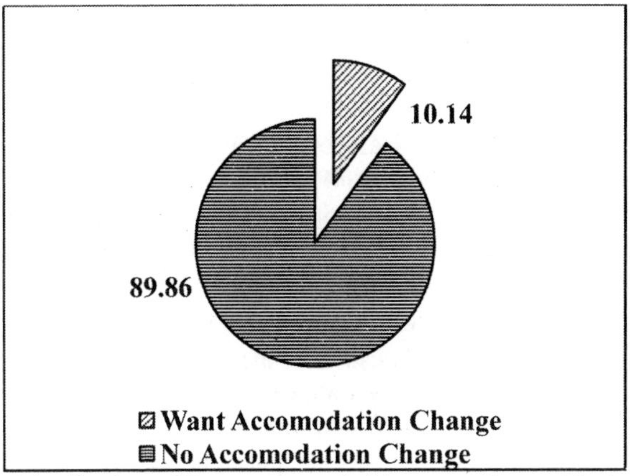

Fig. 4.17a: Distribution of Tenant Households According to their Reason for Accommodation Change

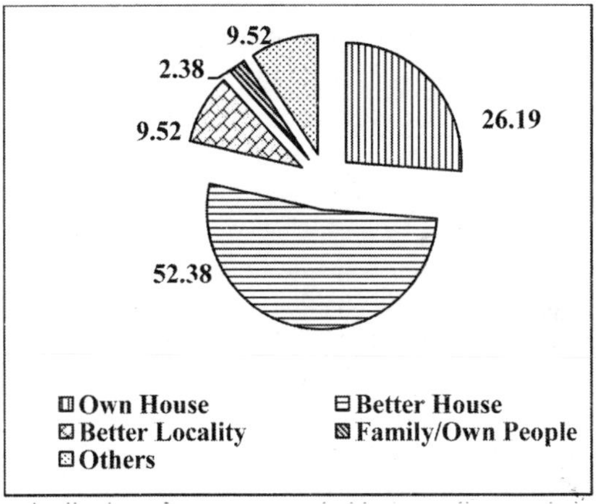

Fig. 4.17b: Distribution of Tenant Households According to their Reason for Accommodation Change

From Fig. 4.17b, it is observed that more than half of the 42 households (52.38 %) who expressed their desire for accommodation change opined that they would like to shift to a better house and 26.19 per cent of them would shift to their own houses. 9.52 per cent of them wanted to shift to a better location and the desire to go near family/own people constitute 2.38 per cent.

4.3 Summary of Observations

From the survey, it is observed that there are more married households in Dimapur town. In respect of religion, it was found that there are more Christians but community-wise there are more Non-Nagas residing in the town. It is observed that a great majority of the households have migrated to the town but the migration was much higher among the tenant households. The survey also shows a very high literacy rate among the respondents with greater shares of graduate and above. Majority of the heads of households are found to be self-employed undertaking their own businesses while a greater proportion of the spouses is unemployed. With regard to the average monthly per capita incomes of the families, it is found that 27.05 per cent of tenant households and 57.89 per cent of owner households earn above Rs. 10,000 per month.It is observed that the modal monthly income of the heads of tenant households is in the income group Rs. 10,000 – Rs. 20,000 while the modal monthly income of the heads of owner households is Rs. 60,000 and above. The survey also revealed that most households possess a personal vehicle but tenant households have more 2 wheelers and owner households have more cars. The survey found that a relatively larger proportion of owner households employ domestic servants compared to tenant households. It is also found that the owner households have a greater average family size and average number of adults but the tenant households have a greater average number of children below the age of 14 years. The average number of families in the same building was found to be much higher in the case of tenant households while the average duration of stay in the town for the owner households was found to be almost double to that of tenant households. In respect of the tenant households, it is observed that housing is becoming scarcer and time taken for first rented accommodation is increasing over the decades. It is also observed that a good number of tenant households have a desire to shift to a better house within the town.

REFERENCES

Akinyode, B.F., Khan, T.H. and Ahmad, A.S.B.H. (2015). Socio-economic factors in measuring the demand for residential neighbourhood in Nigeria. *Asian Social Science*, 11(12), 235-247.

Fields, G.S. (1980). Education and income distribution in developing countries: A review of the literature [Electronic version]. In T. King (Ed.), *Education and income: A background study for world development* (pp. 231-315). Washington, DC: The World Bank.

5
Determinants of Housing Demand in Dimapur

Introduction

Housing is considered to be one of the basic necessities of life as it has a profound impact on health, productivity and welfare of individuals (Akintunde, 2008). It constitutes one of the three basic items of food, clothing and shelter required for minimum survival. Moreover, in recent times, housing is not only considered purely as shelter but an indicator of lifestyle which is closely associated with economic, social and educational needs of human being (Ademiluyi, 2010). It is essential to meet the needs and aspirations of the residents as well as contribute to the physical, mental, social well-being of the people by providing them quiet environment, living and outdoor spaces, privacy, cleanliness, safety and aesthetic satisfaction (Okechukwu 2009; Ademiluyi and Raji, 2008; Aero 2006; Olayiwola *et al.,* 2005).

This chapter is devoted to the identification of factors affecting the demand for housing in Dimapur town of Nagaland. Also impacts of various determinants on the housing demand are examined thoroughly. Here, it may be noted that housing units come as a bundle of attributes and are immovable assets, which involve huge costs. It is not just like any other commodity that satisfies one or two needs. Different attributes like material of construction (determines longevity), size and space, provisions created within the house (that provides comfort), positioning of house with respect to natural direction, neighbouring components (residents, establishments etc. that provides psychological and social status), location with respect to places of visit for daily activities and natural environment (that determines the physical comforts of residents) are the major criteria for the decision to buy or take a house on rent along with the capability of individuals. Thus, different attributes associated with a house provides different amenities and satisfy the required objectives of the people with diversified needs and that also varies across the people of heterogeneous social groups with differential age, occupation and psychological background.

The attributes of housing can be broadly classified into Structural, Locational and Neighbourhood characteristics and those fulfil a number of requirements of the residents. It may also be noted that frequent construction of residential buildings are difficult and it is observed that rarely residential buildings are sold or purchased every year in the study area. Most house owners who inherited their houses are constrained to live there since it is too difficult for many of them to buy or construct a new residential building. Not only that, many a time, several family members having share of the same property (by virtue of inheritance law) stay with difficulty in the same location/building (for locational advantage) instead of moving to a remote area where land is available.

On the other hand, for the tenants, given their income and other preferences, it is relatively easier for them to change accommodation as per their needs and capabilities. A large number of service holders who are from outside the region, prefer to stay in rented accommodation till the service period is over or they get residential accommodation from their employers. The preference pattern in respect of various attributes may differ between the purchase for (construction of) own house and rented accommodation by the tenants. For tenants, it is temporary and some of the attributes they cannot change but accept for the convenience of their work and the owners may like to add many features to their houses for their long term objectives of maintaining livelihood and/or enjoying amenities. Thus, due to the basic differences in respect of demand for housing attributes, the analysis is done separately for Tenants and House Owners.

Since housing comes as a bundle of attributes and it is very difficult to separate them, we shall make an attempt to determine which attribute(s) has significant impact(s) on the demand for housing in the study area. The socio-economic factors of households are expected to influence their residential choice making, as their capability also determine their effective choice for some amenities other than very crucial space of house. A detailed discussion of socio-economic characteristics of the sample households has been made in Chapter 5. This section is devoted to the analysis of the impacts of the various housing attributes on the housing price (or rent) in Dimapur town during 2015-16.

Determinants of the Demand for Housing in Dimapur Town

Today housing is considered more than a mere shelter and is related with lifestyle which encompasses economic, social and educational needs, all of which play their parts in the choice of housing by the individuals (Ademiluyi, 2010). The demand for housing thus depends not only on the capability of individuals, but also on various other attributes associated with the concerned house to meet their needs satisfactorily. People are often found to compromise some of the required amenities for various economic and social reasons. It is generally noticed that people prefer to stay within homogeneous group, with less interference and risk, better opportunities, accessibility, environmental ambience etc., all of which is hardly available from a particular house. Moreover, such preferences are often found to be constrained by economic conditions of the individuals.

In an endeavour to account for the inherent heterogeneity of good in question, that is housing, many recent analyses of housing markets have viewed the housing commodity in hedonic or characteristic terms (Lancaster, 1966 and Rosen, 1974). The dwelling unit in these analyses is conceptualized not as a homogeneous, composite good, but as a bundle of individual attributes, each of which contributes to the provision of one or more housing services. Thus, a housing unit is treated as a heterogeneous commodity, each unit being different from others because of the different attributes inherent in it. When a house is purchased or rented, the various attributes that go with it are also purchased or rented (Akpam, 1994).

Houses differ in terms of both quantitative and qualitative attributes (Goodman, 1989) that contributes to the welfare of the individuals living in it in a number of ways. Depending on the urge for obtaining such benefits, people (potential buyers or tenants) expresses their willingness to pay for them, which may be explained in terms of suitable hedonic price equation, known as the demand function. The market prices (P) of the property in implicit form can thus be expressed as: $P = f(L, S, N)$. The partial derivative of this price function with respect to any attribute is the implicit marginal price of that attribute, *ceteris paribus* (Rosen, 1974). This implicit price of the housing attribute is revealed in the regression coefficient. All buyers may perceive the amounts of attributes embodied in the housing product to be identical, but their subjective valuations of each component attribute may differ depending on their respective choice for such attribute and that depends on various social and economic conditions. The price of the house, then, is the sum of the implicit prices for the attributes that are contained in it. Estimation of such an equation would thus, enable us to test and analyze the possible influence of each of the many attributes on the overall house price in a particular area.

Mode of Analysis

First of all, the ward-wise percentage distribution of various structural attributes and civic amenities in Dimapur town is analyzed. Each attribute has been categorized into a number of available options representing quality of house and availability of facilities. In order to check the correlation among the selected structural attributes, an intra-class correlation has been conducted. This is done to understand whether a housing unit that possess a better structural attribute (say, better wall material), also has better quality of other structural attributes or not. It is expected that a good house with better quality of exterior will also have better quality of interior and so for roof. Also, in middle income families of the backward regions it has been observed that many people use only concrete for the wall, but tin or similar other material for the roof. Similarly, sometimes cemented floor with bamboo wall is also observed to be prevalent in some houses depending on the capability and urgency of requirement of floor, wall, roof and other facilities like type of toilet facilities, size of the room etc. For all the sample families in the area, what is the overall relation among the structural attributes is important to know in order to understand the nature of demand for various attributes.

Tenants or buyers may prefer a few attributes with good quality while may compromise with other attributes depending on their capability, and relative urgency of the facilities inherent in a housing unit. Moreover, if there is a strong relationship among some structural attributes, only one of those may be enough and be included in the regression for estimating the demand equation and avoid the problem of multicollinearity. That variable on the one hand will represent the quality of overall structural parameter and its coefficient will indicate people's willingness to pay for it. As the quality of various such attributes for same set of housing units is correlated, method of intra-class correlation (Fisher's Alpha) is more appropriate than the conventional Pearson's correlation measure (Fisher, 1954).

Thereafter, the ward-wise average monthly rents, land prices and house prices (per square feet) and their average annual growth rates are computed. These are computed on the basis of the primary data as mentioned earlier, collected from the sampled respondents by direct interview using an interview schedule from the 23 wards of Dimapur Municipal area. Dichotomous types of responses have been obtained in regard to the availability of various facilities and from the proportion of positive responses for different items, overall proportion of positive response for a number of structural attributes is computed for all the wards. In other words, from the average percentages so calculated for each attribute, ranking in terms of percentage of the availability of the various structural attributes and civic amenities across the wards has been computed by simple summation of the percentages of all the attributes in a particular category (structural or civic amenities) and dividing it by the number of attributes and amenities. Thereafter, the impacts of the various housing attributes on the housing price (or rent) are analysed using hedonic pricing approach.

Results and Discussion

Ward-wise Percentage of Houses having Various Structural Attributes and Civic Amenities

Various structural attributes under consideration have been categorized into a number of available options representing the structural quality of house, which is described in Table 5.1. The exterior wall material used for the house has been categorized into bamboo or wood, combination of bamboo/wood with concrete (bricks), and the whole concrete. The proportional distribution of houses having best quality material (i.e. concrete) across the ward among those three categories is displayed in Table 5.2. Likewise, other structural attributes such as floor, roof, toilet, house condition, number of floors and carpet area has been categorized for the purpose of analysis. With regard to the material used for roofing, it is observed in the sample survey that only two types of materials were used, viz. tin/asbestos and concrete. However, quality of roof has been divided into three categories such as houses built with tin/asbestos roofing having bamboo/wood wall, tin/asbestos roofing with concrete wall, and houses with concrete roof having total concrete wall. Houses with concrete roof having concrete wall is considered to be the best in qualitative term and on the basis of its longevity. From the opinions of the surveyed respondents regarding the overall condition of the house, their responses have been categorized into the three categories, viz. unsatisfactory, medium and excellent. With respect to size of house, the number of floors (stories) of the building as well as the carpet (floor) area of the housing unit has been used for computation. But a limitation of this criterion is that there are also single-storied houses with good structural quality and also with large carpet area. In the case of carpet area, the size of the carpet area has been categorized into three categories with middle size of 500-800 square feet. This is done on the basis of the median family size of 5 across the surveyed respondents. From personal experience it is understood that a 5-member family require about 500-800 square feet area of house (carpet area) to maintain a comfortable life (average carpet area of all the respondents is observed to be 662 square feet). Less than 500 sq. ft and more than 800 sq. ft areas are considered to be relatively poor and best categories as observed from the sample houses.

Table 5.1: Description of Structural Attributes According to Quality and Size

Category	Attribute	Poor	Moderate	Good
Construction Material	Wall	Bamboo/Wood	Bamboo/Wood and Concrete	Concrete
	Floor	Earth/Wood	Concrete	Marble/Tile
	Roof	Tin/Asbestos with Non-Concrete Wall	Tin/Asbestos with Concrete Wall	Concrete
	Toilet	Not Attached	Not Attached but with Concrete Septic Tank	Attached
	Overall House Condition	Unsatisfactory	Medium	Excellent
Size of House	No. of Floors	One	Two	More than Two
	Carpet Area	Less than 500 sq.ft.	500 - 800 sq.ft.	More than 800 sq.ft.

Note: There are single-storied buildings which are of good structural quality and large in size.

With respect to the civic and other amenities, the response of the respondents for the availability of such amenities is taken into account. The quality of most amenities is difficult to quantify precisely and so irrespective of the differences in quality we considered only its availability. In case of water supply, out of the several options we considered 24 hours water supply availability to the house among the surveyed respondents as the most favourable option. Good or regular supply, just enough and insufficient supply are the other three categories considered here. The type of sewer has been categorized into open, partially open and covered; and the proportion of houses with covered sewer is shown in Table 5.2.

Overall, it is observed that a good proportion of the surveyed respondents live in houses constructed of concrete wall (81.20%), concrete roof (54.21%). The original data however reveals that 54.27 per cent of the houses are double or multiple storied buildings and 70 per cent of the houses have attached toilet inside their housing units. It is also observed that about 77.35 per cent of the surveyed respondents stay in houses made of concrete (cement) floor. Table 5.2 shows that there are significant variations in the structural attributes of the houses across the wards. Among the six main structural attributes presented in Table 5.2, coefficient of variation in the proportion of houses having floor made marble is the highest (68.47%), which is followed by concrete roof (35.43%). The least variation is observed in the case of percentage of sample houses having concrete wall (16.50%). The last column presenting the response on excellent overall house condition and its percentage also varies significantly with coefficient of variation stands at 47.90 per cent.

Table 5.2: Estimated Average, Standard Deviation and Coefficient of Variation of Selected Structural Qualities

	Concrete Wall (%)	**Marble Floor (%)**	**Con-crete Roof (%)**	**Average No. of Floors**	**Average Carpet Area**	**Atta-ched Toilet (%)**	**Excellent House Cond-ition (%)**
Average	81.20	17.38	54.21	1.82	663.46	69.93	27.88
Std. Dev.	13.40	11.90	19.20	0.49	121.47	15.90	13.36
Coeff. of Var	16.50	68.47	35.43	27.16	18.31	22.74	47.90

Source: Field Survey Conducted During 2015-16.

Fisher's intra-class correlation (two-way) among various structural attributes show that all the structural attributes under consideration are significantly correlated at one per cent level of significance except between carpet area and number of floors of the building which is significant at five per cent level of significance (Table 5.3). This result is on expected line since better quality of floor material used (marble/tile being the best) is expected to be significantly correlated with houses made of concrete wall material, and the owners or tenants are expected to belong to the upper stratum of the society. Likewise, roof type is also observed to be significantly correlated with exterior wall type and floor material used in the building. It implies that when a housing unit has better quality wall, the house has a very significant probability of having better other structural attributes such as better floor, roof, carpet area, attached toilet and overall better house condition.

In order to check whether there are significant variations in the attributes considered across the surveyed sample units, a Chi-Square test for variation in each attribute has been computed (Table 5.3). It is observed that there is significant variation in almost all the attributes across the sample houses across the wards in Dimapur town. The test reveals

Table 5.3: Intra-class Correlations between Various Structural Attributes and Estimated Chi-Square Values for Each Attribute

Categories of Structural Attributes	Wall Type	Floor Type	Roof Type	No. of Floor	Carpet Area	Attached Toilet	House Condition
Wall Type	1						
Floor Type	.517**	1					
Roof Type	.476**	.307**	1				
No. of Floor	.403**	.339**	.627**	1			
Carpet Area	.288**	.384**	.177**	.112*	1		
Attached Toilet	.673**	.442**	.570**	.528**	.380**	1	
House Condition	.266**	.253**	.349**	.290**	.191**	.318**	1
Chi-Square Test for Variation in each attribute across the wards	518.92**	743.04**	0.02	355.55**	451.87**	77.76**	273.22**

Source: Field Survey conducted during 2015-16.

Note: ** and * indicate that the coefficient is significant at 1% and 5% level of significance by two-tailed test.

that variations in wall type, floor type, number of floors, attached toilet and overall house condition, are all significant at one per cent level of significance. It is, however, observed that there is no significant difference in roof type across the town. Two-way correlation table also shows that there are significant correlations among various Amenity items. The Chi-Square tests for variation in each attribute across the sample residences also indicate significant inter-household variations in availability and type of fencing, compound, Balcony, Garage, Flower Bed, Water Supply, Sewer Type. The results of individual Chi-Square are displayed in the last row of Table 5.4 and all of which are significant at one per cent level of significant by two-tailed test.

Ward-wise percentage distribution of various structural and civic amenities portrays a wide variation in availability and quality of various structural attributes and amenities in the sampled housing units (Table 5.5). In respect of structural qualities such as wall, floor and roof materials used along with the number of floors, carpet area of the house and attached

Table 5.4: Estimated Intra-Class Correlations between Various Amenities

	Avail of Fencing	**Comp-ound**	**Balcony**	**Garage**	**Flower Bed**	**Water Supply**	**Sewer Type**
Avail. of Fencing	1						
Compound	.460**	1					
Balcony	.243**	.223**	1				
Garage	.408**	.345**	.352**	1			
Flower Bed	.412**	.450**	.347**	.488**	1		
Water Supply	.168**	.170**	.211**	.258**	.233**	1	
Sewer Type	-.023	-.039	.164**	.228**	.119**	.200**	1
Chi-Square Test for Variation in each attribute across the wards	125.01**	131.86**	44.70**	231.51**	53.56**	541.66**	302.09**

Source: Field Survey conducted during 2015-16.

Note: ** indicate that the coefficient is significant at 1% level of significance by two-tailed test.

toilet etc. Ward 17 is observed to have comparatively better and taller buildings. The overall opinion of the respondents (most of whom are tenants) with regard to their housing condition also support this argument. 47.62 per cent of the respondents in Ward 17 opined that their houses are in excellent condition, while 52.38 per cent of them viewed that their housing conditions are moderate and no surveyed respondent stated that their overall housing condition is unsatisfactory. However, in Ward 3, merely 5 per cent of the respondents stated that the overall condition of their houses is excellent, while 90 per cent and 5 per cent of them expressed that their overall housing conditions are respectively moderate and unsatisfactory.

To get a better idea about the variations in structural quality as well as amenities available across the wards, average percentage of houses having best facilities is computed (as per the method mentioned in the previous section). Using that, overall ranking of the wards is made in order of percentage of houses having best facilities (Table 5.5). In terms of the structural quality, Ward 17 ranks first and followed by Ward 19; while Ward 22 ranks the last. It is observed that in Ward 17, 100 per cent of surveyed respondents stay in houses with concrete exterior wall and attached toilet, and 61.9 per cent of them live in houses having marble or

Table 5.5: Ward-wise Percentage of Houses having Various Structural Attributes and Civic Amenities

No. of Ward	Structural Attributes								Civic and Other Amenities								House more than Total Average Age of House
	Concrete Wall	Marble/Tile Floor	Concrete Roof	Average No. of Floors	Average Carpet Area	Attached Toilet	Excellent House Condition	Rank	Fenced	Compound	Veranda/ Balcony	Garage	Flower Bed	24 Hrs Water Supply	Covered Sewer	Rank	
1	90	20	65	2.05	681	85	35	**5**	85	50	70	50	60	80	0	**9**	50
2	66.67	28.57	71.43	1.52	619.52	57.14	19.05	**13**	95.24	95.24	76.19	33.33	42.86	61.9	0	**8**	19.05
3	70	5	30	1.15	777.7	45	5	**20**	90	85	70	30	45	60	5	**10**	20
4	77.27	4.55	54.55	1.32	499.18	68.18	9.09	**17**	90.91	81.82	59.09	31.82	45.45	63.64	0	**13**	22.73
5	95	20	45	1.75	765.4	75	35	**11**	95	75	45	45	35	80	0	**12**	40
6	90.91	13.64	63.64	2.14	514.55	77.27	27.27	**8**	31.82	9.09	31.82	4.55	0	77.27	4.55	**23**	72.73
7	73.91	8.7	30.43	1.52	527.83	60.87	34.78	**19**	100	56.52	52.17	30.43	21.74	60.87	0	**17**	21.74
8	71.43	19.05	47.62	1.76	557.86	61.9	42.86	**16**	100	42.86	76.19	28.57	14.29	52.38	9.52	**18**	19.05
9	95	10	70	2.55	869	90	45	**3**	100	85	80	65	70	55	15	**2**	45
10	81.82	13.64	50	1.55	650.46	68.18	36.36	**14**	95.45	86.36	77.27	45.45	45.45	72.73	0	**4**	50
11	86.36	13.64	63.64	1.68	596.55	72.73	36.36	**10**	100	72.73	77.27	45.45	54.55	68.18	9.09	**5**	50
12	86.36	27.27	63.64	1.77	1023.45	86.36	36.36	**4**	90.91	86.36	95.45	68.18	68.18	86.36	22.73	**1**	9.09
13	90.91	13.64	59.09	1.73	795.73	81.82	40.91	**7**	95.45	86.36	54.55	40.91	54.55	81.82	9.09	**6**	40.91
14	86.36	13.64	72.73	2	651.82	81.82	31.82	**6**	95.45	63.64	72.73	54.55	50	72.73	9.09	**7**	31.82
15	80.95	14.29	38.1	1.57	622.1	61.9	33.33	**18**	90.48	42.86	47.62	19.05	4.76	38.1	0	**19**	42.86

(Contd.)

No. of Ward	Structural Attributes								Civic and Other Amenities								House more than Total Average Age of House
	Concrete Wall	Marble/Tile Floor	Concrete Roof	Average No. of Floors	Average Carpet Area	Attached Toilet	Excellent House Condition	Rank	Fenced	Compound	Veranda/ Balcony	Garage	Flower Bed	24Hrs Water Supply	Covered Sewer	Rank	
16	66.67	9.52	19.05	1.33	630.48	47.62	14.29	**22**	95.24	90.48	76.19	28.57	14.29	57.14	0	**14**	47.62
17	100	61.9	90.48	3.19	709.52	100	**47.62**	**1**	42.86	0	66.67	23.81	0	90.48	9.52	**20**	71.43
18	95.24	9.52	71.43	2.14	552.57	66.67	4.76	**9**	38.1	14.29	33.33	9.52	0	71.43	0	**22**	71.43
19	95.45	31.82	81.82	2.77	605.45	95.45	36.36	**2**	22.73	4.55	72.73	0	0	86.36	9.09	**21**	72.73
20	76.19	14.29	47.62	1.67	637.14	66.67	23.81	**15**	100	80.95	90.48	42.86	47.62	80.95	0	**3**	38.10
21	86.36	13.64	59.09	1.95	664.55	63.64	27.27	**12**	100	77.27	59.09	31.82	50	59.09	4.55	**11**	45.45
22	57.14	19.05	23.81	1.29	605.71	38.1	9.52	**23**	90.48	76.19	57.14	33.33	23.81	42.86	0	**16**	28.57
23	47.62	14.29	28.57	1.43	701.91	57.14	9.52	**21**	100	95.24	52.38	28.57	2.81	57.14	0	**15**	23.81
All	**81.43**	**17.14**	**51.63**	**1.82**	**662.07**	**70**	**27.96**		**84.49**	**63.27**	**65.10**	**34.29**	**33.47**	**67.55**	**4.69**		**40.61**

Source: Field Survey conducted during 2015-16.

tile floors. The average number of floors is also observed to be the highest in this ward (3.19).

In terms of other amenities like availability of fence, compound, veranda/balcony, garage, flower-bed, 24 hours water supply and covered sewer, Ward 12 ranks first, which is followed by Ward 9 and then comes Ward 3. On the other hand, Ward 6 lies at the bottom of the list in terms of available amenities. It is further observed that the highest proportion of houses have garage facility (68.18%) in Ward 12. Also, 68.18 per cent of the respondents have flower-bed and about 95.45 per cent have veranda or balcony and 22.73 per cent of those houses have covered sewer in the same ward. In contrast, it is observed that in the Ward 6, only 9.09 per cent of the surveyed respondents have a compound, 4.55 per cent have garage and covered sewer while none of them has flower-bed in this ward.

On the whole, it is observed that the buildings located in the central market areas have relatively better structural qualities. On the other hand, buildings located in the outskirts have relatively better civic and other amenities. It is further observed that most of the surveyed respondents across the wards have fencing (84.49%) and 24 hours water supply to their housing units (67.55%). Though 63.27 per cent of the respondents have a compound (open space) outside their housing units, it is also observed that only 34.29 per cent and 33.47 per cent of them have provision of garage and flower-bed respectively. It is also observed that barely 5 per cent of the surveyed respondents have covered sewer in and around their housing units. Whereas 27.35 per cent of them have partially covered sewer and majority of them (about 68%) have open sewer. It may be noted that covered sewer in the town is very less. Only 4.69 per cent of all surveyed respondents have stated to have fully covered sewer in and around their housing units.

Table 5.5 also reveals that over 50 per cent of the buildings in 7 wards are older than the overall average age of house in the survey area. It can also be observed that these wards are located in the main town areas and the average age of the houses in that area is much higher than the overall average age of houses, (15.91 years) in the town. This is because of the fact that houses in and around the main town areas were built comparatively earlier and as population increased, new houses have been progressively built farther away from the main town. Both Ward 6 and Ward 19 which are centrally located are observed to have 72.73 per cent of houses each built earlier than 16 years. In contrast, the wards farther away from the main town are found to have a lower percentage of houses aged more that the overall average age. It is observed that in Ward 12, only 9.09 per cent of the houses are older than the overall average age of house followed by both Ward 2 and Ward 8 having 19.05 per cent of such houses.

From the percentage of respondents having various structural attributes and amenities a ward level average percentage of respondent housing possessing various structural attributes and amenities are computed. From their ranking of wards are made in respect of possession of overall structural attributes and overall amenities. The Kendall's Rank Correlation between these two rankings is found to be only 0.115, which is not significant. Thus, despite having strong correlation among ward-wise possession of various structural attributes and that among various amenities, no significant correlation has been observed between the desire to have structural attributes and amenities. The indication is that people first prefer for various structural attributes in a house, which is essential for a decent living in case of tenants and longevity for the owners. Only after satisfactory arrangement of structural items, people go for various amenities and the desire for those items increase with the affluence.

Ward-wise Average Rent, Land Price and House Price and their Annual Growth

For the purpose of examining variation across the space, ward-wise average rent, land price and house price and their simple average annual growth rates have been computed. With regard to monthly rent, the responses of tenant respondents are considered, whereas for land and house prices the response of owner respondents are taken into account. In respect of rent and its average annual growth rates, the monthly house rent paid by the surveyed tenant respondents at the time of interview are taken into account. The rent per square feet has been calculated by considering the current monthly rent paid and divided by the respective carpet (floor) area in square feet. But, since the duration of their stay in the present houses is not uniform (that ranges from less than a year to 48 years), a simple average annual growth is calculated by dividing the percentage growth of rent between the first and current monthly rent paid with their respective duration of stay in the present house in years. Likewise, land price and house price along with its average annual growth with regard to owner-occupied respondents has been calculated. The value of land prices per square feet has been computed by considering the price paid during purchase or the equivalent market rate ten years before and the existing market value of similar type and size of land in their respective neighbourhoods. In respect of house price, since several surveyed owner respondents had got their present houses through inheritance, the equivalent market values of the house at two points of time (ten years period wherever possible) has been taken into account. In case of those who constructed or purchased their present houses, the value (cost) at the time of construction or purchase and the present equivalent market price or value has been considered. But, since a uniform period for all surveyed owner-occupied respondents is also not available with respect to land and house prices, their average annual growth have been calculated by computing the respective percentage growth rate between two points of time and then divided by the applicable number of years.

The ward-wise summary of average monthly rent paid in 2015-16 (Table 5.6) reveals that tenants in Ward 17 pays the highest average monthly rent (Rs. 7,638.89) followed by the average rent existing in Ward 19 (Rs. 7,500), whereas it is about Rs. 3,229 in Ward 16. As mentioned earlier, houses of the best structural quality in the town is observed in Ward 17, which is also centrally located. On the other hand, it is observed that in Ward 16, which is situated in the outskirt of the town, several surveyed tenant respondents stay in houses constructed with bamboo/wood and semi-concrete exterior wall (21.50%) and floor is made of earth or simply cement (88.65%). It has also been observed that most of the houses in Ward 16 are single-storied detached buildings as only 19.05 per cent of the houses have concrete roof and the average number of floors is only 1.33.

However, it is observed that average rent per square feet is the highest in Ward 6 (Rs. 13.49) which is closely followed by Ward 18 (Rs. 13.39). These wards are located in the central or its adjacent area. The lowest average rent per square feet in the survey area is observed in Ward 16 (Rs. 6.40), which is located far away as compared to those former wards. Priority of people is to have a residence nearer the central areas, where administrative offices, major colleges and quality schools, main markets are located. With respect to average annual growth of rent, it is observed that Ward 6 experienced the highest growth rate with figure registered at 6.11 per cent and followed by Ward 19 with a growth rate of 5.98 per cent per annum. In contrast, Ward 13 is observed to experience the lowest average annual growth of rent (2.51%). On the whole, it is observed that the rent paid and its annual growth rate is higher in the main town areas as expected.

With regard to average land price, Ward 19 registered the highest land price (Rs. 3,333.33 per sq. ft.) in the survey, which is followed by Ward 17 (Rs. 3,033.33 per sq. ft.). Whereas, Ward 3 registered the lowest price (Rs. 600 per sq. ft.). On the other hand, it is observed that the average annual growth of land prices is the highest in Ward 13 (28.53%). This can be because Ward 13 is close to the main market area and more new commercial complexes have been coming up in the area in recent years. In contrast, it is also observed that Ward 7 recorded 13.92 per cent of average annual growth of land prices, which is the lowest across the wards surveyed. Moreover, it can be observed that growth of overall land prices is comparatively much higher than growth of house rent.

The average house price per square feet also show wide differences across the wards. The highest average house price per square feet is recorded in Ward 17 (about Rs. 6,610), while the lowest is in Ward 22 (about Rs. 1,650). In terms of the annual average growth rate of house prices (per sq. ft.) of all the surveyed owner-occupied respondents, it is recorded that Ward 8 has experienced the highest growth rate of 5.80 per cent, followed by Ward 22 (5.40%), while Ward 7 registered the lowest growth rate of 2.53 per cent. It may be noted that both Ward 8 and Ward 22 are located close to the main market areas while Ward 7, though not too far from the main market, is mostly like a slum area and is partly flood prone during monsoon season. Hence, this area is not the first choice of many people.

A comparison of the average annual growth of prices (per sq.ft.) of the houses built before and after the year 2000 revealed that houses which were built prior to 2000 witnessed a higher growth (5.41%) than those built after 2000 (4.06%). This implies that houses built before 2000 had lower construction costs and the present value of the houses have increased more rapidly since most of these houses are located close to the central places. A comparison of the average annual growth of house prices on the basis of its structural quality also showed that houses built with bamboo or wood wall experienced the highest growth (8.01%), followed by houses built with concrete wall and tin/asbestos roofing (4.08%) and house built with concrete wall and concrete roofing (3.91%). This result is basically due to the relative differences in their construction costs where the houses of lower cost experienced higher percentage growth. The cost per square feet in multi-floor buildings is considerably higher than the cost per square feet to build single-family detached homes (Glaeser, Gyourko and Saks, 2005).

An overview of Table 6.6 also reveals that average annual growth of rent (4.53%) is higher than the average annual growth of house prices (4.06%). It is also observed that average annual growth of land prices is the highest (17.88%) among all the three categories. This implies that there is acute scarcity of land in Dimapur town. Land can be regarded as the most permanent asset and the study revealed that there is great disparity in land prices depending on its location. Since there is no apartment system in Dimapur town where one can buy only the rooms (flats); sale of land and in very limited number houses (where land is with a house) always

Table 5.6: Ward-wise Summary of Rent, Land Price and House Price and their Average Annual Growth

Ward	Average Rent (2015-16)	Rent/sq.ft. (2015-16)	Average Annual Growth of Rent	Average Land Price per sq. ft.	Average Annual Growth of Land Price	Average House Price per sq. ft.	Avg. Annual Growth of House Price (Built before 1999)	Avg. Annual Growth of House Price (Built after 2000)	Avg. Annual growth of House Price (All Period)
1	5470.59	10.22	5.84	2166.67	20.68	4877.97	–	5.18	5.18
2	4844.44	10.77	4.75	840	14.2	3363.96	3.92	3.20	3.44
3	3358.82	6.9	3.51	600	22.22	2053.7	–	3.72	3.72
4	3633.33	8.59	4.22	1175	15	3232.9	5.00	3.20	3.65
5	4781.25	9.51	4.3	1300	16	4694.44	3.75	4.24	4.12
6	5831.58	13.49	6.11	2600	17.67	4943.31	–	4.14	4.14
7	4305.26	10.15	4.28	1125	13.92	3563.94	–	2.53	2.53
8	4627.78	9.9	3.81	1300	15.14	3970.09	–	5.80	5.80
9	5176.47	9.31	5.14	966.67	16.67	4159.11	5.00	5.36	5.24
10	4947.37	8.92	3.12	1033.33	14.72	4289.72	5.62	2.29	3.40
11	4126.32	8.29	3.75	900	14.48	2561.16	7.14	2.81	4.25
12	4833.33	6.01	4.15	737.5	19.58	2933.33	–	2.97	2.97
13	5361.11	8.83	2.51	975	28.53	2605.75	–	3.87	3.87

(Contd.)

Ward	Average Rent (2015-16)	Rent/sq.ft. (2015-16)	Average Annual Growth of Rent	Average Land Price per sq. ft.	Average Annual Growth of Land Price	Average House Price per sq. ft.	Avg. Annual Growth of House Price (Built before 1999)	Avg. Annual Growth of House Price (Built after 2000)	Avg. Annual growth of House Price (All Period)
14	3689.47	6.92	4.02	900	25.15	3905.37	–	3.02	3.02
15	3666.67	7.42	4.14	1566.67	17.18	3515.11	7.78	3.63	5.01
16	3229.41	6.4	5.54	725	17.71	2500	10.00	4.10	5.58
17	7638.89	12.06	5.85	3033.33	20.02	6609.98	3.25	3.33	3.28
18	5344.44	11.56	5.28	2666.67	16.39	3258.21	8.33	3.75	5.28
19	7500	13.39	5.98	3333.33	18.06	3858.76	–	4.17	4.17
20	3961.11	7.55	5.7	1100	19.62	2940.81	4.41	3.03	3.49
21	4552.63	7.66	5.21	1733.33	14.03	4542.01	–	3.37	3.37
22	3561.11	7.32	3.43	933.33	19.17	1649.51	3.41	5.40	4.73
23	4117.65	8.42	3.54	950	15.06	3247.77	2.78	3.30	3.17
Avg.	4719.96	9.11	4.53	1420.04	17.88	3620.74	5.41	3.76	4.06

Source: Field Survey conducted during 2015-16.

go together. Purchase of land is considered a very secured and profitable investment because it is most durable and along with escalating demand its price is rising rapidly. This is experienced more with increasing demand and changing locational pattern where the commercialised area is growing very fast. Hence, land prices are increasing more rapidly than house prices. The relatively higher average annual growth of rent compared to average annual growth of house prices implies that the rental market in Dimapur town is profitable. This may be a reason why a large proportion of the present households in the town live in rented accommodations (about 68%) since they cannot afford to buy a plot of land to construct their own residential houses.

Table 5.7 shows that there are significant variations in the rent, land price and house price across the wards. It is observed that monthly rent varies from Rs. 800 to Rs. 20,000 with a mean of Rs. 4,728.99. Its standard deviation is estimated to be 2,339.29 and the coefficient of variation is 49.47 per cent. Rent per square feet is also found to vary from Rs. 3.33 to Rs. 20.83 (mean value of Rs. 9.13 per sq. ft.) with a standard deviation of 2.90 and coefficient of variation of 31.71 per cent. In respect to land price per square feet, it is found to range from Rs. 400 to Rs. 4,500 with an average price of Rs. 1,381 per sq.ft. Its standard deviation is estimated to be 851.96 and coefficient of variation is 61.69 per cent. It is also observed that the average house prices per square feet of sample owner-occupied respondents vary significantly ranging from merely Rs. 250 to Rs. 8,333.33 per sq. ft. with an average value of 3467. Its standard deviation is calculated to be 1788.09 and its coefficient of variation is 51.58 per cent. Among the three variables, the variation in land prices per square feet is observed to be the greatest.

Table 5.7: Estimated Average, Standard Deviation and Coefficient of Variation of Rent, Land Price and House Price (in Rupees)

	Rent	**Rent (per sq. ft.)**	**Land Price (per sq. ft.)**	**House Price (per sq. ft.)**
Average	4728.99	9.13	1381	3467
Std. Dev.	2339.29	2.90	851.96	1788.09
Coefficient of Variance	49.47	31.71	61.69	51.58

Source: Field Survey conducted during 2015-16.

Factors Affecting Choice of Housing and its Location

Apart from the housing attributes, residential choices of the people are also influenced by other socio-economic conditions such as income, education, community or ethnicity, religion, location etc. Economic condition acts as an enabling factor to go for various attributes (size, construction material, value added fittings and other facilities), locations (prominent or backward area), while socio-cultural conveniences, security question and environmental preferences compel a person to think for location of her/his residence. Generally, people have a preference to live within homogeneous groups for better sense of security, communication and understanding. In order to check the hypothesis that homogeneity of culture and religion significantly affect the demand for housing and its price, a Chi-square test and independent sample T-test have been computed.[1] This has been done to ascertain whether there are significant differences in the monthly rent (implicit rent in case of owner-occupied respondents) when the religion and community of the neighbours are identical with that of the surveyed respondents. The result is presented in Table 6.8.

With respect to religion of the neighbours, Chi-square test for variation shows that there is no significant difference in monthly rent between surveyed respondents who reside within the cluster of similar religion and those who stay with neighbours of other religion [Assymp. Sig. (2-sided) = 0.628)].

With regard to community of the neighbours however, it is observed that surveyed respondents have a strong preference to reside among the people belonging to their own community and they are even willing to pay higher rent (price) for staying in such areas. The Chi-square value is 80.28, which is significant at one per cent level of significance [Assymp. Sig. (2-sided) = .000)].

To test the hypothesis that homogeneity of religion has statistically positive impact on rent, an independent sample t-test has also been performed and the result is displayed in Table 5.8. The respondents who live near people following similar religion (N = 472) is associated with a mean monthly rent of Rs 5,645.34 (SD = 3234.42). By comparison, the respondents who have no neighbour belonging to their religion (N = 18) is associated with a smaller mean monthly rent of Rs. 4,972.23 (SD = 4,188.47). The assumption of homogeneity of variances is tested and satisfied via Levene's F test, F (488) = .002, $p = 0.963$. The independent t-test is associated with a statistically insignificant effect, t (488) = 0.86, $p = 0.392$. Thus, the willingness to pay for rent does not differ significantly due to the fact whether the respondents live near people of their own religion or with neighbours belonging to other religion. Cohen's *d* is estimated at 0.08, which is a small effect based on Cohen's (1992) guidelines.

Table 5.8: Chi-square Test (Pearson) and Independent Sample T-Test Results for Rent According to Religion and Community of Respondent's Neighbours

Chi-square Test (2-Sided)						
Variable	**Value**			**df**	**Assymp. Sig. (2-sided)**	
Religion	31.71			35	.628	
Community	80.28			35	.000	
Independent Sample T-Test (2-Tailed)						
Variable	**N**	**F (Sig.)**	**t**	**df**	**Sig. (2-tailed)**	**M (SD)**
Religion	1=472 0=18	.002 (.963)	.857	488	.392	1=5645.34 (3234.42) 0=4972.23 (4188.47)
Community	1=383 0=107	17.76 (.000)	8.27	267.17	.000	1=6107.31 (3367.02) 0=3878.50 (2144.15)

Source: Field survey conducted during 2015-16.

Note: 1 represents neighbours with similar religion/community and 0 otherwise.

With respect to community, to test the hypothesis of whether variation in homogeneity of neighbouring community is associated with variation in rent, a similar test has been performed. The respondents who live near people of own community (N = 383) is associated with a mean rent of Rs. 6,107.31 (SD = 3367.02), whereas the respondents who has no neighbour belonging to same community (N = 107) is associated with a numerically smaller mean monthly rent of Rs. 3,878.50 (SD = 2144.15). The assumption of homogeneity of variances has been tested and satisfied using Levene's F test, F (488) =17.78, p = .000. The independent sample t-value is 8.27 with p = .000. The indication is in favour of people's preference for similar neighbouring community, which may be due to the conveniences of verbal communication, security and cultural affinity of the people. Respondents in order to live near the people of same community are even willing to pay significantly higher price/rent as the case may be. Cohen's *d* is estimated at 1.01, which is a large effect based on Cohen's (1992) guidelines.

Table 5.9: Ward-wise Percentage Distribution of Sample Respondents According to their Religion and Religion of Neighbours

	Households by Religion				**Neighbours' Religion**				
Ward	**Chri-stian**	**Hindu**	**Mus-lim**	**Jain**	**Sikh**	**Budd-hist**	**Same**	**Mixed**	**None**
1	55	35	0	5	5	0	5	95	0
2	47.62	47.62	4.76	0	0	0	23.81	76.19	0
3	65	20	15	0	0	0	35	65	0
4	68.18	22.73	9.09	0	0	0	31.82	68.18	0
5	70	25	0	0	5	0	20	75	5
6	19.05	33.33	14.29	14.29	9.52	9.52	4.55	81.82	13.63
7	30.43	60.87	8.7	0	0	0	13.04	82.61	4.35
8	47.62	42.86	4.76	0	0	4.76	14.29	80.95	4.76
9	55	40	0	5	0	0	30	65	5
10	77.27	13.64	9.09	0	0	0	45.45	50	4.55
11	90.91	9.09	0	0	0	0	9.09	90.91	0
12	100	0	0	0	0	0	50	50	0
13	81.82	18.18	0	0	0	0	18.18	81.82	0
14	86.36	4.55	9.09	0	0	0	22.73	72.73	4.55
15	19.05	66.67	14.29	0	0	0	14.29	85.71	0
16	66.67	28.57	4.76	0	0	0	14.29	80.95	4.76
17	0	33.33	4.76	61.9	0	0	14.29	80.95	4.76
18	33.33	42.86	4.76	19.05	0	0	4.76	80.95	14.29
19	22.73	40.91	27.27	4.55	4.55	0	9.09	81.82	9.09
20	80.95	14.29	4.76	0	0	0	14.29	85.71	0
21	63.64	22.73	4.55	9.09	0	0	27.27	72.73	0
22	57.14	23.81	19.05	0	0	0	14.29	76.19	9.52
23	47.62	47.62	4.76	0	0	0	14.29	85.71	0
Total	**55.92**	**30.00**	**7.35**	**5.10**	**1.02**	**0.61**	**19.59**	**76.73**	**3.67**

Note: Neighbours' religion has been classified into 'Same', 'Mixed' and 'None' which represents that all neighbours belong to the same religion as the respondent's religion, mixture with other religion(s) and no neighbour belong to the respondent's religion respectively.

Source: Field Survey Conducted during 2015-16.

Ward-wise percentage distribution of the whole sample respondents according to their religion and religion of neighbours has been presented in Table 5.9. As noted earlier, Christianity and Hinduism are the two major

Table 5.10: Descriptive Summary of Mean Socio-economic Variables and Other Housing Attributes According to Religion

Religion	Family Income (Rs.)	Monthly Rent (Rs.)	No. of Rooms	Family Size	Carpet Area (sq.ft.)	Water Connection	Overall House Condition	Distance from Workplace (metre)
Christian	41788.32	6368.25	3.50	4.45	816.96	1.76	1.16	1051.46
Hindu	21802.72	4152.38	2.14	4.03	426.85	1.16	1.16	662.43
Muslim	14166.67	3152.78	1.75	4.14	331.61	0.75	1.00	457.08
Jain	41000.00	9000.00	3.28	4.88	833.60	2.00	1.36	483.00
Sikh	47000.00	8600.00	3.20	4.20	760.00	2.00	1.20	684.00
Buddhist	25000.00	5666.66	2.33	4.33	413.33	2.00	1.67	240.00

Source: Field Survey Conducted During 2015-16.

religions observed in the survey accounting for about 86 per cent of the surveyed respondents. Christians are found in majority in fifteen wards and Hindus are in majority in four wards. However, it is observed that across the wards, majority of the surveyed respondents, particularly the tenants live alongside people belonging to different religions. It shows that majority of them (76.73%) stay with mixed religious neighbours. However, about 20 per cent of them stay with neighbours of same religion and the percentage varies significantly across the wards. It implies that though a large number of people are contented to live in areas where people of the other religion are also present as neighbours, about one-fifth of the sample respondents prefer to be nearer people belonging to their own religion. However, overall significance of preference for staying with same religious people is very poor as is evidenced by the Chi-square and T-test above. Hence a cosmopolitan characteristic of the township is exhibited here.

A household choose a house depending on the availability of various structural attributes, location, neighbourhood and going market rent across the space coupled with their capability, preference and necessity. A descriptive statistic has been presented in Table 5.10 just to get some insight into certain important socio-economic and structural characteristics of the surveyed respondents according to their religion.

Rent paid by the surveyed respondents is positively related to their income and structural quality of the housing units measured by number of rooms, carpet area and overall condition of house (as shown latter). Religious categorisation shows that, on an average Muslims have the lowest average family income (monthly) and also, they pay the lowest average monthly rent. It is apparent that they live in small and congested houses of moderate quality houses even though they live relatively closer to their workplaces. It is also observed that though Sikhs earn the highest average monthly income, the highest monthly rent is paid by the Jains who are found to stay in relatively larger and better houses.

In order to know how significantly religion of respondent and homogeneity of religion of neighbours affect housing price (rent), following regression models have been estimated.

$$logP_i = \alpha_1 + \sum_{i=1}^{n} \beta_{1i} X_i + \sum_{i=1}^{n} \gamma_{1i} R_i + U_i \quad ....(5.1)$$

$$logP_i = \alpha_1 + \sum_{i=1}^{n} \beta_{1i} X_i + U_i \quad ....(5.2)$$

$$logP_i = \alpha_1 + \sum_{i=1}^{n} \gamma_{1i} R_i + U_i \quad ....(5.3)$$

where P_i represents the monthly rent paid by the ith respondent, X_i represents variables like family income, family size, duration of stay etc. and R_i represents categorical or dummy variables in respect to different religion (with Muslims taken as control group), α_1 represents the intercept, U_i the random disturbance term. Here β_i represents the elasticity of rent (P_i) with respect to X_i and γ_i represents the impact of a marginal change in the ith R variables (religion) on rate of changes in rent (P_i). For each religion a dummy variable is introduced that takes value one for the particular religion possessed by the respondent and zero otherwise. Similarly, for the variable representing the homogeneity of neighbour, if at least one of the neighbours is of the same religion as that of the respondent then it is one and zero otherwise.

From the results of multiple regression analysis for socio-economic variables including religion, it is found that all of the selected variables, except religion of the neighbours, have statistically significant positive impacts on the monthly rent paid (Table 5.1i). The regression model 5.1 represents the impacts of the socio-economic variables including religion on the monthly rent. It is observed that family income, family size, duration of stay has significantly positive impacts on the rent. Families with higher income and size pay higher monthly rent as expected. Families with more members require more rooms or larger space and thus they are expected to pay higher rent. It is also apparent that as people decide to settle down in the town for longer period they move into better houses and/or more conveniently located areas and pay higher rent as indicated by the significant positive coefficient of duration of stay.

With respect to religion, it is observed that all other religious groups pay significantly higher rent as compared to the Muslims. The coefficient of Neighbours' religion is, however, not significant implying that homogeneity of religion of the neighbours does not have much influence on the preference of respondents and thus the rent paid.

The regression model 5.2 represents the impacts of the only socio-economic. It is again found that all the selected variables have significant positive impacts on rent paid. However, the overall religion as compared to Muslim, including that of homogeneity of religious cluster is found to have significant impact. It is examined by applying Truncated Regression Technique and using the following test statistics (Green, 2000):

$$F_{k_{1,n-(k_1+k_2)}} = \frac{\dfrac{\Sigma_1^n e_{2i}^2 - \Sigma_1^2 e_{1i}^2}{k_1}}{\dfrac{\Sigma_1^2 e_{1i}^2}{n-(k_1+k_2)}} \quad \text{……… (5.4)}$$

Here Σ_{1i}^2 and Σ_{2i}^2 represent residual sum of squares of regression of model 5.1 (p_i is regressed on the variables income, family size, duration of stay along with the religions and religion of neighbour) and regression of model 5.2 (p_i is regressed only on income, family size and duration of stay). If F is significant, then the overall impact of religion on rent is significant. Here, the estimated value of $F_{4,480}$ is 5.85 when the model is truncated with the religion of respondents as Christian, Hindu, Buddhist, Jain and Sikh with Muslim as the control factor and homogeneity of neighbour's religion is considered. The test statistics is highly significant at one per cent level of significance. However, if only homogeneity of neighbour's religion is included and excluded keeping all other variables intact the value of $F_{9,480}$ is found to be 0.231, which is insignificant at 5 per cent level implying that homogeneity of religion in the neighbourhood does not impact the choice and rent paid by the individual.

The regression model 5.3 represents the impacts of religion of the respondents and homogeneity of neighbour's religion with Muslim as the control group. It is observed that all the other religious groups pay significantly higher rent compared to Muslims. However, the willingness to pay rent does not differ significantly due to the fact whether the respondents live near people of their own religion or with neighbours belonging to other religion.

Table 5.11: Estimated Regression Coefficients of Respondents by Religion, Neighbours' Religion and Selected Socio-Economic Characteristics

	Model 1	**Model 2**	**Model 3**
	Coefficient	Coefficient	7.847 (75.28)***
(Constant)	2.284 (8.88)***	1.900 (8.42)***	
LnFamily Income	.536 (20.06)***	.576 (24.92)***	
LnFamily Size	.165 (4.49)***	.154 (4.15)***	
LnDuration of Stay	.165 (7.85)***	.178 (8.59)***	
Christian	.211 (2.75)***		.761 (7.13)***
Hindu	.145 (1.95)*		.310 (2.83)***
Buddhist	.406 (1.88)*		.780 (2.27)**
Jain	.443 (4.29)***		1.207 (7.98)***
Sikh	.378 (2.16)**		1.193 (4.36)***
Neighbours' Religion	-.150 (-1.53)		.005 (.084)
R^2, Adj. R^2 & F-stat. (Sig.)	0.70, 0.69 & 121.96 (.000)	0.68, 0.68 & 345.82 (.000)	0.22, 0.21 & 22.15 (.000)

Note: (1) *, ** & *** indicate significance at 10 per cent, 5 per cent and 1 per cent level respectively.
(2) Values in the parentheses represent t-values.
(3) Muslim is taken as the Control Group.
Dependent Variable: LnMonthly Rent.

Source: Field Survey Conducted during 2015-16.

Table 5.12: Ward-wise Percentage Distribution of Sample Respondents According to their Group of Community and Neighbours' Community

Ward	Naga	Respondents' Community		Community of Neighbours		
		Bengali/ Assamese/ Nepali/NE Tribes	Marwari/ Bihari/ Others	All Same	Mixed	None
1	50	20	30	10	90	0
2	42.86	19.05	38.1	9.52	90.48	0
3	65	40	15	20	80	0
4	68.18	9.09	22.73	4.55	90.91	4.55
5	65	15	20	0	100	0
6	18.18	9.09	72.73	22.73	77.27	0
7	21.74	47.83	30.43	8.7	91.3	0
8	38.1	38.1	23.81	0	100	0
9	40	35	25	10	85	5
10	72.73	4.55	22.73	27.27	72.73	0
11	90.91	0	9.09	4.55	95.45	0
12	95.45	4.55	0	22.73	77.27	0
13	72.73	9.09	18.18	4.55	90.91	4.55
14	81.82	18.18	0	22.73	77.23	0
15	19.05	61.9	19.05	0	95.24	4.76
16	57.14	33.33	9.52	19.05	80.95	0
17	0	14.29	85.71	66.67	33.33	0
18	33.33	23.81	42.86	28.57	71.43	0
19	22.73	13.64	63.64	9.09	90.91	0
20	76.19	9.52	14.29	4.76	95.24	0
21	50	27.27	22.73	4.55	95.45	0
22	57.14	38.1	4.76	0	100	0
23	47.62	38.1	14.29	4.76	95.24	0
Total	**51.63**	**22.04**	**26.33**	**13.27**	**85.92**	**0.82**

Note: Neighbours' community has been classified into 'Same', 'Mixed' & 'None' which represents that all neighbours belong to the same community as the respondent's community, mixture with other community(s) and no neighbours belong to totally other than that of respondent's community respectively.

Source: Field Survey Conducted During 2015-16.

Community-wise distribution of surveyed respondents and that of their neighbours across the Wards is presented in Table 5.12. For the convenience of analysis, the community of the respondents have been classified into three categories. Naga is taken as one group because of its larger proportion in the survey area. Bengali, Assamese, Nepalese and North East Tribes are considered under a category on account of their closer cultural affinity as evidenced in better adjustability and understanding among them. If they do not find accommodation with their exactly own community, their next preference is the other communities in this group. All other respondents belonging to other states and region have been combined together in the third category. Among the three categories, it is observed that Naga accounts for more than 50 per cent in the survey area and they are in clear majority in sixteen wards. But in respect to community of the neighbours, it is observed that the study area exhibits a highly cosmopolitan nature as indicated by the high proportion of surveyed respondents living among mixed communities. However, it may be pointed out that in Ward 17, majority of the surveyed respondents live among members of the same category of community. Also, in some wards there are prevalence of people preferring to stay with neighbours of homogeneous community and those are Wards 18, 10, 12, 14, 6, 3 and 16 where about 20 per cent of families stay with similar neighbours. Overall, it is observed that 85.92 per cent of the total respondents live in areas where, along with members of their own category of community, they live near people belonging to different communities. Merely 0.82 per cent of the respondents are found to live in areas where there is no neighbour of her/ his community.

The descriptive statistic of the surveyed respondents in terms of socio-economic groups as presented in Table 5.13 reveals that Naga community on a average earn the highest average monthly income and pay the highest average monthly rent despite the fact that on average their distance from workplace is also the highest. Distance from workplace may not be problem here because apart from being a small town, among the three categories, a relatively larger proportion of Nagas are found to possess one or multiple personal vehicles (65.61%). It is apparent that Nagas have larger family size and so they require bigger houses with more rooms with relatively better water connection facilities. In contrast, the category of Bengali/Assamese/Nepalese/other NE tribes is observed to have the lowest average family income and paying the lowest monthly rent among these three groups. Though they have a larger average family size than Marwari/Bihari/Others category, because of their lower income they are found to live in smaller and poorer quality houses measured in terms of size and overall conditions. It is also observed that majority of the respondents belonging to Marwari/Bihari/Others category who are primarily businessmen live in the central areas and their overall house condition is relatively better and distance from workplace is found to be the least.

Table 5.13: Descriptive Summary of Mean Socio-Economic Variables and Other Housing Attributes According to Community

Community	Family Income (Rs.)	Monthly Rent (Rs.)	No. of Rooms	Family Size	Carpet Area (sq. ft.)	Water Connection	Overall House Condition	Distance from Workplace (metre)
Naga	43181.82	6572.33	3.59	4.49	846.20	1.79	1.16	1068.97
Bengali/ Assamese/ Nepali/ Other NE Tribes	22264.15	3850.94	2.21	4.25	445.88	1.09	1.13	772.50
Marwari/ Bihari/ Others	24541.98	5212.21	2.29	4.05	481.39	1.36	1.20	502.38

Source: Field Survey Conducted During 2015-16.

In order to know how significantly community and other socio-economic factors affect housing price (rent), a similar linear regression of the type as used in case of religion is performed. For each community group a dummy variable is introduced that takes value one for the particular community group in which the respondent belongs and zero otherwise. Similarly, if any neighbour is of the same community/group as that of the respondent then it is one and zero otherwise. From the results of multiple regression analysis for socio-economic variables including community, it is found that all of the selected variables have statistically significant positive impacts on the monthly rent paid (Table 5.14). The regression model 5.1 represents the impacts of the socio-economic variables including community with Bengali, Assamese, Nepali, and Other NE-Tribe group as the control group and the homogeneity of the neighbouring community on the monthly rent. It is observed that for a unit increase in income, family size and duration of stay, there is a corresponding significant increase in the rent paid. It may be noted that here coefficient of family income is the highest that implies income is the most important contributory factor in variation of housing price among the variables considered.

With regard to community, as mentioned above, the category consisting of Bengali, Assamese, Nepali and other NE Tribes has been taken as the control group. It is found that both the other two categories of community, viz. Naga and Marwari, Bihari and others, pay significantly higher rent than the control group. Moreover, it is observed that respondents pay more to live with people belonging to their own category of community as indicated by the significant positive coefficient of neighbours' community.

The regression model 5.2 represents the impact of only the socio-economic variables on rent paid. It is observed again that all selected variables have significantly positive impacts on monthly rent. Here the estimated value of $F_{4,483}$ is 6.69 when the model is truncated with the community of Naga and Marwari, Bihari and others with Bengali, Assamese, Nepali and other NE-Tribes as the control factor and homogeneity of neighbour's community is considered. The test statistics is highly significant at one per cent level of significance. However, if only homogeneity of neighbour's community is included and excluded keeping all other variables intact the value of $F_{6, 483}$ is found to be 1.12, which is significant at 5 per cent level implying that homogeneity of community in the neighbourhood significantly affect the choice and rent paid by the individual.

Table 5.14: Estimated Regression Coefficients of Respondents by Community, Neighbours' Community and Selected Socio-Economic Characteristics

	Model 1	**Model 2**	**Model 3**
Variable	**Coefficient**	**Coefficient**	
Constant	1.950 (8.08)***	1.900 (8.42)***	7.756 (79.13)***
LnFamily Income	.544 (20.83)***	.576 (24.92)***	
LnFamily Size	.164 (4.52)***	.154 (4.15)***	
LnDuration of Stay (Year)	.179 (8.65)***	.178 (8.59)***	
Naga	.162 (3.54)***		0.527 (7.68)***
Marwari/Bihari/ Others	.184 (3.90)***		0.205 (2.63)***
Neighbours' Community	.115 (2.47)**		0.326 (4.25)***
R^2, Adj.R^2 & F-stat (Sig.)	0.70, 0.69 & 185.82 (.000)	0.68, 0.68 & 345.82 (.000)	0.15, 0.15 & 29.59 (.000)

Note: (1) ** and *** indicate significance at 5 per cent and 1 per cent level respectively.
(2) Values in the parentheses represent t-values.
(3) Bengali/Assamese/Nepali/ NE Tribes is taken as the Control Group.

Dependent Variable: Monthly Rent.

Source: Field Survey Conducted During 2015-16.

The regression model 5.3 represents the impact of the respondent's community along with the homogeneity of the neighbour's community on rent paid (with same control group). It is observed that Naga and Marwari, Bihari and others pay significantly higher rent as compared to the control group. Respondents in order to live near the people of same community are even willing to pay significantly higher price/rent.

In order to check whether the impacts of various locational and neighbourhood attributes on monthly rent vary across heterogeneous socio-economic categories, separate regressions have been run for different groups of such categories. For the purpose, we considered community, education and status of occupation of the head of household and monthly family income. Community is broadly classified as Naga and Non-Naga, while education and family income are classified or grouped on the basis of less than or greater than their respective averages. For occupation, we considered private service, business/self-employed and government service since they are well represented in the survey. The results are shown in Tables 5.15 and 5.16.

Quality of approach road is found to significantly influence rent positively for all socio-economic categories except for the higher educated, higher income and those in Government service (Table 5.15). This is because they reside in better residential areas, which already have better roads and the question does not arise. Distance from workplace also has significantly positive influence on rent for all categories except the higher income group. However, the coefficient in this study is found to be positive in contrast to most other studies. This may be because Dimapur is a small town and hence, average distance to workplace is found to be 0.853 km with an average travel time of about 11 minutes only, and the preference to be nearer to other destinations dominates over the workplace. This is also reflected in positive impact of overall locational convenience index.

A weighted *locational convenience index* (LCI) was constructed on the basis of seven locational convenience options for choosing the place of residence (explained later in pages 161-162). It is observed that except for Naga, higher income group and business community, LCI has significant positive impact on rent. Except for higher income group, private service and government service holders, distance from railway station has an inverse relationship with rent. Moreover, distances from market and crematorium and flood prone area during monsoon are also found to have significantly negative impact on rent for most socio-economic categories.

On the whole, type of access road surface, locational convenience and distances from workplace and market have significant positive impact, while distance from railway station and flood during monsoon have a

Table 5.15: Results of Regression of Monthly Rent of Various Locational Attributes by Socio-economic Categories

Category	Naga		Non-Naga		Edu < Av		Edu > Av		Income < Av	
Variable	**Coef.**	**Sig.**	**Coef.**	**Sig.**	**Coef.**	**Sig.**	**Coef.**	**Sig.**	**Coef.**	**Sig.**
1	**2**	**3**	**4**	**5**	**6**	**7**	**8**	**9**	**10**	**11**
Constant	4460.9	.000	7.12	.994	2455.5	.001	3623.1	.001	2127.5	.000
Flood	-954.1	.161	-1447.9	.006	-942.7	.024	-630.0	.388	-361.15	.236
Approach Road–Type	1034.6	.005	578.73	.019	844.36	.000	479.08	.154	681.58	.000
Distance to Workplace	.678	.004	1.134	.000	1.108	.000	.571	.004	.538	.002
Distance to Market	1.003	.029	-.827	.045	-.290	.455	.126	.761	-.508	.071
Distance to Rail Station	-1.043	.013	-.787	.088	-.782	.081	-.720	.070	-.514	.112
View	124.15	.837	977.10	.076	280.25	.578	839.81	.131	115.92	.743
Locational Convenience	305.67	.460	2514.52	.000	651.66	.059	1527.8	.000	766.52	.001
Dist. to Crematorium/ Cemetery	-.422	.352	1.68	.001	.257	.605	.388	.358	.423	.197
R^2 & F-stat (Sig.)	0.14 & 4.57 (.000)		0.37 & 18.30 (.000)		0.32 & 9.12 (.000)		0.10 & 4.20 (.000)		0.26 & 10.60 (.000)	
No. of respondents	228		262		165		325		251	

(Contd.)

Category	Income > Av		Pvt Service		Business		Govt Service		All Respondents	
Variable	**Coef.**	**Sig.**	**Coef.**	**Sig.**	**Coef.**	**Sig.**	**Coef.**	**Sig.**	**Coef.**	**Sig**
1	**12**	**13**	**14**	**15**	**16**	**17**	**18**	**19**	**20**	**21**
Constant	7884.8	.000	1624.6	.035	2534.9	.037	4917.4	.010	-576.06	.445
Flood	-462.36	.667	-609.86	.235	-1239.2	.057	-1587.7	.156	-871.21	.038
Approach Road–Type	-116.12	.770	693.55	.004	1093.2	.001	-320.65	.534	991.01	.000
Distance to Workplace	.299	.185	.524	.011	.845	.012	1.14	.000	.929	.000
Distance to Market	.244	.604	.157	.723	-.602	.230	.098	.878	.052	.860
Distance to Rail Station	-.710	.094	-.565	.205	-.800	.144	-.311	.544	-.714	.018
View	585.28	.358	184.28	.719	1260.4	.045	760.76	.362	635.12	.108
Locational Convenience	633.68	.172	979.74	.004	634.47	.148	1554.8	.015	5815.3	.000
Dist. to Crematorium/ Cemetery	-.011	.982	.210	.617	.700	.232	.155	.813	.421	.191
R^2 & F-stat (Sig.)	0.05 & 1.40 (.197)		0.26 & 4.83 (.000)		0.20 & 6.75 (.000)		0.19 & 3.37 (.002)		0.27 & 22.28 (.000)	
No. of respondents	239		121		230		125		490	

Source: Field survey conducted during 2015-16.

Table 5.16: Results of Regression of Monthly Rent of Various Neighbourhood Attributes by Socio-economic Categories

Category	Naga		Non Naga		Edu < Av		Edu > Av		Income < Av	
Variable	**Coef.**	**Sig.**	**Coef.**	**Sig.**	**Coef.**	**Sig.**	**Coef.**	**Sig.**	**Coef.**	**Sig.**
1	**2**	**3**	**4**	**5**	**6**	**7**	**8**	**9**	**10**	**11**
Constant	2967.6	.161	-1738.2	.192	818.05	.573	499.34	.823	2925.6	.007
Distance to Govt. Office	.488	.443	.885	.016	1.085	.008	1.234	.006	.592	.053
Distance to Departmental Shop	-.003	.994	.156	.402	-.630	.062	.177	.432	-.944	.000
Crime Rate	116.86	.820	-122.03	.720	-100.21	.763	-753.9	.036	-40.12	.867
Neighbours' Community	-444.05	.756	-233.63	.823	48.598	.691	456.15	.805	-197.9	.812
Education of Neighbours	544.34	.138	1423.1	.000	1141.25	.000	568.79	.068	557.4	.002
Occupation of Neighbours	269.17	.456	1214.2	.000	171.06	.528	935.63	.004	98.06	.626
Pollution	-140.79	.884	987.81	.145	558.36	.450	421.76	.579	608.7	.272
Distance to Worship Place	1.899	.003	1.485	.000	-1.049	.001	-.131	.774	-.652	.005
R^2 & F-stat (Sig.)	0.07 & 1.92 (.059)		0.45 & 26.28 (.000)		0.36 & 10.90 (.000)		0.10 & 4.29 (.000)		0.26 & 10.72 (.000)	

(Contd.)

Category	Income > Av		Pvt Service		Business		Govt Service		All Respondent	
Variable	**Coef.**	**Sig.**	**Coef.**	**Sig.**	**Coef.**	**Sig.**	**Coef.**	**Sig.**	**Coef.**	**Sig.**
1	**12**	**13**	**14**	**15**	**16**	**17**	**18**	**19**	**20**	**21**
Constant	3044.2	.373	2427.1	.246	1059.5	.560	2914.6	.238	-1741.6	.236
Distance to Govt. Office	1.78	.000	-.480	.315	.946	.032	1.93	.062	1.20	.000
Distance to Departmental Shop	.329	.147	-.496	.175	.241	.264	-.076	.903	.048	.801
Crime Rate	-577.03	.285	-563.91	.117	-517.40	.222	-460.28	.589	-390.6	.197
Neighbours' Community	453.86	.883	-462.40	.786	325.52	.825	-1318.4	.334	154.6	.897
Education of Neighbours	379.96	.278	1058.26	.000	1494.9	.000	755.12	.166	1385.5	.000
Occupation of Neighbours	458.50	.214	-94.94	.745	161.47	.646	560.82	.332	942.7	.002
Pollution	72.02	.932	964.59	.192	786.68	.347	-1235.8	.355	634.4	.268
Distance to Worship Place	.095	.853	-.615	.070	-1.48	.000	.721	.377	-.750	.009
R^2 & F-stat (Sig.)	0.09 & 2.66 (.008)		0.33 &6.91 (.000)		0.27&10.37) (.000)		0.10 & 1.61 (.130)		0.24 & 18.89 (.000)	

Source: Field survey conducted during 2015-16..

significant negative bearing on rent for all the social and economic groups in the study. Generally, distance from workplace and market is found to have significant negative impact on housing price (or rent), but in the present study distance both are observed to have significant positive impact on rent. From the sample, it is observed that a large number of individuals came in recent years and it is difficult for them to get accommodation in the vicinity of their workplace or central areas. Travel time, which is used as a measure of accessibility to important places, is recorded as quite insignificant and the average time to commute by the respondents on foot is about ten minutes (with average distance of 300 metres) only and by car average travel time is observed to be about 15 minutes (with average distance of 1500 metres). Besides, it is also observed that 58.98 per cent of the respondents possess a personal vehicle which eases their accessibility. More importantly, the *location convenience index* for choosing the current place of residence is found to have significantly positive impact on rent. This indicates that for most of them, the importance of proximity to workplace and market is overshadowed by other factors.

In case of neighbourhood attributes (Table 5.16), educational level of immediate neighbours showed significant positive impact on rent for all categories except Nagas, those with higher income and business groups. Distance from worship place is found to have significant negative influence on rent except higher income; higher educated and Government service residents, but it positively affects rent for Naga communities. Except for those in private service distance from Government office complex has significant positive impact on rent. However, distance from departmental shop has a significant inverse link with rent for Non-Nagas, less educated people and lower income families. High crime rate is found to significantly reduce rent for the higher educated category, which is on expected line. Occupation profile of the immediate neighbours has significant positive impact for the less educated ones and Non-Naga communities.

Available literature suggests that pollution negatively impact house prices (or rent) but the present study found that it is not a significant factor. This is probably because of either ignorance on the part of the residents or other advantages like proximity to market and workplace overshadow such negative externalities.

Impact of Various Housing Attributes on Housing Price (Rent)

The analysis is made on the basis of the primary data collected during July 2015 to May 2016. From the data collected, we first selected some important structural, locational and neighbourhood attributes based on earlier empirical studies. Then by using SPSS we checked the data for the problem of multi-collinearity and we had to drop some variables with high Variance Inflation Factor (VIF) value even though they were considered important in other studies (Maddala, 2001). Next, in order to reduce the problem of heteroskedasticity a double-log form of the hedonic price function is chosen for the estimation by transforming the quantitative data into their natural log form (Wooldridge, 2013). Thus, the hedonic price equation with *n* housing attributes is given by

$$\log P_i = \alpha_1 + \sum_{i=1}^{n} \beta_i \log z_i + \sum_{i=1}^{n} \gamma_i X_i + U_i \;\ldots\ldots\ldots \quad (5.5)$$

where P_i represents the monthly rent paid by the ith respondent, z_i represents quantitative explanatory variables like age of house, carpet area, distances to places of importance etc. and X_i represents categorical variables like floor material, quality of approach road, security standard etc., α_1 represents the intercept and U_i the random disturbance term with usual classical regression properties. Here β_i represents the elasticity of P_i with respect to ith explanatory variable Z, while γ_i the impact of a marginal change in the ith categorical variable on the rate of changes in P_i.

The regression results in Table 5.17 represent the impacts of structural attributes on the rent. In case of the tenants, number of floors or stories, floor material, water connection, house condition, age of house and carpet area of the house is found to have significantly positive impacts on monthly rent. The R^2 of 0.85 reveals that 85 per cent of the total variation in the dependent variable is explained by the regression equation. Even after adjusting for the degrees of freedom, 84 per cent is explained by the equation. The p-value of 0.081 of the observed R-squared value in White heteroskedasticity test does not reject the hypothesis of no heteroskedasticity at 5 per cent level of significance. The positive coefficients of the structural attributes in the regression result is on expected lines because multi-storied buildings with better construction materials and bigger size of house commands higher rent. Though there is no floor premium observed in the survey, taller buildings are often found to be of better structural quality and hence, command higher monthly rent. Floor types consist of earth, wood, concrete and marble/tile which are ranked in ordinal form and better quality of floor is found to be positively related to rent as expected.

Water is one of the essential items of survival and people face significant problem in collecting water from various sources in most small and hilly towns and sometimes have to even buy from vendors. Hence, a house having good water connection inside the housing unit with adequate water supply is expected to charge more rent. The overall condition of the housing units was classified according to the respondent's opinion as unsatisfactory, medium or excellent and the positive coefficient is on expected line.

In the present study, age of house is found to have a significant positive impact on the monthly rent. This implies that people who desires to stay at the heart of the town are mostly compelled to choose the older houses as those were built early adjacent to the central places. Even if some modern facilities are missing those houses generate more rent due to majority of other facilities required in daily life.

Generally, houses which have larger floor area or size carry higher rent and the result of the regression also found a positive relationship between the two. However, availability of veranda or balcony is observed to have negative significant impact on rent. This may be due to the fact that though people may like to have veranda or balcony, many buildings in the main town area do not have such amenities due to scarcity of space. There is some sort of compromise for other advantages like proximity to market, better accessibility etc. and several higher income businessmen are observed to be willing to pay higher monthly rents even without such amenities if the other structural attributes meet their requirements satisfactorily.

With respect to owner-occupied households, the implicit monthly rent (market equivalent monthly rent) is used to measure the house price. It is observed that number of floors, floor quality, water connection, age of house, carpet area of the house and exterior wall material has significant positive impacts on house prices. The model R^2 is 0.71, adjusted R^2 is 0.67 and F-Statistics 20.41 with p-value of 0.000. The White heteroskedasticity test gives a p-value of 0.845of the observed R-squared value and supports the hypothesis of no heteroskedasticity (Table 5.17). Greater number of floors with better construction materials (floor type and exterior wall material) and larger size of house involves higher costs and so the positive coefficients are as expected. Availability of adequate water at greater ease also positively affect house price.

Several empirical studies have established negative impact of age of house on house price except due to vintage effects (Li and Brown, 1980; Rodriguez and Sirmans, 1994). But in the present study, age of house is observed to have significantly positive impact on the housing price like that of rent equation. This implies that house prices have a location premium since the older houses are mostly located near the central commercial areas. The negative coefficient of house condition (though not significant) also substantiates this implication as these older houses in the central places command higher (rental) value.

Table 5.17: Estimated Coefficients of Regression of LnRent on Structural Attributes According to Status of Ownership

Variable	Tenants			Owners		
	Coeff.	t-Stat	Prob.	Coeff.	t-Stat	Prob.
(Constant)	2.965	19.27	0.000	4.078	8.168	0.000
House Condition	0.051	1.99	0.048	-0.039	-1.143	0.257
Floor Type	0.131	5.41	0.000	0.184	3.507	0.001
Veranda/ Balcony	-0.06	-2.31	0.021	0.016	0.133	0.895
Water Connection	0.126	5.48	0.000	0.245	2.588	0.012
LnNo. of Floors	0.071	4.73	0.000	0.065	1.798	0.077
LnAge of House	0.123	5.58	0.000	0.08	2.044	0.045
LnCarpet Area	0.719	27.61	0.000	0.486	7.237	0.000
Exterior Wall Material	0.007	0.3	0.765	0.221	2.350	0.022
Dependent Variable: LnMonthly Rent						
	R^2 = 0.85, Adj. R^2 = 0.84, F-Stat. = 280.34 (0.000)			R^2 = 0.71, Adj. R^2 = 0.67, F-Stat. = 20.41 (0.000)		
White Heteroskedasticity Test:						
	F-stat. = 1.572 (0.078) & Obs* R-squared = 23.159 (0.081)			F-stat. = 0.57 (0.878) & Obs* R-squared = 8.785 (0.845)		

Dependent Variable: Squared Residual.
Source: Field Survey conducted during 2015-16.

The impact of the locational attributes on the monthly rent is given in Table 5.18. Here two indexes are calculated for better analysis of various qualitative data. First, a weighted view quality index was calculated by combining the view availability from house of green cover, forest cover and good architectural building. Next, a weighted locational convenience index was also constructed on the basis of seven locational convenience options for choosing the place of residence. The index has been constructed by assigning weights to opinion expressed by each respondent on each option for choosing the present location of residence such as for more space, nearer to workplace, children school, location inconvenience of the earlier house, better neighbourhood quality, natural environment and security. These weights have been computed by calculating the ratio of the sum of each option (for all the respondents) to the sum total score of the seven options. Presence or absence of each option is accrued value 1 or 0. Then value of each option corresponding to every respondent is multiplied by the weight of that particular opinion and then added up to get overall index for the corresponding respondent. Symbolically, locational convenience index (LCI) = $\sum W_iX_i$, where W_i is the weight of the ith value of individual locational variable. In the same way view index is constructed.

With regard to the tenant respondents, the quality of approach road connected to house, distance from workplace and location convenience are found to have significant positive impact on the monthly rent paid by the tenants, whereas distance from market as well as train station have significant negative impact on the rent. The White heteroskedasticity test gives a p-value of 0.06 of the observed R-squared value. Availability of approach road to house across the wards ranges from about 86 per cent to 100 per cent with 13 wards comprising 100 per cent respondents having approach road connected to their housing units. The respondents whose house is connected with approach road is distinguished on the basis of the surface quality such as earth, stone and earth, and concrete or black-topped. The quality of approach roads improves accessibility and comfort of travel. Hence, the positive impact of quality of approach road on the monthly rent paid is on expected line.

Generally, distance from workplace is expected to have significant negative impact on housing price (or rent) but in the present study distance from workplace is observed to have significant positive impact on rent. From the sample, it is observed that a large number of individuals came in recent years and it is difficult for them to get accommodation in the vicinity of their workplace. Moreover, Dimapur being a small town, distance from workplace is not much as indicated by the average distance of 0.85 km and distance to workplace is found to range between 0 to 6 km. Travel time, which is used as a measure of accessibility to job places, is also found to be quite insignificant and the average time to commute by the tenant respondents on foot is about eight and half minutes (with average distance of 292 metres) only and by car average travel time is observed to be 13 minutes (with average distance of 1335 metres). Those who shuttle on foot everyday actually travel lesser distance or take short cut road, while the distance for the car users is comparatively more. Besides, it is also observed in the sample that 53.38 per cent of the tenants possess a personal vehicle, which eases their accessibility. More importantly, the *locational convenience index* for choosing the current place of residence is found to have significantly positive impact on rent. This indicates that for most tenants, the importance of proximity to workplace is overshadowed by other factors. People, especially the servicemen and business community, like to stay near town and railway station and intend to pay more rent in order to avoid difficulty in communication to market, rail station etc. Hence, the negative coefficient of distance from market as well as train station is on expected line.

Table 5.18: Estimated Coefficients of Regression of LnRent on Locational Attributes According to Status of Ownership

Variable	Tenants			Owners		
	Coeff.	t-Stat	Prob.	Coeff.	t-Stat	Prob.
(Constant)	8.379	9.576	0.000	8.394	22.346	0.000
Located near River/Lake	-0.042	-0.611	0.541	-0.017	-0.182	0.856
Approach Road type	0.291	8.786	0.000	0.176	2.474	0.016
LnDistance–Workplace	0.077	4.548	0.000	0.000	0.865	0.390
LnDistance–Market	-0.089	-4.075	0.000	0.000	1.0181	0.312
LnDistance–Forest cover	-0.058	-0.725	0.469	-7.89E-06	-0.156	0.877
LnDistance–Rail Station	-0.099	-2.164	0.031	-6.73E-05	-0.812	0.419
View Quality Index	0.029	0.43	0.668	0.311	2.008	0.049
Location Convenience Index	1.073	8.658	0.000	0.345	1.449	0.152
Dependent Variable: LnMonthly Rent						
	R^2 = 0.40, Adj. R^2 = 0.39, F-Stat. = 33.97 (0.000)			R^2 = 0.18, Adj. R^2 = 0.08, F-Stat. = 1.81 (0.091)		
White Heteroskedasticity Test						
	F-stat.= 1.42,(0.047) & Obs* R-squared = 58.72 (0.06)			F-stat.=0.90,(0.63) & Obs* R-squared = 41.65 (0.53)		

Dependent Variable: Squared Residual.
Source: Field Survey conducted during 2015-16.

In case of owner-occupied respondents, quality of approach road and view quality index is observed to have significantly positive impact on housing price. The White heteroskedasticity test gives observed R-squared value of 41.69 with a p-value of 0.529. Locations with better quality of approach roads are generally close to the central market areas and so the positive coefficient of approach road quality is as expected. However, owners do not like to stay in congested and crowded places but prefer some degree of privacy and open space as indicated by the positive coefficient of the view quality index. The view index has also been computed by computing weights (as in the case of locational convenience) for availability of view from the house such as green cover, forest area and good architectural building. Though distance to workplace, market and other amenities are important, it is observed that such amenities do not significantly impact housing price in case of owners. As mentioned in case of tenants, distance may not be an important factor since the average distance to workplace on foot is recorded to be about 179 metres which takes an average time of about six minutes, and by vehicle the average distance and time is found to be 1563 metres and 15 minutes respectively. Average distance from market is also recorded to be only about 1284 metres and it is observed that a great majority (89.47%) of the owner-respondents own personal vehicle.

It is observed in model 5.1 of the regression that monthly family income, possession of personal vehicle, median distance from places of importance which are visited more frequently and the quality of house construction have significant impacts on rent and thereby choice of housing (Table 5.19). It may be noted that housing choice in respect of locational attributes is not determined by distance from, say workplace alone, but by the combined distances from places of travel on a regular basis. On the whole, it is observed that house construction quality impacts housing price (rent) most significant as indicated by the highest coefficient.

In the regression model 5.2, the numeric variables like monthly rent, family income and average distance to workplace, market, school and government office have been transformed into their natural log. It is observed all the variables which significantly impact rent in model 5.1 have significant impact on rent in model 5.2 besides *locational convenience index.*

Table 5.19: Estimated Regression Coefficients of Respondents by Selected Socio-Economic Characteristics, Median Distance, House Construction Quality& Locational Attributes

Variable	Model 1	Model 2
(Constant)	1301.73 (3.29)***	4.039 (10.82)***
Occupation of Head	-164.820 (-1.6)	0.002 (0.10)
Monthly Family Income*	.084 (10.84)***	0.420 (11.31)***
Vehicle	268.712 (3.40)***	0.044 (3.48)***
MedianDist–WMSGO*	-.669 (-2.38)**	-0.104 (-3.53)***
House Construction quality	1381.174 (6.663)***	0.292 (6.92)***
Location near River	—	-0.025 (-0.52)
Approach Road Type	—	0.027 (.97)
View Quality Index	—	-0.030 (-0.59)
Locational Convenience Index	—	0.453 (4.73)***
R^2, Adj.R^2 & F-stat. (Sig.)	0.57, 0.57 and 128.64 (.000)	0.68, 0.67 and 112.89 (.000)

Note: (i) MedianDist–WMSGO represents the median distance from workplace, market, school & Govt. Office.

Dependent Variable: Monthly Rent (Model 1) & LnMonthly Rent (Model 2).

(ii) * represents variables in Model 2 are in log form.

(iii) *** and ** indiate that the coefficient is significant at 1% and 5% level of significance by two tailed test.

Source: Field Survey conducted during 2015-16.

Table 5.20 displays the estimated coefficients of regression of rent paid on neighbourhood attributes. In respect of the tenants, median distance from worship place, hospital and departmental shop, when neighbour's house structure is of temporary in nature (i.e. made of bamboo walls), and proximity to garbage/waste dumping yard have significantly negative impact on monthly rent whereas educational level of immediate neighbours has significant positive impact on rent. The White heteroskedasticity test gives observed R-squared value of 17.89 with a p-value of 0.084 representing no heteroskedasticity. Places of regular visits like worship place, hospital and departmental shop are important for most tenant respondents and some of them are willing to pay more rent to be closer to such places of regular visits for more convenience.

The quality of the neighbours' houses is also found to significantly impact monthly rent paid. In the present study, it is observed that monthly rent significantly decreases when the neighbours' houses are made of temporary structure (bamboo walls). This is because when the respondent's neighbouring houses are made of temporary structures; in most cases the respondent's housing is also made of temporary structure for which the monthly rent is relatively cheaper as compared to permanent or concrete structures. Besides, houses made of temporary structures are mostly found on the peripheral areas of the town where monthly rents are also observed to be relatively lower. Most people, especially those with young children, prefer to reside near educated neighbours. Hence, it is observed that the tenants are willing to stay near higher educated neighbours by paying higher monthly rent.

Garbage or waste dumping sites are places of environmental hazards and it is observed that presence of such sites/yards in close proximity to residential houses have significant negative impact on the monthly rent paid. However, it is observed that residing in close proximity to heavy traffic roads which emanate high degree of noise pollution has no significant impact on the monthly rent. This implies people's preference to reside near central market places.

In case of owner-occupied respondents, the educational attainment of immediate neighbours is observed to have significantly positive impact on housing price. The White heteroskedasticity test gives observed R-squared value of 14.16 with a p-value of 0.166. Educated people generally prefer to live among other equally or more educated neighbours and the positive coefficient of education of the immediate neighbours is as expected. It is observed that 85.53 per cent of owner-occupied respondents have higher secondary and above level of educational attainment. In fact, it is also observed that 60.53 per cent of them are at least graduates.

For owner-occupied households also, distances to neighbourhood amenities such as worship place, departmental shop etc. are found to have insignificant impact on price. This may be either because the distance is not much of a concern as the average distance to their worship place and departmental shop are merely 0.52 km and 1.03 km respectively. Moreover 89.47 per cent of them own a personal vehicle. For owners, staying within homogeneous group is observed to be not important. Though for overall sample we found neighbourhood community is significant in the choice of residence. Actually, 98.68 per cent of owner-occupied respondents are already living in a neighbourhood where at least one household belong to their own community.

Table 5.20: Estimated Coefficients of Regression of LnRent on Neighbourhood Attributes According to Status of Ownership

Variable	Tenants			Owners		
	Coeff.	**t-Stat**	**Prob.**	**Coeff.**	**t-Stat**	**Prob.**
(Constant)	9.333	24.89	0.000	8.733	14.22	0.000
LnMed–Dist WpDsH	-0.209	-4.86	0.000	-0.021	-0.29	0.770
Security Standard	0.040	1.30	0.194	0.098	1.63	0.108
Neighbour House–Temporary	-0.299	-4.59	0.000	0.150	1.26	.0213
Neighbours' Community	-0.030	0.49	0.625	0.091	0.94	0.349
Education of Neighbours	0.241	6.06	0.000	0.134	1.69	0.096
Proximity to Garbage Yard	-0.174	-3.61	0.000	-0.076	-0.60	0.549
Proximity to Heavy Traffic Noise	0.077	1.56	0.120	0.014	0.16	0.871
Note: MedDist–WpDsH represents the median distance from worship place, departmental shop and hospital. Dependent Variable: LnMonthly Rent.						
R^2, Adj. R^2 and F-stat. (Sig.)	0.40, 0.39 and 37.99 (0.000)			0.12, 0.03 and 1.34 (0.247)		
White Heteroskedasticity Test						
F-stat. (Sig.) and Obs* R-squared	1.65 (0.083) and 17.89 (0.084)			1.49 (0.164) and 14.16 (0.166)		

Dependent Variable: Squared Residual.
Source: Field Survey conducted during 2015-16.

The regression results in Table 5.21 represent the combined impacts of all the three housing attributes on the housing prices (or rent). With respect to the tenants, it is observed that floor quality, water connection and carpet area of the house positively impact the monthly rent whereas distance from train station and proximity to heavy traffic noise negatively impact the monthly rent at one per cent level of significance. Also, the number of floors of the building, age of house (in years), house exterior wall material and the location convenience index positively affect the monthly rent, while coefficient of median distance from workplace, market, school and government office, and view quality index is negative and significant.

On the whole, it is observed that six structural attributes significantly affect the monthly rent, four locational attributes and one neighbourhood attribute have significant impacts on the monthly rent. Structural characteristics play the most dominant role in the housing price followed by the locational characteristics. All the coefficients of the variables or attributes which significantly impact the monthly rent are found to have the expected signs except for view quality index. Though most people prefer to enjoy good scenic views from their house, it appears that there is some compromise in choosing their place of residence in favour of other structural and locational attributes to stay within the main town area.

Neighbourhood attributes, which also significantly influence people in their housing choices, is observed to be insignificant except for proximity to main roads when all the housing attributes are combined. This may be because neighbourhood qualities are not significantly different across the different wards of the town.

In case of owner-occupied respondents, it is found that carpet area, quality of floor, water connection and exterior wall material have significantly positive impacts on housing price (implicit rent). All the coefficients of the variables or attributes which significantly affect the housing price are found to have the expected signs. Overall, it is observed that only structural attributes impact housing price. Though locational attributes such as distance from workplace and market, quality of view from house etc. are also important in housing choices, the regression revealed that coefficients of these attributes are not significant for the owners. This may be because the average distances from workplace and market are not much. The average distance to workplace for those who commute on foot is recorded to be about 179 metres (with an average time of six minutes) and for vehicle users it is 1563 metres (with an average time of 15 minutes). The average distance to market is recorded to be 1280 metres and most owner-occupied respondents are found to possess a personal vehicle (89.47%) as mentioned earlier. Moreover, it is also observed that owner-occupied respondents have an average view quality index of 0.527 as against the overall average of 0.478. This implies that since most of them have quite a good scenic view, its coefficient is found to be insignificant when other important attributes are also considered together. Coefficients of neighbourhood attributes are also found to be insignificant in this case when all housing attributes are taken together. The education level of the immediate neighbours which is found to be significant in Table 5.20 has been found to be insignificant here. As some of the explanatory variables already captured the variation in price (Dependent variable), the coefficients of neighbourhood variables became insignificant as they offer little more explanation only.

Table 5.21: Results of Regression of Log of Rent Paid on All Housing Attributes According to Status of Ownership

		Tenants	Owners
	Variable	**Coefficient**	**Coefficient**
	(Constant)	4.048 (8.31)***	4.193 (4.16)***
Structural	LnNo of Floors	0.039 (2.03)**	0.048 (0.97)
	Floor Type	0.106 (4.60)***	0.165 (2.72)***
	Veranda/Balcony	-0.007 (-0.31)	0.063 (0.48)
	Water Connection	0.124 (5.74)***	0.279 (2.42)**
	House Condition	0.027(1.13)	-0.042 (-0.85)
	LnAge of House	0.054 (2.51)**	0.054 (1.00)
	LnCarpet Area	0.745 (28.94)***	0.482 (5.77)***
	House Exterior Material	0.040 (1.73)*	0.199 (1.88)*
Locational	Located Near River/ Lake	-0.009 (-0.30)	-0.009 (-0.13)
	Quality of Approach Road	-0.016 (-0.90)	0.031 (0.54)
	LnMedDist–WMSGO	-0.058 (-1.72)*	0.013 (0.14)
	LnDist–Forestcover	0.029 (0.78)	-5.7E-06 (-0.17)
	LnDist–Trainstation	-0.114 (-5.04)***	-5.3E-06 (-1.14)
	View Quality Index	-0.062 (-1.94)*	0.127 (1.19)
	Location Convenience Index	0.115 (1.81)*	0.012 (0.06)
Neighbourhood	LnMedDist–WpDsH	0.016 (0.56)	-0.028 (-0.39)
	Security Standard	0.019 (1.33)	0.010 (0.22)
	Neighbour House Structure is Temporary	-0.027 (-0.85)	0.013 (0.16)
	Neighbours' Community	-0.034 (-0.50)	-0.009 (-0.13)
	Education Level of Neighbours	-0.031 (-1.48)	-0.020 (-0.35)
	Near Garbage/Waste Yard	-0.018 (-0.79)	0.055 (0.54)
	Near Heavy Traffic Noise	0.066 (2.73)***	0.082 (1.24)

(Contd.)

Dependent Variable: LN Monthly Rent		
Notes: (1) *, ** and *** indicate significance at 10 per cent, 5 per cent and 1 per cent level respectively; (2) Values in the parentheses represent t-values; (3) MedianDist–WMSGO represents the median distance from workplace, market, school and Government Office; and (4) MedDist–WpDsH represents the median distance from worship place, departmental shop and hospital.		
R^2, Adj. R^2 and F-stat. (sig.)	0.88, 0.88 and 135.82 (.000)	0.74, 0.63 and 6.70 (.000)
White Heteroskedasticity Test		
F-Statistic (prob.)	1.57 (0.001)	1.14 (0.342)
Obs* R-squared (prob.)	309.52 (0.070)	40.04 (0.337)

Dependent Variable: Squared Residual.
Source: Field Survey conducted during 2015-16.

The regression results in Table 5.22 represent the combined impacts of socio-economic factors along with all the three housing attributes and spatial variation in the housing prices (or rent). Here, the analysis is conducted for the entire sample units without segregating the respondents into tenants and owner-occupied households. The model has a R^2 value of 0.93, adjusted R^2 value of 0.93 and F-Statistic of 129.14 with p-value of 0.000. It is observed that among the socio-economic variables, monthly family income, family size and duration of stay in Dimapur town have significant positive impact on the monthly rent paid.

With regard to structural attributes, number of floors, external wall material, floor quality and carpet area has significantly positive impacts on monthly rent. Among the locational attributes, only locational convenience has significantly positive impact on the monthly rent. With respect to neighbourhood attributes, it is observed that monthly rent significantly decreases when the neighbours' houses are made of temporary structure (bamboo walls). This is because, as stated earlier, when the respondent's neighbouring houses are made of temporary structures; in most cases the respondent's housing is also made of temporary structure for which the monthly rent is relatively cheaper as compared to permanent or concrete structures. Besides, houses made of temporary structures are mostly found on the peripheral areas of the town where monthly rents are also observed to be relatively lower. Though public sewer or drain have environmental hazards, the positive significant impact indicates that people have a strong preference to stay in central places due to other benefits and conveniences.

The monthly rents across the wards also show significant variations with Ward 1 taken as the control group. Ward 1 is also centrally located and it is observed that households staying in wards which are closer to the main market area (CBD) pay significantly higher rent whereas households living in wards farther away from the central market pay significantly lower rent. It may be noted that tenants pay lesser rent (compared to implicit rent of owners) though it is not statistically significant.

From the above discussions, it appears that demand for housing is influenced by several factors and structural factors on the supply side along with availability of water, connectivity and communication facilities, location of house are some very crucial attributes. On the demand side income of the household, family size, education and cultural as well as neighbourhood characteristics affects the choice and payment of rent or house prices. Among them income is the major determinant of the type of housing a household demand. Besides, it is also found that tastes and preferences based on social factors such as community and its neighbours influence the demand for housing in the study area. Moreover, spatial variation in monthly rent is observed across the wards and it is found that households residing in wards closer to the main market pay significantly higher rent compared to those who live in wards farther away from such central places.

Table 5.22: Regression Results when LnRent is Regressed on all Socio-economic, Structural, Locational and Neighbourhood variables with Spatial Dummies

	Variable	Coeff.	t	Sig.
	(Constant)	3.316	11.97	.000
Socio-Economic	LnFamily Income	.081	3.74	.000
	LnFamily Size	.060	2.68	.008
	LnDuration of Stay	.023	1.88	.060
	Vehicle	.009	1.33	.183
	Education of Head	.004	.41	.686
Structural	LnNo. of Floor	.079	3.15	.002
	External Wall Material	.084	4.63	.000
	Floor Type	.115	6.26	.000
	Veranda/Balcony	-.010	-.469	.640
	Water Supply	.026	1.56	.120
	House Condition	.009	.510	.611
	LnAge of House	.027	1.52	.130
	LnCarpet Area	.648	22.80	.000

(Contd.)

Locational	Located near River	-.014	-.56	.573
	Approach Road Type	.002	.12	.908
	LnAvgDist–WMSGO	-.052	-2.11	.36
	View Index	.031	1.11	.267
	Location Convenience Index	.094	1.83	.069
Neighbour-hood	Security Standard	.004	.29	.769
	Neighbour House Structure–Temporary	-.067	-2.467	.014
	Neighbours' Religion	-.078	-.35	.860
	Neighbours' Community	-.006	-.24	.814
	Education of Neighbour	.002	.11	.914
	Near Garbage Yard	-.003	-.17	.868
	Near Public Sewer/Drain	.048	2.70	.007
Variation in Rent Across Wards	D2	.155	2.64	.009
	D3	-.137	-2.18	.030
	D4	-.062	-1.05	.292
	D5	-.070	-1.21	.227
	D6	.165	2.82	.005
	D7	.130	2.24	.026
	D8	.104	1.75	.082
	D9	-.106	-1.82	.070
	D10	.063	1.07	.284
	D11	-.169	-2.97	.003
	D12	-.267	-4.51	.000
	D13	-.074	-1.29	.198
	D14	-.241	-4.19	.000
	D15	-.210	-3.52	.000
	D16	-.292	-5.12	.000
	D17	.043	.70	.487
	D18	.066	1.11	.267
	D19	.180	2.91	.004
	D20	-.167	-2.85	.005
	D21	-.155	-2.73	.007
	D22	-.094	-1.59	.112
	D23	.025	.42	.672

(*Contd.*)

	Tenant Dummy	-.035	-1.17	.243
	R^2 = 0.93, Adj. R^2 = 0.93 and F-stat.= 129.14 (.000)			

Notes: (1) Ward 1 is taken as control group.
(2) LnAvgDist-WMSGO represents median distances from workplace, market, school and government office.
(3) Tenant dummy indicates 1 for tenant and 0 otherwise.

Source: Field Survey Conducted during 2015-16.

Summary of Observations

The analysis of the determinants of the demand for housing in the study area has revealed several important insights. With regard to various structural various structural and civic amenities, it is observed that there are significant variations in the availability and quality of such attributes across the wards. Fisher's intra-class correlation (two-way) among the structural attributes show that all the structural attributes considered are significantly correlated, which implies that a housing unit with a better floor material is also found to have better wall, roof etc. The results of the Chi-square test reveal that there are significant variations in all the structural attributes, except roof type, across the sample houses. Overall, it is observed that the buildings located in the central market areas have relatively better structural qualities whereas buildings located in the outskirts have relatively better civic and other amenities.

The ward-wise summary of average monthly rent reveals that there is wide variation across the wards. Monthly rent varies from Rs. 800 to Rs. 20,000 with a standard deviation of 3271.49 and coefficient of variation of 58.21 per cent. Rent per square feet is also found to vary significantly from Rs. 3.33 to Rs. 20.83 with a standard deviation of 2.85 and coefficient of variation of 31.70 per cent. In respect to land price per square feet, it is found to range from Rs. 400 to Rs. 4,500 with standard deviation of 851.96 and coefficient of variation of 61.69 per cent. It is also observed that prices of owner-occupied house vary significantly ranging from merely Rs. 2,00,000 to Rs. 1,00,00,000 with standard deviation of 19,03,944.20 and coefficient of variation of 44.20 per cent. In terms of average annual growth rates, it is observed that average annual growth of rent (4.53%) is higher than the average annual growth of house prices (4.06%). It is also observed that average annual growth rate of land prices is relatively much higher (17.88%). This implies that there is acute scarcity of land in Dimapur town. The relatively higher average annual growth rate of rent compared to that of house prices implies that the rental market in Dimapur town is profitable.

Apart from the housing attributes, residential choices of the people are also observed to be influenced by other socio-economic conditions such as income, community or ethnicity, religion, among other factors. With respect to religion, the Chi-square test and Independent t-test reveal that there is no significant difference in monthly rent between surveyed respondents who reside within the cluster of similar religion and those who stay with neighbours of other religion. In respect of community, it is observed that surveyed respondents have a strong preference to reside among the people belonging to their own community and they are even willing to pay higher rent (price) for staying in such areas.

On the factors affecting housing choices, given the housing attributes and its prices, it is observed that people make their decisions depending on their capability, necessity and preferences. It is observed that rent paid by the surveyed respondents is positively related to their income and structural quality of the housing unit. The results of multiple regression analyses for socio-economic variables including religion and community revealed that income, religion and community along with other socio-economic variables have statistically significant impacts on the monthly rent paid.

A hedonic approach with a double log form of regression has been used to estimate the impacts of various housing attributes on housing price (rent) for both tenants and owner-occupied respondents. In respect of structural attributes, it is observed that in case of the tenants, number of floors, floor material, water connection, overall house condition, age of house and carpet area of the house have significantly positive impacts on monthly rent. On the other hand, for owner-occupied households, number of floor, floor quality, water connection, age of house, carpet area of the house and exterior wall material has significant positive impacts on house prices.

With respect to the impact of locational attributes on the housing prices, it is observed that for tenant respondents, the quality of approach road connected to house, distance from workplace and location convenience are found to have significant positive impact on the monthly rent paid, whereas distance from market as well as train station have significant negative impact on the rent. In case of owner-occupied respondents, quality of approach road and view quality is observed to have significantly positive impact on housing price.

In respect of neighbourhood attributes, in case of tenants, distances to worship place and departmental shop, and temporary neighbour's house have significantly negative impacts on the monthly rent, while educational level of immediate neighbours has significant positive impact on rent. In case of owner-occupied respondents, security standard in the neighbourhood and the educational attainment of immediate neighbours is observed to have significantly positive impact on housing price.

The combined impacts of all the three housing attributes on the housing prices (or rent) reveals that with respect to tenants, six structural attributes and four locational attributes significantly affect the monthly rent. In case of owner-occupied respondents, however, only three structural attributes have significant impacts on housing price.

Spatial variation in monthly rent is also observed across the wards and it is found that households residing in wards closer to the main market pay significantly higher rent as compared to those living in wards farther away from such central places.

NOTE

1. Here analysis has not been done separately for the owners and tenants since owners mostly belong to the same religion, though there are some different community people in their neighbourhood. It may be because when they choose to own a house, the long-term consideration of staying for generations compel them to prefer to stay within own religious group. In many cases also the house ownership came due to inheritance and thus the neighbours are of the same religion by default. But people from other state who comes for service, business etc. rarely prefer to own a house permanently. Tenants who mostly hailed from other regions and other parts of the state, stay during their service period or short-term assignments or business mostly prefer to stay in locations with their homogenous community in order to avoid many inconveniences. But that may not be feasible always due to lack of immediate availability of rented accommodation. Also, vicinity of workplace and preference for communication as well as budget constraint compel many of them to stay in the mixed (religious and community) populated area.

REFERENCES

Ademiluyi, I.A. (2010). Public housing delivery strategies in Nigeria: A historical perspective of policies and programmes. *Journal of Sustainable Development in Africa*, 12 (6), 153-161.

Ademiluyi, I.A. and Raji, B.A. (2008). Public and private developers as agents in urban housing delivery in Sub-Saharan Africa: the situation in Lagos State. *Humanity & Social Sciences Journal*, 3 (2), 143-150.

Aero, T. (2006). Residential choice from a lifestyle perspective. *Housing, Theory and Society*, 23 (2), 109-130, DOI: 10.1080/14036090600773139. Retrieved from http://dx.doi.org/10.1080/14036090600773139 on 1/4/2016.

Akintunde, K.O. (2015). Housing needs and land administration in Nigeria: Problems and prospects. In Smith, I.O. (Ed.) *Land and real property rights in Nigeria*. Available at: https://ssrn.com/abstract=1122303. (Accessed on 2/4/2016).

Akinyode, B.F., Khan, T.H. and Ahmad, A.S.B.H. (2015). Socio-economic factors in measuring the demand for residential neighbourhood in Nigeria. *Asian Social Science*, 11 (12), 235-247. DOI: 10.5539/ass.v11n12p235. Retrieved from: http://dx.doi.org/10.5539/ass.v11n12p235 on 31/3/2016.

Akpom, U.N. (1994). Housing attributes and the cost of private rental buildings in Lagos Nigeria: A Hedonic Price Analysis. *The Review of Regional Studies*, 26 (3), 351-365.

Cohen, J. (1992). A power primer. *Psychological Bulletin*, 112(1), 155-159.

Fields, G.S. (1980). Education and income distribution in developing countries: A review of the literature [Electronic version]. In T. King (Ed.), *Education and income: A background study for world development* (pp. 231-315). Washington DC: The World Bank.

Fisher, R. A. (1954). *Statistical methods for research workers*. 12th ed. Oliver and Boyd, Edinburgh; Hafner Publishing Co., Inc., New York.

Goodman, A.C. (1989). Topics in empirical urban housing Research. In Arnott, R. (Ed.) *Regional and urban economics Part 2* (pp. 781-876). Massachusetts, USA: Psychology Press.

Greene, W.H. (2003). *Econometric analysis*. Pearson Education India.

Lancaster, K.J. (1966). A new approach to consumer theory. *Journal of Political Economy*, 74 (2), 132-157.

Li, M.M. and Brown, H.J. (1980). Micro-neighbourhood externalities and hedonic housing prices. *Land Economics*, 56 (2), 125-141.

Maddala, G.S. (2001). *Introduction to Econometrics* (2nd Ed.). New York, Macmillan Publishing Company.

Ndubueze, O.J. (2009). *Urban housing affordability and housing policy dilemmas in Nigeria*. (Doctoral dissertation, University of Birmingham, 2009).

Olayiwola, L.M., Adeleye, O. and Ogunshakin, L. (2005). Public housing delivery in Nigeria: Problems and challenges.*Paper presented at the XXXIII IAHS World Congress on Housing*, September 2005, Pretoria, South Africa.

Rodriguez, M. and Sirmans, C.T. (1994). Quantifying the value of a view in single-family housing markets. *The Appraisal Journal*, Vol. 62. 600-603.

Rosen, S. (1974). Hedonic prices and implicit markets: Product differentiation in pure competition. *Journal of Political Economy,* 82(1), 35-55.

6
Conclusion and Policy Implications

Findings of the Study

In this volume, the determinants of the demand for housing in Dimapur town, Nagaland has been explained in successive chapters. The nature of the trends of residential properties, amenities and prices of housing in Dimapur town have been analyzed and it is observed that with rapid population growth over the decades, availability and quality of residential properties and amenities have been growing. This trend has reflected in the growing demand for housing, which has resulted in increasing prices of various categories of land in the survey area. The analysis is based on both secondary and primary data and after having an idea of trend of town population, residential properties, general prices of land and house property etc., socio-economic and demographic characteristics of the sampled respondents have been analysed. Thereafter, factors affecting housing choices and location, and the determinants of the demand for housing in Dimapur town is analysed by using suitable techniques.

The contribution of this study is the inclusion of difference of preferences for housing attributes between tenant and owner-occupied respondents. Also, the overall impact of religion and community of the respondents including homogeneity of neighbours' religion and community on housing price (rent) has been explored by relating those variables to the variations observed in the monthly rent paid. Homogeneity of community of individual tenants and their neighbours is found to have significant impact on the variation in rent. Though variation in religion across respondent significantly determines rental variation due to their locational variations with activity pattern, earning capability; homogeneity of religion or neighbour's religion does not matter in the rental payment by the individuals. Further, spatial variations in the housing prices across the wards is examined by using ward level dummies and the result reveals that significantly higher housing prices (rents) are paid by the respondents staying in wards nearer to the main commercial areas or centre of administrative activities as compared to those living in wards farther away from the central areas. It is despite the fact the people from farthest area of the town does not require much more time to the central areas. It is the premium paid by the business people for enjoying commercial advantage, administrative activities and other socio-cultural and environmental benefits.

Dimapur town is considered as the economic gateway of Nagaland state and is one of the fastest growing towns in North-Eastern region of India. The progress of the town in economic and educational fields has been attracting new entrants continuously. Over the past few decades, there has been significant growth of population with people flocking to the town. Increasing number of households require growing housing facilities. This phenomenon is exerting immense pressure on the housing sector in the town and without sufficient new supply of dwellings; it pushes up the prices for both renting and purchasing houses. Due to lack of proper planning, it has resulted in congestion and overcrowding of people and buildings in certain pockets of the town. Though the growth rate of population and density has decelerated, absolute growth of population and density has been increasing, which is expected to exert pressure on the housing requirements of the population. Growth of area also ceased after 1991. Of course, pattern of demand for categories of houses might have changed due to the growing density and variation in socio-economic composition of population across the wards. Here educational status, which has also been increasing, is an important factor that affects the choice of housing of the individual through changing occupational locations.The residential houses and housing amenities have, however, shown qualitative improvement during the period 2001-2011.

Due to non-existence of apartment/flat system in Dimapur, it is extremely difficult to segregate house prices and land prices. But the pressure of increasing demand for housing is most visible in the rapidly growing land prices in Dimapur. At constant price, the average annual growth rate of land price has varied from 1.74 per cent to 11.17 per cent across the wards and it also varies significantly across various categories of land. Growth of price of homestead land is the highest because the price per unit of area is relatively low while special commercial areas recorded the lowest growth rate because its price has already reached almost a saturation level. Also, due to very low price and after rising scarcity in the commercial areas, demand for the outskirt barren areas has increased. Spatial variation in land prices and population density also exhibits people's preference of suitable location of residence and willingness to pay for that.

Social and economic factors like religion, community, education, family size and age profile of the households, their gender and marital status, nature of employment and level of income are expected to significantly affect the nature of housing units sought by them. From the survey, it is observed that by religion, Christians are in majority but community-wise there are more non-Nagas residing in the town. It is also observed that a great majority of the households have migrated to the town but the proportion of migrants is greater in the case of tenants compared to the owners. The survey also shows a very high literacy rate among the respondents with greater shares of graduate and above. Majority of heads of households are found to be self-employed, undertaking their own businesses, while a greater proportion of their spouses are unemployed. With regard to the average monthly per capita incomes of the families, it is found that 27.05 per cent of tenant households and 57.89 per cent of owner households earn above Rs. 10,000 per month.The survey also revealed that most of the households possess a personal vehicle but tenant households have more 2 wheelers and owner households have relatively more cars. Average number of families living in the same building is found to be much higher in the case of tenant households, while the average duration of stay in the town for the owner households was found to be almost double to that of tenant households. In respect of the tenant households, it is observed that housing is becoming scarcer and time taken for first rented accommodation is increasing over the decades.

With regard to various structural and civic amenities, it is observed that there are significant variations in the availability and quality of such attributes across the wards. Overall, it is observed that the buildings located in the central market areas have relatively better structural qualities, whereas buildings located in the outskirts have relatively better civic and other amenities.

The ward-wise analysis of average monthly rent, land price and house price reveals that there are significant variations across the wards. The relatively higher average annual growth of rent compared to average annual growth of house prices implies that the rental market in Dimapur town is profitable.

Apart from the housing attributes, residential choices of the people are also observed to be significantly influenced by other socio-economic conditions such as income, community, religion, among other factors. It is observed that income, religion and community along with other socio-economic variables have statistically significant impacts on the monthly rent paid. It is also observed that the respondents have a strong preference to live within homogeneous social groups but it is not significant in respect of religion as indicated by the analysis. Moreover, choice of housing is influenced by the median distance from places of regular visits. Quality of house construction is observed to affect housing price (rent) most significantly in the study area.

Significant variations in impacts of locational and neighbourhood attributes on housing prices are found across various socio-economic groups. Overall, in respect of locational attributes, quality of approach road to the house, locational convenience and distances from workplace and market have significant positive impacts, while distance from railway station and flood during monsoon have significant negative impacts on rent for all the categorised social and economic groups in the study. Generally, distance from workplace and market is found to have significant negative impact on housing price (or rent) but in the present study both distances are observed to have significant positive impact on rent. This indicates that for most of them, importance of proximity to workplace and market is overshadowed by other factors as locational convenience is found to have significant positive impact on rent.

With respect to neighbourhood characteristics, all the attributes considered here have significant impact on rent for most of the categories of respondents surveyed as expected except for pollution. This is probably because of either ignorance or other advantages of staying in the central places, though associated with higher level of pollution, overshadow such negative externalities.

The hedonic pricing approach has been used to estimate the impacts of various housing attributes on housing price (rent) for both tenants and owner-occupied respondents. When the housing attributes are considered separately with respect to tenant and owner-occupied households, it is observed that the inherent attributes affect housing prices differently in both cases. With regard to structural attributes, it is found that in case of tenants, number of floors of the building in which they stay, floor quality, water connection, overall house condition, age of house and carpet area have significant positive impacts on rent paid. In addition to those, the material and thus quality of external wall have significantly positive impact on housing prices (implicit rent) in case of owner-occupied respondents.

With respect to locational attributes, quality of approach road, distance from workplace and location convenience have significantly positive impacts on rent whereas distance from market and distance from train station have significantly negative impact on rent in case of tenants. On the other hand, only quality of approach road and view quality from house has significantly positive impacts on housing prices in case of owners. For neighbourhood attributes, it is observed that median distance from worship place, hospital and departmental shop, when neighbours' house is made of temporary structure and proximity to garbage/waste dumping yard have significantly negative impacts on rent paid for tenants. However, educational attainment of immediate neighbours has significant positive impact on housing price for owners.

It is observed that when all housing attributes are considered together, structural attributes affect the housing prices most significantly for both tenants as well as owner-occupied respondents. Overall, six structural attributes, four locational attributes and one neighbourhood attribute significantly affect housing prices in case of tenants. On the contrary, it is found that only structural attributes (four attributes) significantly affect housing prices in case of owners.

The regression of house price on socio-economic factors along with all the three housing attributes and spatial variation in the housing prices (or rent) when considered for the entire sample units without segregating the respondents into tenants and owner-occupied households also shows more or less similar results. It is observed that among the socio-economic variables, monthly family income, family size and duration of stay in Dimapur town have significant positive impacts on the monthly rent paid. With regard to structural attributes, number of floors, external wall material, floor quality and carpet area have significantly positive impacts on monthly rent. Among the locational attributes, it is observed that only locational convenience has significant positive impact on the monthly rent. With respect to neighbourhood attributes, it is observed that monthly rent significantly decreases when the neighbours' houses are made of temporary structure (bamboo walls). Housing prices (rents) across the wards also show significant variations when Ward 1 (centrally located) is taken as the control group. It is observed that households staying in wards which are closer to the main market area (CBD) pay significantly higher rent whereas households living in wards farther away from the central market pay significantly lower rent. It is also noticed that tenants pay lesser rent (compared to implicit rent of owners) though it is not statistically significant.

Therefore, from the preceding discussions, it appears that demand for housing is influenced by several factors and structural factors on the supply side along with availability of water, connectivity and communication facilities, location of house, which are some very crucial attributes required for leading a comfortable life. On the demand side income of the household, family size, education and cultural as well as neighbourhood characteristics affect the choice and payment of rent or house prices. Among them income is the major determinant of the type of housing a household demand. Besides, it is also found that tastes and preferences based on social factors such as community and its neighbours influence the demand for housing in the study area. Moreover, spatial variation in monthly rent is observed across the wards and it is found that households residing in wards closer to the main market pay significantly higher rent as compared to those who live in wards farther from such central places.

All the hypotheses considered have been proved correct in case of both tenants and owners except for homogeneity of religion and distance from workplace. For the respondents in the study area, housing price is observed to be not significantly affected by homogeneity of neighbours' religion but only by the homogeneity of neighbours' community. Moreover, as mentioned earlier, the positive coefficient of distance from workplace can be because average distance from workplace is recorded to be insignificant and also for most of the respondents it is not only the distance from workplace alone but the combined average of distance to places of regular visits which affect their housing price as expected inversely.

Even though the environmental quality matters in housing choice, distance from forest is not found to be significant which is overshadowed by the livelihood considerations. Only the large house owner likes to be nearer to the neighbourhood forest at the outskirt indicating their preference for quiet and lesser pollution.

Policy Implications

From the overall analysis and the knowledge gathered from the survey, certain important policy implications may be highlighted:

(1) Apartment/Flats system of housing may be promoted to mitigate the rising scarcity of housing in Dimapur if horizontal expansion is not feasible.

(2) As distance from workplace, market and other places of importance affects house price significantly, proper distribution of such facilities can distribute the housing preferences across the areas and help in avoiding congestion of some central areas.

(3) Good communication facilities can reduce the travel time further and development of all wards with major common amenities can make the pricing space neutral.

(4) Proper waste disposal management is essential since presence of garbage dumping sites in close proximity to residential houses significantly reduces house price (rent). As there is willingness to pay for cleanliness in the form of more rent or price that can be charged from the residents and the revenue can be utilized for the proper garbage treatment.

(5) Proper records of all house/land transactions should be maintained for better future research and policy making.

Scope for Further Study

This study is not without any limitations and there is much scope for further research and improvement in this area.

House prices are observed to be sensitive to variations in housing attributes but non-availability of proper records and sufficient information on house prices over different time periods have rendered this study handicapped in analyzing temporal variations in house prices in Dimapur. Studies can be extended to examine the impacts of variations in housing attributes and other factors on actual housing prices.

Analysis is done only for a town. However, the same analysis may be extended to more towns with different characteristics like monocentric or multicentric; houses of business people in town or residential building etc. A comparative analysis may be helpful in generalizing the results. Also, respondents' perceptions of various attributes especially those related to environmental issues including pollution and other hazards may be further researched.

Bibliography

Books

Alonso, A. (1964). *Location and land use: toward a General Theory of Land Rent*. Harvard University Press, Cambridge, Massachusetts.

Fisher, R. A. (1954). *Statistical methods for research workers*. (12th Ed.) Oliver and Boyd, Edinburgh; Hafner Publishing Co., Inc., New York.

Garrod, G. and Willis, K.G. (1999). *Economic Valuation of the Environment: Methods and case studies*, Edward Elgar Publishing Ltd., UK.

Government of India, UNDP Project. (2013). *District Human Development Report, Dimapur*, Nagaland. Government of Nagaland, Department of Planning and Coordination.

Greene, W.H. (2003). *Econometric analysis*. Pearson Education India.

Maddala, G.S. (2001). *Introduction to econometrics* (2nd Ed.). New York, Macmillan Publishing Company.

Menger, C. (1871). *Principles of Economics*. Reprinted in 2007 by the Ludwig von Mises Institute, Alabama, USA, 2007.

Mills, E.S. (1972). *Studies on the structure of the urban economy*. John Hopkins University, Baltimore.

Muth, R.F. (1969). *Cities and Housing: The Spatial Pattern of Urban Residential Land Use*. Chicago, University of Chicago Press.

Shiller, R.J. (2008). *The Subprime solution: How today's global financial crisis happened, and what to do about it*. Princeton: Princeton University Press.

Town Planning Organization. (1975). *The Master Plan for Dimapur*, Department of Urban Development, Government of Nagaland.

Wooldridge, J.M. (2015). *Introductory econometrics: A modern approach*. Nelson Education.

Journal, Articles and Reports

Abiodun, J.O. (1976). Housing problems in Nigerian cities. *The Town Planning Review*, 47(4), 339-347.

Ademiluyi, I.A. (2010). Public housing delivery strategies in Nigeria: A historical perspective of policies and programmes. *Journal of Sustainable Development in Africa*, 12 (6), 153-161.

Ademiluyi, I.A. and Raji, B.A. (2008). Public and private developers as agents in urban housing delivery in Sub-Saharan Africa: the situation in Lagos State. *Humanity & Social Sciences Journal*, 3 (2), 143-150.

Aero, T. (2006). Residential choice from a lifestyle perspective. *Housing, Theory and Society*, 23 (2), 109-130, DOI: 10.1080/14036090600773139. Retrieved from http://dx.doi.org/10.1080/14036090600773139 on 1/4/2016.

Ahlfeldt, G.M. and Maennig, W. (2011). Arenas, arena architecture and the impact on location desirability: the case of 'Olympic Arenas' in Prenzlauer Berg, Berlin. *Urban studies*, 46 (7), 1343-1362. DOI: 10.1177/0042098009104569.

Akintunde, K.O. (2015). Housing needs and land administration in Nigeria: Problems and Prospects. In Smith, I.O. (Ed.) *Land and real property rights in Nigeria*. Retrieved from: https://ssrn.com/abstract=1122303 on 2/4/2016.

Akinyode, B.F., Khan, T.H. and Ahmad, A.S.B.H. (2015). Socio-economic factors in measuring the demand for residential neighbourhood in Nigeria. *Asian Social Science*, 11(12), 235-247.

Akpon, U.N. (1994). Housing attributes and the cost of private rental buildings in Lagos Nigeria: A hedonic price analysis. *The Review of Regional Studies*, 26 (3), 351-365.

Aluko, O.E. (2010). The impact of urbanization on housing development: The Lagos experience, Nigeria. *Ethiopian Journal of Environmental Studies and Management*, 3(3), 64-74.

Anderson, R.J. Jr. and Crocker, T.D. (1971). Air pollution and residential property value. *Urban Studies,* 8, 171-180.

Augustina, O. (2015). Housing infrastructural facilities as determinants of rental values of residential properties in Osogbo, Osun State – Nigeria. *Journal of Research in Business, Economics and Management*, 1(1), 7-14.

Bartik, T.J. (1987). The estimation of demand parameters in hedonic price models. *Journal of Political Economy*, 95(1), 81-88.

Bajari, P. and Benkard, C.L. (2005). Demand estimation with heterogeneous consumers and unobserved product characteristics: A hedonic approach. *Journal of Political Economy*, 113(6), 1239-1276.

Becker, G.S. (1965). A theory of the allocation of time. *Economic Journal,* 75(299), 493-517.

Bello, M.O. and Bello, V.A. (2007). The influence of consumers behaviour on the variables determining residential property values in Lagos, Nigeria. *American Journal of Applied Sciences*, 4(10), 774-778.

Benson, E.D., Hansen, J.L., Schwartz, A.L. Jr. and Smersh, G.T. (1998). Pricing residential amenities: The value of a view. *Journal of Real Estate Finance and Economics*, 16 (1), 55-73.

Black, S.E. (1999). Do better schools matter? Parental valuation of elementary education. *Quarterly Journal of Economics*, 114 (2), 577-599.

Blomquist, G.C., Berger, M.C. and Hoehn, J.P. (1988). New estimates of quality of life in urban areas. *The American Economic Review*, 78(1), 89-107.

Bourassa, S.C. and Peng, V.S. (1999). Hedonic prices and house numbers: The influence of Feng Shui. *International Real Estate Review*, 2(1), 79-93.

Braden, J.B., Feng, X. and Won, D.H. (2011). Waste sites and property values: A meta-analysis. *Environmental and Resource Economics*, 50(2), 175-201.

Brasington, D.M. and Hite, D. (2005). Demand for environmental quality: A spatial hedonic analysis. *Regional Science and Urban Economics*, 35, 57-82.

Brown, J.N. and Rosen, H.S. (1982). On the estimation of structural hedonic price models. *Econometrica*, 50(3), 765-768.

Carroll, T.M., Clauretie, T.M. and Jensen, J. (1996). Living next to Godliness: Residential property values and churches. *Journal of Real Estate Finance and Economics*, 12(3), 319-330.

Chattopadhyay, S. (1999). Estimating the demand for air quality: New evidence based on the Chicago housing market. *Land Economics*, 75(1), 22-38.

Chau, K.W., Ma, V.S.M and Ho, D.C.W. (2001). The pricing of 'luckiness' in the apartment market. *Journal of Real Estate Literature*, 9(1), 31-40.

Chau, K.W., Ng, F.F. and Hung, E.C.T. (2001). Developer's goodwill as significant influence on apartment unit prices. *Appraisal Journal*, 69(1), 26-34.

Chau, K.W., Wong, S.K. and Yiu, C.Y. (2004). The value of the provision of a balcony in apartments in Hong Kong. *Property Management*, 22(3), 250-264.

Chay, K.Y. and Greenstone, M. (1998). *Does air quality matter? Evidence from the housing market.* NBER Working Paper 6826. Retrieved from: citeseerx.ist.psu.edu/viewdoc/download?doi=10.1.1.199.480&rep=rep1&type=pdf on 25/6/2015.

Clapman, E., Englund, P., Quigley, J.M. and Redfoearn, C. (2006). Revisiting the past and settling the score: Index revision for house price derivatives. *Real Estate Economics*, 34(2), 275-302.

Clauretie, T.M and Neill, H.R. (2000). Year-round school schedules and residential property values. *Journal of Real Estate Finance and Economics*, 20 (3), 311-322.

Cochran, W.G. (1963). *Sampling Techniques*, Wiley, New York.

Cohen, J. (1992). A power primer. *Psychological Bulletin*, 112(1), 155-159.

Cohen, J.P. and Coughlin, C.C. (2008). *Changing noise levels and housing prices near the Atlanta Airport*. Working Paper 2005 – 060D. Federal Reserve Bank of St. Louis. Retrieved from: www.http:// research.stlouisfed.org/wp/2005/2005-060.pdf on 23/6/2015.

Colwell, P.F. and Dilmore, G. (1999). Who was first? An examination of an early hedonic study. *Land Economics*, 75(4), 620-626.

Conroy, S., Narwold, A. and Sandy, J. (2013). The value of a floor: Valuing floor level in High-Rise condominiums in San Diego. *International Journal of Housing Markets and Analysis*, 6(2), 197-208.

Corell, M.R., Lillydahl, J.H. and Singell, L.D. (1978). The effects of Greenbelts on residential property values: Some findings on the Political Economy of open space. *Land Economics*, 54(2), 207-217.

Court, A.T. (1939). Hedonic price indexes with automotive examples. *The Dynamics of Automobile Demand*, General Motors Company, New York, pp. 99-117.

Court, L.M. (1941). Entrepreneurial and consumer demand theories for commodity spectra. *Econometrica*, 9(2), 135-162.

Cropper, M.L., Deck, L.B. and McConnell, K.E. (1988). On the choice of functional form for hedonic price functions. *The Review of Economics and Statistics*, 70(4), 668-675.

De, U.K. and Vupru, V. (2018), Role of Neighborhood Socio-Cultural & Religious Homogeneity in Housing Choice at Dimapur Town, India, *Journal of Developing Areas,* 53(2), 123-138.

De, U.K. and V. Vupru (2017), Location and Neighbourhood Conditions for Housing Choice and Its Rental Value: Empirical Examination in an Urban Area of North-East India, *International Journal of Housing Markets and Analysis*,10 (4), 519-538.

Deaton, B.J. and Hoehn, J.P. (2002). The effect of hazardous waste sites on property values in zones of high industrial activity: a hedonic approach. *Paper submitted for the AAEA 2002 Annual Meeting,* Long Beach, California. Retrieved from: http://ageconsearch.umn.edu/bitstream/19612/1/sp02de01.pdf on 25/1/2014.

Deaton, B.J. and Hoehn, J.P. (2004). Hedonic analysis of hazardous waste sites in the presence of other urban disamenities. *Environmental Science & Policy*, 7, 490-508.

Des Rosiers, F., Lagana, A., Theriault, M. and Beaudoin, M. (1996). Shopping centres and house values: An empirical investigation. *Journal of Property Valuation and Investment*, 14(4), 41-62.

Di Pasquale, D. and Wheaton, W.C. (1992). The markets for real estate assets and space: A conceptual framework. *Journal of the American Real Estate and Urban Economics Association*, 20(1), 181-197.

DMC official website – dmcnagaland.nic.in/SSL/login.aspx.

Edmonds, R. (1984). A theoretical basis for hedonic regression: A research primer, *AREUEA Journal*, 12(1), 72-85.

Eichholtz, P. and Lindenthal, T. (2014). Demographics, human capital and the demand for housing. *Journal of Housing Economics*, 26, 19-32.

Els, M. and Fintel, D.V. (2008). *Residential property prices in a sub-market of South Africa: Separating real growth from attribute growth.* Stellenbosch Economic Working Paper: 14/08, University of Stellenbosch. Retrieved from: https://ideas.repec.org/p/sza/wpaper/wpapers62.html on 11/4/2015.

Epple, D. (1987). Hedonic prices and implicit markets: Estimating demand and supply functions for differentiated products. *Journal of Political Economy,* 95(1), 59-80.

Espey, M. and Lopez, H. (2000). The impact of airport noise and proximity on residential property values. *Growth and Change*, 31, 408-419.

Fields, G.S. (1980). Education and income distribution in developing countries: A review of the literature [Electronic version]. In T. King (Ed.), *Education and income: A background study for world development* (pp. 231-315). Washington, DC: The World Bank.

Fleischer, A. (2011). A room with a view – A valuation of the Mediterranean Sea view. *Tourism Management*, 30, 1-5.

Follain, J.R. and Calhoun, C.A. (1997). Constructing indices of the price of multifamily properties using the 1991 Residential Finance Survey. *Journal of Real Estate Finance and Economics*, 14 (1), 235-255.

DOI: 10.1023/A:1007748807628. Retrieved from: link.springer.com/article/10.1023/A:1007748807628 on 27/2/2015.

Follain, J.R. and Jimenez, E. (1985). Estimating the demand characteristics: A survey and critique. *Regional Science and Urban Economics*, 15, 77-107.

Forrest, D., Glen, J. and Ward, R. (1996). The impact of a Light Rail system on the structure of house prices: A hedonic longitudinal study. *Journal of Transport Economics and Policy*, 30(1), 15-29.

Fortin, N.M., Hill, A.J. and Huang, J. (2013). Superstition in the housing market. IZA Discussion Paper No. 7484, *Paper presented at the Institute for the Study of Labor*, Bonn, Germany. Retrieved from: faculty.arts.ubc.ca/nfortin/Superstition.pdf on 11/2/2014.

Fortin, M. and Leclerc, A. (2000). *Demographic changes and real housing prices in Canada*. Working Paper No. 00-06. University of Sherbrooke. Retrieved from http://citeseerx.ist.psu.edu/viewdoc/download?doi=10.1.1.198.9803&rep=rep1&type=pdf on 23/5/2015.

Francke, M.K., Vos, G.A. and Janssen, J.E. (2000). Standardised price indices for the regional housing market: A comparison between the Fixed-Sample Index and Hedonic Index. *Paper Presented at the 7th European Real Estate Society Conference*, Bordeaux, 2000.

Freeman, A.M. (1979). Hedonic prices, property values and measuring environmental benefits: A survey of the issues. *The Scandinavian Journal of Economics*, 81(2), 154-174.

Frew, J. and Jud, G.D. (2003). Estimating the value of apartment buildings. *Paper presented at the 2002 American Real Estate Society Annual Meeting*. Retrieved from: aux.zicklin.baruch.cuny.edu/jrer/papers/pdf/past/vol25n01/05.77_86.pdf on 15/6/2014.

Frew, J. and Wilson, B. (2002). Estimating the connection between location and property value. *Journal of Real Estate Practice and Education*, 5 (1), 17-25.

Frischtak, C. & Mandel, B.R. (2012). *Crime, House Prices, and Inequality: The Effect of UPPs in Rio*. Staff Report No. 542, Federal Reserve Bank of New York. Retrieved from https://www.newyorkfed.org/medialibrary/media/research/staff_reports/sr542.pdf on 18/9/2016.

Garrod, G. and Willis, K.G. (1992). Valuing goods' characteristics: An application of the Hedonic Price Method to environmental attributes. *Journal of Environmental Management*, 34(1), 59-76.

Gibler, K.M. and Nelson, S.L. (2003). Consumer behaviour applications to real estate education. *Journal of Real Estate Practice and Education*, 6(1), 63-83.

Glaeser, E.L., Gyourko, J. and Saks, R.E. (2005). *Urban Growth and Housing Supply*. Discussion Paper No. 2062, Harvard Institute of Economic Research. Retrieved from: http://post.economics.harvard.edu/hier/2005list.html on 22/5/2015.

Glossop, C. (2014). *Housing and Economic Development: Moving forward together*. Centre for Research and Market Intelligence. Retrieved from www.centreforcities.org/wp-content/uploads/2014/09/08-11-06-Housing-and-economic-development.pdf on 21/02/2017.

Goodman, A.C. (1978). Hedonic prices, price indices and housing markets. *Journal of Urban Economics*, 5(4), 471-484.

Goodman, A.C. (1989). Topics in empirical urban housing research. In R. Muth and A. Goodman (eds.), *The Economics of Housing Markets*, Harwood Academic, Chur, Switzerland, 49-146.

Government of India, *Census of India, 1961, 1971, 1981, 1991, 2001 and 2011*. Retrieved from: censusindia.gov.in

Government of India, *Census of India 2011*, New Delhi. Retrieved from: www.census2011.co.in/census/city/183-dimapur.html on 12/11/2013.

Griliches, Z. (1961). Hedonic price indices for automobiles: An econometric analysis of quality change, in *The Price Statistics of the Federal Government, General Series No. 73*. 137-196, Columbia University for the National Bureau of Economic Research, New York.

Grimes, A. and Liang, Y. (2009). Spatial Determinants of Land Prices: Does Auckland 's Metropolitan Urban Limit Have an Effect?*Applied Spatial Analysis and Policy*, 2 (1), 23-45.

Haas, G.C. (1922). *A statistical analysis of farm sales in Blue Earth County, Minnesota as a basis for farmland appraisal*. Masters Dissertation, the University of Minnesota, 1922.

Habitat for Humanity, Ireland. (2015). *The importance of housing*. Retrieved from www.habitatireland.ie/2015/01/importance-housing/ on 22/11/2016.

Hansen J. (2006). *Australian house prices: A comparison of Hedonic and Repeat Sales measures*. Research Discussion Paper: 2006-03, Reserve Bank of Australia. Retrieved from: http://www.rba.gov.au/publications/rdp/2006/pdf/rdp2006-03.pdf on 4/3/2015.

Haurin, D. and Brasington, D. (1996). *The impact of School quality on real house prices: Interjurisdictional effects*. Working Paper 010, Ohio State University. Retrieved from: www.econ.ohio-state.edu/pdf/haurin/haurin.pdf on 11/2/2014.

Hendershott, P.H. (1991). *Are real house prices likely to decline by 47 per cent?* NBER Working Paper No. 3880. DOI: 10.3386/w3880. Retrieved from: http://www.nber.org/papers/w3880.pdf on 8/6/2015.

Ho, J. (2008). *The economics of luckiness: The impact of number superstition on condominium prices in Singapore*. Honours dissertation, Department of Economics, Amherst College, 2008.

Holly, S. and Jones, N. (1997). House prices since the 1940s: Cointegration, demography and asymmetries. *Economic Modelling*, 14, 549-565.

Houthakker, H.S. (1952). Compensated changes in quantities and qualities consumed. *Review of Economic Studies*, 19(3), 155-164.

Hsueh, L.M. (2000). The relationship between housing price, tenure choice and saving behaviour in Taiwan. *International Real Estate Review*, 3(1), 11-33.

Hugalu, T. *et al.* (2016). *A hedonic house Price Index for Turkey*. Working Paper No. 16/03, Central Bank of the Republic of Turkey. Retrieved from: https://www.unece.org/fileadmin/DAM/stats/documents/ece/ces/ge.22/2016/Session_6_Hedonic_House_Price_Index_for_Turkey.pdf on 22/08/2016.

Huh, S. & Kwak, S.J. (1997). The choice of functional form and variables in the hedonic price model in Seoul. *Urban Studies*, 34(7), 989-998.

Jayasekare, A.S., Herath, S., Wickramasuriya, R. and Perez, P. (2019). The price of a view: estimating the impact of view on house prices. *Pacific Rim Property Research Journal*, 25(2), 141-158, DOI: 10.1080/14445921.2019.1626543.

Jim, C.Y. and Chen, W.Y. (2006). Impacts of urban environmental elements on residential housing prices in Guangzhou (China). *Landscape and Urban Planning*, 78, 422-434.

Jud, G.D and Watts, J.M. (1981). Schools and housing value. *Land Economics*, 57(3), 459-470.

Kain, J.F. and Quigley, J.M. (1970). Measuring the value of housing quality. *Journal of the American Statistical Association*, 65(5), 532-548.

Karantonis, A. (2008). *Population growth and housing affordability in the modern city—Sydney a case study*. University of Technology, Sydney. Retrieved from: http://www.prres.net/papers/Karantonis_Population_Growth_and_Housing_Affordability.pdf on 22/5/2015.

Ketkar, K. (1992). Hazardous waste sites and property values in the state of New Jersey. *Applied Economics*, 24, 647-659.

Kiel, K.A. (1995). Measuring the impact of the discovery and cleaning of identified hazardous waste sites on house value. *Land Economics*, 71(4), 428-435.

Kockelman, K.M. (1997). The effects of location elements on home purchase prices and rents: Evidence from the San Francisco Bay area. *Transportation Research Record No. 1606*, pp. 40-50.

Koomen, E. and Buurman, J. (2002). Economic theory and land prices in land use Modeling. *Paper presented at the 5th AGILE Conference on Geographic Information Science, Palma* (Balearic Islands, Spain) 2002.

Kruse, S.A. and Ahmann, J. (2009). *The value of Lake adjacency: A hedonic pricing analysis on the Klamath River, California*. Ecotrust Working Paper Series No. 5. Retrieved from: www.ecotrust.org/workingpapers on 18/1/2014.

Lancaster, K.J. (1966). A new approach to consumer theory. *Journal of Political Economy*, 74(2), 132-157.

Lansford, H. Jr. and Jones, L.L. (1995). Marginal price of Lake recreation and aesthetics: An hedonic approach. *Journal of Agricultural and Applied Economics*, 27 (1), 212-223.

Lee, G.S., Dengler, P.S., Felderer, B. and Helmenstein, C. (2001). Austrian demography and housing demand: Is there a connection. *Empirica*, 28, 259-276.

Lee, T.H. (1968). Housing and permanent income: Tests based on a three-year reinterview survey. *The Review of Economics and Statistics*, 50(4), 480-490. Retrieved from: http://www.jstor.org/stable/1926817 on 8/6/2015.

Lee, T.H. and Kong, C.M. (1977). Elasticities of housing demand. *Southern Economic Journal*, 44(2), 298-305.

Leggett, C.G. and Bockstael, N.E. (2000). Evidence of the effects of water quality on residential land prices. *Journal of Environmental Economics and Management*, 39, 121-144. Retrieved from: http://www.idealibrary.com on 24/11/2013.

Li, M.M. and Brown, H.J. (1980). Micro-neighbourhood externalities and hedonic housing prices. *Land Economics*, 56 (2), 125-141.

Lindh, T. and Malmberg, B. (2008). Demography and housing demand– What can we learn from residential construction data? *Journal of Population Economics*, 21, 521-539.

Lorenz, D.P., (2006). *The application of Sustainable Development Principles to the theory and practice of property valuation.* Doctoral Dissertation, University of Karlsruhe, Germany, 2006.

Maisel, S.J., Burnham, J.B. and Austin, J.S. (1971). The demand for housing: A comment. *The Review of Economics and Statistics*, 53(4), 410-413.

Mankiw, N.G. and Weil, D.N. (1989). The baby boom, the baby bust, and the housing market. *Regional Science and Urban Economics*, 19, 235-258.

Maurer, R., Martin P. and Sebastian, S. (2004). Hedonic price indices for the Paris housing market. *Allgemeines Statistisches Archiv*, 88 (3), 303-326. Retrieved from: http://papers.ssrn.com/sol3/papers.cfm?abstract_id=691242 on 23/1/2014.

Mayo, S.K. (1981). Theory and estimation in the economics of housing demand. *Journal of Urban Economics*, 10, 95-116.

Max, S. (2004). Schools, what is it good for? When it comes to home prices, school matters. Buyers will pay a premium to live near top schools. CNN.com, August 27, 2004. Retrieved from http://money.cnn.com/2004/08/27/real_estate/buying_selling/schools/ on 12/2/2014.

McMillen, D. and McDonald, J.F. (1998). Suburban subcenters and employment density in metropolitan Chicago. *Journal of Urban Economics,* 43(1), 157-180.

McMillan, M.L., Reid, B.G. and Gillen, D.W. (1980). An extension of the hedonic approach for estimating the value of quiet. *Land Economics*, 56 (3), 315-328.

Michaelsen, M.M. and Haisken-DeNew, J.P. (2015). Migration magnet: The role of work experience in rural-urban wage differentials. *IZA Journal of Migration*, 4 (21). DOI 10.1186/s40176-015-0046-7. Retrieved from: https://izajom.springeropen.com/articles/10.1186/s40176-015-0046-7 on 23/5/2015.

Millhouse, J.A. (2005). *Assessing the effects of architectural design on real estate values: A qualitative approach.* Masters Dissertation, Rice University, 2005.

Mishra, S.K. and Ngullie, M.L. (2003). Quality of life in Dimapur Nagaland (India). *SSRN Electronic Journal*. Retrieved from: https// www.researchgate.net/publication/249960907on 8/6/2015.

Mishra, S.K. and Ngullie, M.L. (2008). Hedonic demand for rented house in Kohima, Nagaland. *Munich Personal RePEc Archive.* MPRA Paper No. 10076. Retrieved from: http://mpra.ub.uni-muenchen.de/10076 on 23/8/2013.

Mok, H.M.K., Chan, P.P.K. and Cho, Y.S. (1995). A hedonic price model for private properties in Hong Kong. *Journal of Real Estate Finance and Economics*, 10, 37-48.

Morris, E.W., Woods, M.E. and Jacobson, A.L. (1972). The measurement of housing quality. *Land Economics*, 48(4), 383-387.

Mulder, C.H. (2006). Population and housing: A two-sided relationship. *Demographic Research*, 15(13), 401-412. DOI: 10.4054/DemRes.2006.15.13. Retrieved from http:www.demographic-reseach.org/Volumes/Vol15/13on 22/05/2015.

Murty, M.N. and Gulati, S.C. (2004). A generalized method of hedonic prices: Measuring benefits from reduced urban air pollution. *Natural Resources Accounting*, CSO, GOI. Retrieved from: http://www.iegindia.org/workpap/wp254.pdf on the 24/11/2013.

Musa, U. (2016). *Impact of housing attributes on rental values of residential properties in Minna, Nigeria*, Master Dissertation, Universiti Tun Hussein Onn Malaysia.

Muth, R.F. (1966). Household production and consumer demand functions. *Econometrica*, 34 (6), 699-708.

Nakamura, S. (2018). Spatial distributions of job accessibility, housing rents, and poverty in Nairobi, Kenya, *World Bank Policy Research Working Paper No. 8654*. Downloaded from https://papers.ssrn.com/sol3/papers.cfm?abstract_id=3290987. Accessed on 25.08.2014.

Ndubueze, O.J. (2009). *Urban housing affordability and housing policy dilemmas in Nigeria*. Doctoral dissertation, University of Birmingham, 2009.

Nelson, J.P. (1980). Airports and property values: A survey of recent evidence. *Journal of Transport Economics and Policy*, 14(1), 37-52.

Nelson, J.P. (1982). Highway noise and property values: A survey of recent evidence. *Journal of Transport Economics and Policy*, 16(2), 117-138.

Nunns, P., Hitchins, H. and Balderston, K. (2015). *The value of land, floor space and amenities: a hedonic price analysis of property sales in Auckland 2011-2014*. Auckland Council Technical Report, TR2015/012. Retrieved from: http://knowledgeauckland.org.nz/assets/publications/TR2015-012-Value-of-land-floorspace-and-amenitics-Auckland.pdf on 22/8/2016.

Olayiwola, L.M., Adeleye, O. and Ogunshakin, L. (2005). Public housing delivery in Nigeria: Problems and challenges. *Paper presented at the XXXIII IAHS World Congress on Housing*, September 2005, Pretoria, South Africa.

Oluwatoyin, O.J., Sunday, S.K. and Folake, A. (2013). Population growth and health facilities in Nigeria (A case study of Ondo State). *International Journal of Scientific and Technology Research*, 2(8), 108-113.

Ottensmann, J.R., Payton, S. and Man, J. (2008). Urban location and housing prices within a hedonic model. *The Journal of Regional Analysis and Policy*, 38(1),19-35.

Peng, T.C. & Chiang, Y.H. (2015). The non-linearity of hospitals' proximity on property prices: Experiences from Taipei, Taiwan. *Journal of Property Research*, 3(4), 341-361, DOI: 10.1080/09599916.2015.1089923.

Retrieved from http://dx.doi.org/10.1080/09599916.2015.1089923 on 18/9/2016.

Pennington, G., Topham, N. and Ward, R. (1990). Aircraft noise and residential property values adjacent to Manchester International Airport. *Journal of Transport Economics and Policy*, 24(1), 49-59.

Quigley, J.M. (1995). A simple Hybrid Model for estimating real estate Price Indexes. *Journal of Housing Economics*, 4(1), 1-12.

Rahadi, R.A. *et al.* (2012). Relationship between consumer preferences and value propositions: A study of residential product. *Procedia– Social and Behavioral Sciences,* 50, 865-874.

Ridker, R.G. and Henning, J.A. (1967). Determinants of residential property values with special reference to air pollution. *The Review of Economics and Statistics*, 49 (2), 246-257.

Rodriguez, M. and Sirmans, C.T. (1994). Quantifying the value of a view in single-family housing markets. *The Appraisal Journal*, 62, 600-603.

Rohani, M. (2012*). Impact of Hauraki Gulf amenity on the land price of neighbourhood properties. An empirical Hedonic Pricing Method case study North Shore, Auckland.*Auckland Council Working Paper 2012/001.

Rosen, S. (1974). Hedonic prices and implicit markets: Product differentiation in pure competition. *Journal of Political Economy*, 82(1), 35-55.

Rosen, S. (1977). *Labour quality, the demand for skill, and market selection*. NBER Working Paper No. 162, Center for Economic Analysis of Human Behaviour. Retrieved from: http://www.nber.org/papers/w0162.pdf on 26/5/2015.

Samarasinghe, O. & Sharpe, B. (2010). Flood prone risk and amenity values: A spatial hedonic analysis. *The Australian Journal of Agricultural and Resource Economics*, 54(1), 457-475.

Selim, S. (2008). Determinants of house prices in Turkey: A hedonic regression model. *Dogus University Journal*, 9(1), 65-76.

Shimizu, C. (2014). Estimation of hedonic single-family house price function considering neighbourhood effect variables. *Sustainability*, 6, 2946-2960. DOI: 10.3390/su6052946.

Shimizu, C. and Nishimura, K.G. (2007). Pricing structure in Tokyo metropolitan land markets and its structural changes: Pre-bubble, bubble, and post-bubble periods. *Journal of Real Estate Finance and Economics*, 35, 475-496.

Sirpal, R. (1994). Empirical modeling of the relative impacts of various sizes of shopping centres on the value of surrounding residential properties. *Journal of Real Estate Research*, 9(4), 487-505.

So, H.M., Tse, R.Y.C. and Ganesan, S. (1997). Estimating the influence of transport on house prices: Evidence from Hong Kong. *Journal of Property Valuation & Investment*, 15(1), 40-47.

Soderberg, B. and Janssen, C. (2001). Estimating distance gradients for apartment properties. *Urban Studies*, 38(1), 61-79.

Srour, I.M., Kockelman, K.M. and Dunn, T.P. (2002). Accessibility indices: A connection to residential land prices and location choices. *Paper Presented at the 81st Annual Meeting of the Transport Research Board,* March-April 2002, Washington. Retrieved from: citeseerx.ist.psu.edu/viewdoc/download?doi=10.1.1.80.7338&rep=rep1&type=pdf on 16/1/2014.

Swan, C. (1995). Demography and the demand for housing: a reinterpretation of the Mankiw-Weil demand variable. *Regional Science and Urban Economics*, 25, 41-58.

Thaler, R. (1978). A note on the value of crime control: Evidence from the property market. *Journal of Urban Economics*, 5(1), 137-145.

Tiwari, P. and Rao, J. (2016). *Housing markets and housing policies in India*. ADBI Working Paper 565. Tokyo: Asian Development Bank Institute. Retrieved from: http://www.adb.org/publications/major-challenges-facing-small-and-medium-sizedenterprises-asia-and-solutions/ on 21/02/2017.

Tse, R.Y.C. (2002). Estimating neighbourhood effects in house prices: Towards a new hedonic model approach. *Urban Studies*, 39(7), 1165-1180.

Tse, R.Y.C. and Love, P.E.D. (2000). Measuring residential property values in Hong Kong. *Property Management*, 18(5), 366-374.

Tyrvainen, L. (1997), The amenity value of the urban forest: An application of the hedonic pricing method. *Landscape and Urban Planning*, 37, 211-222.

Vessali, K.V. (1996). Land use impacts of rapid transit: A review of the empirical literature. *Berkeley Planning Journal*, 11(1), 71-105.

Vor, F. de and Groot, H.L.F. de (2011). The impact of industrial sites on residential property values: A hedonic pricing analysis from the Netherlands. *Regional Studies*, 45(5), 609-623, DOI: 10.1080/00343401003601925.

Waddell, P.(2011). Integrated land use and transport planning and modelling: Addressing challenges in research and practice. *Transport Review*, 31(2), 209-229.

Walden, M.L. (1990). Magnet schools and the differential impact of quality on residential property values. *Journal of Real Estate Research*, 5(2), 221-230.

Waugh, F.V. (1928). Quality factors influencing vegetable prices. *Journal of Farm Economics,* 10(2), 185-96.

Welch, T.F. (2010). *Estimating the effects of transportation infrastructure proximity using multiple longitudinal regression methods: The case of Atlanta.* Master's Dissertation, Florida State University, 2010.

Zabel, J.E. and Kiel, K.A. (2000). Estimating the demand for air quality in four U.S. cities. *Land Economics*, 76(2), 174-194.

Zou, G. (2015). The effect of Central Business District on house prices in Chengdu Metropolitan area: A hedonic approach. *Paper Presented at the International Conference on Circuits and Systems*, August 2015, Paris, France. Retrieved from: www.atlantis-press.com/php/download_paper.php?id=23016 on 22/8/2016.

Index